Jay Rayner's Last Supper

Jay Rayner's Last Supper

*One meal, a lifetime
in the making*

JAY RAYNER

First published by Guardian Faber in the USA in 2019
Guardian Faber is an imprint of Faber & Faber Ltd,
Bloomsbury House, 74–77 Great Russell Street,
London WC1B 3DA

First published in the UK as *My Last Supper*

Guardian is a registered trademark of
Guardian News & Media Ltd,
Kings Place, 90 York Way, London N1 9GU

Typeset by Ian Bahrami
Printed and bound by CPI Group (UK) Ltd, Croydon CRO 4YY

The right of Jay Rayner to be identified as author of this work
has been asserted in accordance with Section 77 of the Copyright,
Designs and Patents Act 1988

A CIP record for this book
is available from the British Library

ISBN 978–1–78335–221–0

2 4 6 8 10 9 7 5 3 1

For Edith, Molly and Todd Baker

Contents

Dying for Something to Eat

After a while you get used to people wishing you dead. In my case it helps that the ones making the suggestion do so lightly, like they were proposing an ice cream or a cuddle. Often there's the catch of a laugh in their voice. It's that stifled amusement, the giggle before the darkness, which alerts me to what's coming.

I am standing on a stage in a small theatre or comedy club, the meat of my live show behind me, and I am taking questions. I am working my way from upstretched hand to upstretched hand, trying to be the most entertaining version of myself that I can.

'Jay, so . . . Ha!' Here we go. 'What would be your death-row dinner?'

The audience laughs. The audience always laughs. By asking the question the balance of power appears to have shifted, and brilliantly. There I am up on stage, owning the space. And now here's a member of the audience bringing me back down to earth by asking me to imagine that I am about to be put to death for some crime of which I am obviously guilty. Then again, they have heard the question only once; I have heard it dozens of times.

I reply. Some members of the audience laugh. Some of them look a little puzzled. Others look utterly furious. As far as they're concerned, I really haven't played the game at all.

The idea of last suppers, be they caused by the judicial system, suicide or misfortune of health, has long fascinated me. It seems such a simple question. You are about to die. What do you choose to eat? But it isn't simple at all. For a start, we eat to keep ourselves alive. That's the whole point of consuming food. It's literally a bodily function. But if

1

you knew your death was imminent, the basic reason for the meal would have gone. You'll be long dead before you starve. So now it's about something else.

Do you choose comfort food, something that reminds you of the good times when you weren't about to die? Do you allow your meal to parent you, to enfold you in the biggest hug possible? Or do you go for ingredients as statement? Your last meal should surely be a time to wade into luxury and excess. Gold leaf on desserts is obviously stupid, but if ever there was a time for stupidity, surely it's now? And how big a part does memory play in all this? Those of us who are more obsessed with our lunch than is strictly necessary build our stories around mealtimes. We construct our narrative one plateful at a time. We eat, therefore we are.

What's more, now you can eat what the hell you like because there are no consequences. Usually, too much deep-fried, sugar-rich food would result in you feeling queasy and worrying about your heart, about what type of person your appetites were turning you into. But now, who cares? Too much spicy, salty food might leave you with a dry mouth; too many Jerusalem artichokes might leave you farting for hours. None of these things matter any more.

But there's a problem, a very large one. Let's call it the mood issue. I am a man of appetites. I have appetites like Minnesota has lakes. (Minnesota has an awful lot of lakes.) But even I would be hard pushed to shove the thought of my impending death out of my head and get down to eating.

Which is exactly what I tell the people who ask me about my death-row dinner.

'I might be a greedy bastard,' I tell the audience, 'but even I would lose my appetite if the next morning I was to be the victim of an appalling miscarriage of justice. How dare the state take my life? The fact is, sometimes there are more important things than dinner.'

They wanted an account of unfettered, careless indulgence.

They wanted me to make them feel okay about their own greed.

Instead I've raised an issue of jurisprudence.

In 2007 photographer Melanie Dunea published a book called *My Last Supper*, in which fifty big-name chefs from around the world gave an account of what they would eat for their last meal on earth. They were then photographed looking thoughtful about their own mortality. In his introduction, the late Anthony Bourdain, the one-time chef turned writer and broadcaster, made the point that these were people who had already had the opportunity to eat anything and everything. You name it, they'd almost certainly been served it. Hence, when asked to describe a final meal, these chefs would probably go after something that reminded them of harder, leaner, simpler times before the glamour and pressure of superstardom. And there is a bit of that. Jamie Oliver chooses spaghetti all'arrabbiata. Both Gordon Ramsay and April Bloomfield, the British-born chef who made her name in New York at the Spotted Pig, want a roast Sunday lunch.

But they are in the minority. Thomas Keller, once regarded as the greatest chef in America for his nerdy, intense cooking at the French Laundry, wants half a kilo of osetra caviar, then *otoro*, the hyper-expensive fatty belly of the endangered bluefin tuna. He follows that with a roast chicken, which sounds rustic enough, but then he goes all in with a Brie with truffles. All of this is to be served with a 1983 vintage champagne. Masa Takayama, the king of New York sushi chefs, wants sashimi of the *fugu* (blowfish), famed for the toxins in its liver, which can kill you if the fish is not prepared properly. He also wants a risotto with white truffles and a blowfish-testicle pudding with a thousand-year-old balsamic vinegar. Maybe for Masa the bollocks of the blowfish really are a taste of the simple life, though God knows what he'd do if he was going for complicated. The New York chef Mario Batali lists a multi-course affair which even he describes as a 'shellfish extravaganza'.

For a reality check you have to look at the work of the New Zealand-born photographer Henry Hargreaves, an opponent of the death penalty. In 2013 he put together a portfolio of photographs recreating various real death-row dinners. Some seemed obvious. The serial killer John Wayne Gacy, convicted of thirty-three murders and executed by lethal injection in 1994, asked for fried shrimps and a bucket of Kentucky Fried Chicken. The Oklahoma bomber Timothy McVeigh went for a whole tub of mint chocolate ice cream. These could indeed be interpreted as attempts by troubled adults to reach back to the innocent comforts of childhood. More curious was the request of murderer and rapist Victor Feguer, who asked for just one olive, stone in. Many subsequently tried to work out what this request meant, what it signified (especially the inconvenience of the damn stone), while apparently failing to recognise that this was the choice of a man guilty of monstrous crimes. The weirdness of his last meal was as nothing compared to the appalling and abnormal way in which he had lived his life.

In 2012 the academic journal *Appetite*, which considers the impact of cultural, psychological and social issues on what we eat and drink, published a paper analysing 'death row nutrition'. The authors, Brian Wansink, Kevin Kniffin and Mitsuru Shimizu, looked at the contents of 247 last meals served in the US between 2002 and 2006, where the budget for the final meal ranged between $20 and $50, depending on the state. Some states allowed the food to be ordered in from nearby restaurants; others insisted it be made from what was in the prison store cupboard. Perhaps unsurprisingly, they found the average meal was a hefty 2,756 calories, which is more than the recommended daily intake for an adult male. The requests from death-row inmates in two states, Texas and Oklahoma, were for meals that were between 750 to 1,000 calories more than in most of the others. Four of them were 7,200 calories or more. (One person ordered a dozen pieces of fried chicken, two rolls with butter, mashed potato and gravy, two soft drinks, plus a pint each of strawberry and vanilla ice cream.) More strikingly, the average meal had 2.5 times the daily recommended serving of protein and fat. Chicken was the most popular meat, accounting for 37.3 per cent of requests, usually served deep-fried, followed by both hamburger and steak at just north of 20 per cent. Nearly 70 per cent wanted fried food. In pursuit of the familiar, there were a few requests for named brands. They wanted McDonald's and KFC. Sixteen per cent of those heading towards execution wanted to drink Coke. Curiously, three of them wanted Diet Coke. Maybe they just liked the taste.

Wansink, Kniffin and Shimizu are painfully aware that this impeccably academic paper could come across as mere prurience dressed up as intellectual endeavour. They acknowledge that talking about last meals has become 'increasingly fashionable in popular American culture', and so they are eager to give this ragbag of numbers a meaning. One of the conclusions they reach is that being made acutely aware of your impending death encourages overeating. They point to a 2009 paper from the Forum for Health Economics and Policy which looked at economic insecurity and its impact on eating habits. It reported that in the weeks immediately following the terrorist attacks of 11 September 2001, a significant proportion of the population reacted to the gloomy sense of unpredictability by eating more. There were increased weight gains across the population of Manhattan. Which is perhaps more interesting than it is surprising.

The authors are honest in admitting that while they have detailed information on what death-row inmates ordered, they have no idea whether they actually ate any of it. They do say, early on, that 21 per cent of the sample refused the offer of a last meal altogether. But rather than let that bring down the calorific average, they simply removed them from the study. Anecdotally, however, there is evidence that many death-row inmates reacted to the question of what they'd like to eat before they died much as I did when faced by the question in the abstract: by losing their appetite. In a 2014 paper for the *Journal of American Folklore* entitled 'Last Meals and the Crutch of Ritual', the American writer and academic Michael Owen Jones quotes a number of inmates and prison officials who report food being left uneaten in the hours before execution. (Most wretched is the story of Ricky Ray Rector. After shooting dead a police officer, he tried to shoot himself, but instead was left with severe brain damage and in a childlike state. When officials came to take him away for execution in 1992, they noted he had left his pecan pie. He told them he was saving it for 'later'.) In his 1990 book *Death Work: A Study of the Modern Execution Process*, the writer Robert Johnson says that prisoners generally 'eat little or nothing at all', and that 'your appetite goes with your hope'. So it really isn't just me, then.

There are other candidates for last meals. There are the suicidals, like Ernest Hemingway, who went for a New York strip steak, a baked potato, a Caesar salad and a glass of Bordeaux before shooting himself in the head. It sounds like a nice enough dinner, but is it unreasonable to suggest, given what he did afterwards, that this last meal was not an especially happy affair?

Then there are the terminally ill. With the moment of death uncertain, timing is an issue, as is the ability to eat. Very few last meals eaten by the dying are like that served to François Mitterrand, the president of the French republic, who died of cancer in 1996. His last meal started with foie gras, oysters and capon, the stations of the cross for the committed French gastronome. But all of that was merely an overture to the consumption of ortolan, a yellow-throated songbird, the eating of which was frowned upon by the majority of his fellow Frenchmen at the time and would eventually be made illegal. Even in a country which has always been ahead of the pack when it comes to ritualising dinner, the process of eating ortolan goes beyond what is strictly necessary. Traditionally, they should first be placed in the dark for a month, so that, thinking it is their night-time feeding period, they fatten themselves up. (Legend has it that the Romans saved on darkening cages by picking out their eyes, thus plunging them into darkness. One might think this would put the poor birds off their lunch, but presumably not or their owners wouldn't have done it.) Next, they are drowned in Armagnac. Finally, they are roasted for eight minutes, plucked and eaten whole, head and all, the idea being that the sharp bones puncture the inside of the mouth so that the diners' blood mingles with that of the bird. There can surely be no meal more sodden with Catholic ritual, with the relentless dance of sin and punishment. You are supposed to eat them with a napkin over your head so that the Lord may not see your sin, or so your fellow diners may not see you spitting out the bones. One or the other.

Which is more extraordinary: the details of the last meal or the fact that this was the last meal of an exceedingly ill man? Illness murders appetite. Medication blunts and steals taste buds. Entirely reasonable existential angst, a fear of the end, can fill the belly with nothing but lead. The grandiose Mitterrand might have been able to pull off this final, shameless flourish, but I am certain that, were I in that situation, I could not.

This may be because I have an example very close to me, one that casts a dark shadow over the lightness of gallows humour. In February 2014 my father Des, then eighty-five, started complaining of acute headaches. Within a few weeks he was in hospital, where he was diagnosed with a neurological condition which would have to be treated with a form of chemotherapy. The headaches caused are so violent and intense that we were warned the condition had a 25 per cent mortality rate through suicide. The doctors acknowledged the condition as literally insufferable. His intake of food dropped dramatically. In time they would get the pain under control, but it made little difference to his appetite. Then again, unlike his younger son, Des had never really been that interested in the variety of the table, and every greedy man needs someone like that in their lives. He wasn't so much disdainful of my appetites as bemused. It was useful for a long speech of mine on the joys of, say, the latest faux rustic French *paysanne* bistro to be met with the 'And?' of a raised eyebrow. Des was always there to remind me that there are actually more important things in life than lunch.

But then the simple pleasures would come along – well-made fish and chips, good chocolate, a salt-beef sandwich – and he would be in there with the best of them. Especially with the salt-beef sandwich. Though he was in no way religious, it linked him to a kind of Jewish community now all but lost. He was born in 1928, the same year as Mickey Mouse and talking pictures, amid the last gasp of Hackney's Jewish East End; long enough ago to remember an uncle from the old country who spoke only Yiddish and laughed at the punchlines to jokes my dad couldn't hope to understand. It was an Ashkenazi community with the smell of chicken fat in its hair.

Des travelled far from those beginnings, a serious schlep by taxi to the cherry-blossomed suburbs of north-west London. I do not idealise him: he had so many neuroses he must have bought them wholesale. But it drove me nuts that he never quite understood the scale of his achievements, for achievements they were. He had taken advantage of the promise of free higher education after National Service to train as an actor at the Guildhall School in London's City. He ended up in B-movies, was part of Anthony Quayle's company at Stratford-upon-Avon (a precursor to the Royal Shakespeare Company) and had taken a supporting role in the first television series of *Hancock's Half Hour*. His later careers were as a fashion PR, as my mother's manager and, most importantly, as a gifted artist, with the steadiest of hands and fiercest of eyes for detail, and whose work was still being exhibited in London's West End just months before his death. And yet through all this he never forgot where he had started. He still had a taste for a good salt-beef sandwich.

Within a few days of being admitted to hospital he was complaining about the food. It actually wasn't bad; it just wasn't what he needed. I was powerless to make him feel better, but this, I was sure, was something I could deal with. After all, if a restaurant critic couldn't feed his old dad, well, what was he for? I have a friend who runs a salt-beef bar called Monty's Deli, which does everything properly. They salt their own beef and soak it and boil it and cut it thick, and ask you if you want it fat on or fat off. It's now in east London, but back then it was in a railway arch in the south of the city. I went to Monty's Deli and asked for the makings: the salt beef, the bread, the mustard. I took it to the hospital, a food flat-pack waiting to be assembled, but it never came out of the bag. Des didn't want it. In truth, he didn't want to be here any more. He'd done an extraordinary job of living on for three years after my mother's death in 2010, and now he'd had enough. No bloody sandwich was going to do the job.

He made it home, ate very little and shrank into his clothes, so they looked as if they had once belonged to someone else, which in a way they had. He knew the end was close and he did not, at any point, start rhapsodising about what he should eat for his last meal. Des died a few weeks later, in the middle of the night, from a heart attack. It's not a romantic story. There's no foodie angle. It's just the way things happen and stop happening.

One of the secrets to a long, fulfilling life is not being dead, something I have tried hard to achieve. But dying can feel like an abstract notion. It's a concept rather than something tangible. I've always thought the best thing about artist Damien Hirst's 1991 piece, the whole shark suspended in a tank of formaldehyde, is its name: *The Physical Impossibility of Death in the Mind of Someone Living*. Thinking about no longer being here is hard. Still, we can try to put some meat on those mortal bones. Here, then, are my top three near-death experiences, from least to most serious.

It is the autumn of 1990 and I am in Palm Springs, California, reporting for the *Observer* on an attempt by the actor Ralph Waite, who played the patriarch in the long-running American TV series *The Waltons*, to win a seat in Congress as a Democrat. It's a tough challenge. Palm Springs is a manicured desert town of over-irrigated golf courses the colour of pool-table baize. There is outdoor air conditioning puffing billows of condensation into the hundred-degree heat. The hot, dusty sidewalks stink of money and entitlement and power. But this, I know, is not the only story in California's 37th District. Just down the road is Indio, a dirt-poor dormitory town, for the most part populated by the janitors and maids who serve the rich white folk up in Palm Springs. I want to get their view of Mr Waite's campaign for Congress.

I am out here working with a tiny French-born photographer called Catherine Leroy, who has already shown me the complex geography of her shrapnel-wound scars, souvenirs from her time covering the Vietnam War for *Life* magazine nearly twenty years before. She plainly finds Palm Springs bourgeois and dull. She has already alienated the apparently genial Waite, who, the day before, had thrown her out of his house for being too demanding.

She perks up at the idea of a trip to what she calls 'the ghetto'. As befits the first accredited journalist to participate in a combat parachute jump, she is well up for it. She drives us across to Indio, and on the edge of town spies a cluster of mobile homes the colour of rust, alongside a bunch of filthy, grey, breeze-block sheds. Without a hint of irony, this place is called Noble's Ranch, the poorest African American quarter of a very poor town. Many homes here do not have air-conditioning units, despite the desert heat, so their doors are open. We park up and walk over to where a guy is standing next to a supermarket trolley full of watermelons. He has a ghetto blaster to his ear. He tells me his name is Marvin. In my best, most pronounced English accent – I've been told it can be disarming – I ask him about Ralph Waite. He says, 'He ain't fighting for no one, man,' and 'There are people trying to buy this district up to turn it into a shopping mall. They want to move everyone out. What's he going to do for us?' I take furious notes. Leroy, just behind me, shoots off pictures. Marvin flinches at the whirr and click of the shutter. I raise my eyebrows at her to suggest she should ask permission. But this is a woman who has taken pictures of US soldiers mid-combat in Vietnam. She is in the zone, figuratively and, given her state of mind, possibly literally. She is back on the front line. She's been in places far heavier than this. She knows what she's doing.

Which is when Marvin asks for payment, money I cannot give. We do not pay for interviews.

Which is when he begins to advance upon me, big meaty hands balled, and I start to back away.

Which is when I notice Leroy is no longer behind me.

Which is when I think I see the flash of what I'm sure is a blade.

I am running now, and he is behind me, a big guy, thumping out the metres of concrete with his fat sneakered feet. Leroy has got into the car and is driving straight at me, which at first secures her in my mind as a complete nutter. Not only am I being chased, my colleague is looking to run me down. Somehow, at the last moment, she throws the car round, while simultaneously reaching across and throwing open the passenger door. I dive in head first and we drive off, the door still open, the cracked oatmeal concrete road flashing past below the open door. Marvin is still running at us, but he can't catch us now. Leroy is laughing. I am not.

It is the summer of 1984. I am seventeen years old and I am alone on a beach in Tangier, on Morocco's northern tip. The late afternoon is shading into dusk. I came here with six friends, our Interrail cards securing the forty-eight-hour train journey from Florence. A few days before we had sat down by the Duomo in the centre of Florence with the *Thomas Cook International Train Timetable*, the bible for all Interrailers. We wanted to work out what the most extreme, unlikely journey we could undertake would be. We had not long finished our A-levels, and we were collecting adventures, like autograph hunters filling the pages of a notebook with signatures. That summer I knew dozens of people who were filling the long gap between school and university by training their way across Europe. We saved on hotels by taking overnights and sleeping on the floors in the corridors; ten of us crammed into a compartment designed for six. We survived on cheap, sweaty, waxy cheese and bread with a crust like leather.

We knew that many of our friends were striking out for Brindisi, on Italy's southern tip, and the overnight ferry to Greece, but that seemed too predictable. We had studied the timetable and decided to head in exactly the opposite direction. We would head north to Provence, skirt the south of France, go through the rail-gauge change at Portbou, on the Spanish border, and then head down the entire length of Spain to Algeciras. An overnight stay with a relative of one of our party in the deep south, then the ferry to Tangiers. And here we now are, in a town where us impoverished backpackers can afford rooms in a four-star hotel on the beach.

I feel intrepid. I have travelled. So why not travel a little more? While my friends sleep or explore the narrow alleys behind the hotel, I go alone to the beach. Bobbing on the steel-grey waters a little way offshore is a diving platform. What fun. I would go for a swim, a proper grown-up bit of exercise with a destination.

I am fifteen minutes into the swim when I realise the mistake I have made. The diving platform is much bigger than I had thought, which means perspective and distance have played their tricks. I have completely underestimated the length of the swim. It is a quarter of a mile from the beach, perhaps more. Currents are pulling in different directions. The waves are getting up as an evening breeze kicks in, and I am tiring quickly. But I am now closer to the platform than to the shore. I stop for a moment and tread water, looking back at the empty beach. Behind it, lights are coming on in the restaurants and bars that cluster the corniche. Life is continuing. The pavements are crowded. Not a soul knows I am out here.

I turn and push for the platform, and somehow, ten minutes later, drag myself up onto it. I sit there shivering, despite the warmth of the North African winds, trying to drag air into my exhausted lungs and looking back at the beach. While I can see the people thronging the front, I can't hear them. Which means they cannot hear me. I try shouting anyway, but soon give up. I look around to see if there are any boats passing by, but there are none. I know I have no choice. I take a deep breath, drop off the side of the platform and push for the shore. The waves are no longer a gentle bob and heave. They are peaks and troughs that make the beach disappear from view. I try to focus on the lights, the symbols of undramatic life continuing, but they are rising and falling as I do and disappearing behind walls of water that, at their tops, shade now into a sky fading to the colour of ink. All I can do is kick. And kick. And kick again.

My legs are just one long length of cramping muscle. My shoulders are sore and with every third stroke I am getting a mouthful of water. My eyes sting and a nausea – part seawater, part fear – is closing my throat. Now there are only the lights and the surf and the sea and the wind and the salt and the words 'Not like this.'

Twenty minutes later, my feet drag against the sandy seabed. Now the balls of my feet are digging in. I can hear the surf breaking on the beach. I crawl the last five feet, clawing at the sand until I am up and out of the water. I turn and, in the darkness, drop onto my arse, my back to the corniche, looking out at the platform I have come from, my arms resting on my knees. I drop my head and sob.

It is a few weeks later, and I am back home in north-west London, driving across suburbia to a friend's house. I take a roundabout a little too fast and, as I do so, a small object drops onto my feet. I glance down. It is my brass dope pipe, tied up in a small square of soft leather. I have taken to stowing it in a tight void where the steering column meets the dashboard of this Volvo 340, in case I should be stopped by the police for speeding. I've already been suspended from school for dope-smoking, and that was messy enough. Courtesy of my mother's fame as an agony aunt, the media had gone to town on me: front-page headlines reading 'Problem Son of Problem Page Claire' and 'Claire's Agony' and the rest. They'd given me the works. I didn't want to add a criminal conviction to the charge sheet.

I must have left the pipe there the night before. Today I don't need it. I may be a devoted stoner, but the person I'm visiting doesn't smoke and I can go without. Better not to be carrying it at all, and I'm not that far from home. At the next roundabout I go all the way round and turn back on myself. I decide to take a short cut through the local suburban estate, via the grandly named Mall. It's a broad road with wide verges, fringed by substantial semi-detached houses. It has a nice gentle curve which I know can be taken at speed, and I am in a hurry. Except it turns out it can't be taken at speed, not today. It has not long stopped raining after a dry stretch and the road is greasy. I take the bend at around fifty-five miles an hour because I am seventeen years old and an idiot.

I know within a fraction of a second that I no longer have control of the car, that my steer to the right is doing nothing to alter the vehicle's direction. The line is all wrong. The kerb is advancing on me. And then, all of a sudden, I can see grass going under the car. I didn't feel the bump, but it's obvious I have mounted the verge. It doesn't seem to have slowed me.

I hit a concrete lamp post smack in the centre of the bonnet. The car leaps up into the air and does a 180-degree turn, landing half on the pavement and half in someone's front garden, balanced on a low garden wall. There is a deep V in the bonnet. The distance between the two ends of the front bumper, where it crumpled, will turn out to be just a hand span. I sit in silence for a moment, then stumble from the car. The car hisses and steams and smells of oil. The windscreen is cracked. The lamp post is leaning at an angle of forty-five degrees, as if trying to decide whether to fall over. I am wearing tight stretch jeans that day of a sort no fat boy should ever choose. No matter. Under the stress of the impact, of my knees pulling up to my chest, they have exploded and now dangle around me in rags. Otherwise I appear to be fine (save for mild whiplash, which will be diagnosed the next day).

A few people have come out of their houses to see what the noise was or, to be more exact, to confirm what they already knew. This corner is apparently notorious for this kind of crash. A man comes and stands next to me. He says, 'A Volvo.'

I frown. The make of destroyed car in front of us doesn't seem that relevant to me, but it turns out that it really is. These are the days before universal car safety, before almost every make and model came with crush zones and airbags as standard. The Volvo I was driving was ahead of the field. 'That and a Rover,' the man says. 'The only two models of car that you can survive a crash like that in. Anything else and you'd be dead.'

A police car has arrived, with a fire engine and ambulance not far behind. I am in a daze but I have space in my head for one thought: I will never drive anything other than a Volvo. For the next thirty years I keep to that.

A lot of thoughts went through my head during these three experiences. There was the accelerated terror of the car crash, the slow-motion terror of my fight against the North African waves, the raging paranoia and anxiety of my encounter in the Californian desert (when, in truth, I probably wasn't in much danger at all, although the adrenaline junky accompanying me wished we were). I thought about my parents and my friends and, in California, my then girlfriend, now my wife. I thought about all the things I wanted to do and hadn't. I thought about my own stupidity, my complicity in my own downfall. Each of these events convinced me that I had a pronounced ability to do stupid things. To be fair – if only to me, and only briefly – what links them all is my age. I was on the very edge of adulthood, there but not quite, an age when errors of judgement are a necessary part of the human condition.

Not once did I think about food. Not once did I think, 'If only I'd eaten properly last night,' or 'If I'd known this was coming, I'd have been more serious about dinner,' or 'Oh, for one more spare rib.' And afterwards I didn't have much appetite either. A real brush with death can impact upon you in many ways. But take it from me: it doesn't make you hungry.

* * *

The bottom line is this: last suppers are a brilliant idea. They are the culinary idea to end all ideas. But they are wasted on the very people who are the most eligible for them. The more I thought about this, the more it seemed to me extremely unfair. I was excluded from enjoying this blissful meal by the piffling detail of not actually being that close to death.

And so I came up with a plan: I would stage my own last supper now, when I was fit and well and able to enjoy it.

Because this really is the right time.

While my own death may not be imminent, I have been forced in recent years to think about my mortality. 2019 marks my twentieth anniversary as a restaurant critic, a job I took deep into both my career and my thirties. I have earned part of my living courtesy of thousands of meals, both expensive and less so. I have given my body to my job, and it hasn't always thanked me for it. But there are upsides too, not least the massive privilege of having food memories that stretch across years and continents: some good, some bad, some bizarre, all of them perfect material from which to construct a final meal.

The long service – I ate many of those lunches and dinners so you wouldn't have to – also means one thing: I am no longer a young man. It is not simply that my beard is the colour of roadside slush mid-thaw, that I am now beyond fifty and aware there is almost certainly less to go than there has been. Both my parents are gone. While my mother lay dying a few years ago I ghost-wrote her last words, another ritual of departure for which the dying are rarely match fit. The memory of my father's last salt-beef sandwich, offered but never eaten, hangs heavy.

With both of them gone, I am now unavoidably adult. There is no one else in the waiting room ahead of me. I also have that other marker of adulthood, a family. There's my wife of over twenty-five years, Pat, whom I met when I was at university and still a teenager, and I have my two boys – Eddie, who as I write is nineteen, and Dan, who is fifteen. Neither is fully launched into adulthood, but both are there on the launch pad, listening to various versions of the countdown. This is surely the perfect moment in which to take stock. And how better to do so than by coming up with a definitive answer to the question I have been asked, and dodged, so many times? At least this way, when the moment to take my leave actually does come, I won't be left feeling that there's unfinished gastronomic business. I will have done the final meal properly.

Much more importantly, though, the idea presents me with the opportunity to indulge in one of the rarely discussed but true pleasures of the table: anticipation. Anybody with even just a passing interest in lunch will have daydreamed about what it will be, thought in detail about the process of getting the ingredients, then preparing and cooking and bringing them to the table. I can imagine my way through a whole meal to come, stopping every now and then to edit and improve. With my plan to build and then serve my last supper I was giving myself the licence to dream for a whole year. And not only dream. I would have to test and taste and test again. I would need a main course, but also something to start. And something to finish. And maybe an extra course as well. Or even two. There would be side dishes. And bread. And butter. The right kind of butter, the stuff you can eat neat without the support of bread. And wine. Quite a lot of wine. Quite a lot of different kinds of wine.

But even dreamers need rules, or if not rules, then a code by which to live. I realised early on that the creation of my last meal would be the coming together of all my memories, hopes and appetites, shameful or otherwise. I was not creating the perfect meal or even *my* perfect meal. Perfection suggests balance and poise. I had no intention of being balanced and poised. I would be bloody outrageous and over the top. I would refuse to think about consequences or the next morning, for when you eat your last supper there isn't meant to be a next anything. In this I would be lying to myself, because of course I would live on, unless something went terribly wrong (or, depending on your point of view, terribly right). I wouldn't even be looking for the perfect ingredients. They might turn out to be so, but only accidentally. Or because I'm burdened with exquisite taste. Happily, this journey can end only one way: with a set-piece meal surrounded by friends. It will be a major event. After all, how many dinners are there which really are a lifetime in the planning? How many dinners are there which, through each course, attempt to distil the memories of the person who organised it? Will it be a massively expanded version of Proust's madeleine, a journey through my life one course at a time? Or will it, like the banquet at the end of *La Grande Bouffe*, be a complete overload of fat and salt and sugar? Will it, in short, be an obscenity? Perhaps it will demand our attention simply because of how long it took in the planning. Or will it simply be dinner? Indeed, is it even possible to capture the essence of one's life through food?

The only way to find out is to start cooking.

Which reminds me. By now you are hungry – or should be. You want something to eat, so here's a recipe. I'll give you a few of these as we go along. They won't be a part of the final last supper; think of them as something to keep you going. This one is a dark, sticky take on *huevos rancheros*. It's weirdly satisfying to make and even more fun to eat. It should also take your mind off the whole death thing.

Chorizo, tomatoes and eggs

Feeds three to four as a snack or just you if you've had a crappy day and are wondering what the point of it all really is.

INGREDIENTS

One medium onion, chopped

250g cooking chorizo, skinned (piquant or not, depending on taste)

Two 400g tins of chopped tomatoes. Buy the expensive ones if it makes you feel better about yourself, but the cheap ones will do the job

200g grated cheddar

100g torn-up mozzarella

Three eggs

Bunch of coriander

200g jar of pickled jalapeños

Heat the oven to 200°C.

Gently fry the chopped onion in olive oil in a deep-sided frying pan until soft.

Break the chorizo into thumbnail-sized nuggets and fry with the onion.

When the chorizo is browned, add the tomatoes, mix all the ingredients together, turn down the heat and let it simmer gently on the hob for twenty minutes or so until almost all the liquid has been boiled off. Stir occasionally to stop it sticking to the bottom of the pan.

Decant half the mixture into an oven-proof casserole dish. Cover with half the mixed cheese. Add the rest of the tomato and chorizo mixture and cover with the remaining cheese.

Put in the oven and leave until the cheese has started to brown and the liquid around the edges is bubbling.

JAY RAYNER'S LAST SUPPER

Take the dish out of the oven and turn on the grill. Meanwhile, crack the three eggs across the top. Put under the grill for about five minutes or until the eggs are cooked through.

Scatter with the coriander and the pickled jalapeños.

Eat this by scooping with tortilla chips. Get a bag of Doritos if you like. They do the job perfectly and I won't judge you. Actually, if you can't be fagged to do the cooking, just get the Doritos. That will deal with the whole hunger issue, and it's much easier to carry on reading this book while eating them.

Bread and Butter

My mother wasn't like all the other mothers. She worked. In the late 1960s and early '70s this was less common in our cherry-blossomed corner of north-west London than it should have been. She disguised it well. The office was at home, a narrow corridor of parquet-floored space, just beyond the stairs; a room so narrow that once, when the gerbil's cage was stowed in there, it was able to reach through the mesh and eat her woollen cardigan as it hung over the back of her chair. She typed on, oblivious. The noise of manual typewriters filled the space from first until last as she and her rotating team of secretaries worked to stem the unending flow of letters sent in to her various magazine and newspaper problem pages. Tissue-thin airmail paper or tattered pages ripped from spiral-bound notebooks, covered in an anguished scrawl, came in. Cool, typewritten letters, the chaos of life tided up courtesy of typography, went out. They were full of comfort and empathy, assurance that the writer was not alone, that their emotional or sexual problem was not unique.

She was rarely at the school gate. There were au pairs for that, Scandinavian girls with hair the colour of corn or slightly baffled dark-eyed women from Italy. My parents were never convinced by the idea of the British au pair. Such an exotic title should be applied to someone not from here. I think she preferred a language barrier. It made life simpler. There was just the one Scottish au pair who told my mother, when I was eighteen months old, that she was 'missing the best years of [my] life' by working so much. Claire replied that if she thought that were true, she'd 'slit his throat now'. I didn't resent her absence, or at least not much. She was both there and not there. She was, like all writers, lost a little inside her own head, in no hurry to find a way out.

She could escape if she wanted to, though. I knew when Claire was in work mode: she had her glasses on. When she took them off she was my mother again, and in my first food memory she is without them. I am three or four years old and am in bed, ill, tucked in under sheets and blankets. This is before my mother's first big book deal in 1972, which she spent on duvets for the whole family and on freeing my father from the day job in public relations he so hated. What my dad did during the day was of little interest to me. The duvets, when they turned up, were a revelation.

For now, though, I am under the blankets. I am slightly overheated and a little itchy, but it's okay because I am being fed something from a cup that I very much like: still-warm crushed boiled eggs and torn pieces of thickly buttered toast, mashed together. Even now I can recall the light bounce of the egg white and the crumbliness of the yolk, softened to a paste by the generous amount of salty, melting butter, and then the two-sided crunch of the squares of toast buried within. It will have been white bread from inside a greaseproof wrapper, probably purchased from the J. Sainsbury on Kenton Road, which back then was still a department store with counter service.

It makes sense that my first food memory should involve bread, because it is also one of humanity's first processed foods. Today, that 'P' word is a culinary expletive. If it's processed, it's bad. Whatever made it most virginal and pure has been taken from it by us. It has been denatured, as though we have actively violated the raw product's 'goodness' in pursuit of shameful longevity and, therefore, cheapness. But that is to misunderstand the very food processes that underpin humanity. So many of our foods are processed before we get anywhere near eating them: milk into cheese, grapes into wine, fruit into jam. Even raw beef, hung until it is tender enough to be chewed, is processed. The American food historian Rachel Laudan explained this in her insightful essay 'A Plea for Culinary Modernism', first published in *Gastronomica I* in February 2001. Our ancestors, she says, were forever looking for ways to make nature's bounty edible. Or, as Laudan puts it, 'to make food tasty, safe, digestible and healthy, our forebears bred, ground, soaked, leached, curdled, fermented, and cooked naturally occurring plants and animals until they were literally beaten into submission'. It is a line I never tire of quoting.

That processing started with grain. There is evidence of grass seeds first having been ground down some 100,000 years ago, about 90,000 years before we domesticated grasses for their seeds. In that case it was sorghum. Anthropologists continue to argue back and forth as to whether we first ground the seeds down to make porridge, beer or bread, but either way the latter was one of the first processed foodstuffs. Grinding grains removed the inedible husk and released the protein and carbohydrate contained within the grass seeds. This gave us the basis for a sustainable diet, which makes the swivel-eyed claims of the Paleo diet lobby – that we should eat no carbs because our ancient Palaeolithic forebears ate only hunks of raw, bloody mammoth – a little tricky to defend.

Bread was one of humanity's first foods, and it was also one of this particular human's first foods, as it was for my own children once they graduated to solids. Bread is tactile. It can be placed in small hands to be rotated and torn. It can be stuffed between lips and chewed to a pleasing mulch. It is not just one texture, but many. And it is an obvious vehicle for brilliant things, such as butter spread thickly, melting through the holes and crevices that develop as a yeast culture releases bubbles of carbon dioxide within the dough when it's proving.

My early childhood memories are of white bread, cut thin and toasted the right shade of golden, with butter pooling to the edges. This was in the days when we had a cooked breakfast every single morning: fried eggs, bacon, white toast the colour of a sunset. Even now I still find this amazing. A cooked breakfast. Every. Single. Morning. The grease glinting in the sunlight. Until just a few years before I was born my mother had been a nurse. She knew a thing or two about health. This, it seems, was the way we did breakfast in the late 1960s and '70s.

23

Until we didn't. At some point in the mid-1970s my mother discovered fibre. She proposed a form of the F-Plan diet to her readers long before anybody else had given it a name. Eventually, she would take to diluting bran tablets, like mini-hockey pucks, in a glass of orange juice, so it went from a bright Technicolor to something that looked like it had already been through the digestive tract. Then the bread changed too. The white disappeared. Now we ate wholemeal, something coarse, heavy and dense. The butter either sat on top of it or sank through so it would become soggy and claggy, like a Fermanagh peat bog. At home bread was rarely pleasurable; out of the home I came to associate mass-produced white bread and its higher sugar content with the forbidden. It was filthy, something to be both enjoyed and a little ashamed of. In time, though, I grew up, abandoned my guilt around food and developed a modicum of good taste. I discovered sourdough.

My plan is to find the very best sourdough in the world. All sourdoughs are made in the same way: with a 'live starter', a mixture of flour and water that ferments with natural yeasts and bacteria from the air to produce lactic acid (and, if you leave it long enough, ascetic acid for a full-on, teeth-baring tang). It's pretty straightforward but has somehow become food item as cult, a standard-bearer for words like 'artisan' and 'craft' and 'individuality'. Sourdough is the small, nerdy, self-absorbed world of food sticking it to the corporatist industrial food complex, one loaf at a time. Its advocates will whisper stories about sourdough starters that have lived for decades, that have been passed from grandmother to grandson and crossed continents. A loaf of sourdough can easily have more traceable heritage than I have.

I got into it around 2012, when the Brick House Bakery opened in my corner of south-east London and started selling their product at a newly launched farmers' market practically at the bottom of my road. They make a domed, golden-crusted loaf which they call a Country White and I call bloody lovely. It has a wide, springy, open crumb and a crisp crust, and it tastes deep and encouraging, without being too sour. It is good to eat by itself and toasted with butter and Marmite and with cheese melted through the holes. It makes terrible sandwiches because it is impossible to cut thin, but who needs sandwiches? I wanted bread to have with dinner, something I could tear at nonchalantly like the sophisticated diner I considered myself to be. I could sneer for England at self-absorbed foodism, the culture of 'sourcing' ingredients rather than buying them, of venerating the small-scale over the large-scale, as if size of production were more important than quality. And then I would go and buy a Brick House Country White and somehow think myself a better person.

It wasn't the first notable sourdough in London, not by a long chalk. Chef Fergus Henderson's famed 'nose to tail' restaurant, St John, had run a major sourdough baking operation from the moment it opened in 1994, which eventually led to a stand-alone bakery. They needed something to toast and serve alongside their famed roast bone marrow. In 2002 the French bakers Poilâne introduced their huge grey boulder of a loaf to Britain. They made headlines because each one cost £9.60. I bought some and made all the right, obsessive noises about it being a living thing that changes as it ages, that it weighed much more and lasted much longer than a normal loaf, thus justifying the price. But the truth is I found eating Poilâne tiresome. It was relentless and I wasn't sure my teeth were up to the job. A loaf of Poilâne was scary.

Anyway, we didn't need French imports. Britain was soon in the grip of what felt like a sourdough war. The bakers wouldn't have characterised it as such. Being an artisan baker was too noble a craft to be besmirched by grubby competition. But everyone knew there was a fight going on out there. The bakeries had names like Bertinet and Dusty Knuckle, Bread Ahead and Moore Artisan. For a while people talked in hushed tones about the bread being made by an angry Swede who liked to argue with the customers at his restaurant in west London. Then the chatter moved to the bread coming out of the kitchen at the restaurant attached to Bonham's, the auctioneers. When the Fat Duck relaunched after a refurbishment in 2015, the new menu included a bread course. It involved thick slices of their own freshly baked sourdough. It had to; nothing else would do.

Around the same time, over in Bellevue, just outside Seattle, an entire laboratory was being brought to bear on the subject. In 2000 Nathan Myhrvold, the former chief technology officer at Microsoft, had left the company and used his vast wealth to found Intellectual Ventures, a high-tech workshop for the exploitation of patents and inventions. Myhrvold had long had an interest in food; while still at Microsoft he'd taken a sabbatical to obtain a culinary diploma in France. It was only a matter of time, then, before he turned his resources to his lifelong obsession. He created a food lab inside Intellectual Ventures and in 2011 self-published *Modernist Cuisine: The Art and Science of Cooking*. It was a five-volume work costing hundreds of dollars which investigated what was going on in the kitchen when we cook, right down to the molecular level, and proposed a bunch of hacks to improve the outcomes. It sold over 200,000 copies, despite the price. Soon, working with Francisco Migoya, recruited from the Culinary Institute of America, he turned his attention to baking. *Modernist Bread* was meant to be a couple of volumes.

It didn't turn out like that. One day, in response to a few enquiries, they sent me a copy. It arrived in a cardboard box that didn't make the delivery man happy. It had run to five hardback, large-format volumes, plus a technical manual, and weighed as much as a hefty five-year-old who should get more exercise and lay off the pies. The section on sourdough went on for dozens of pages. One evening I spoke to Migoya over the phone. Bread, he said, was an extraordinary subject to investigate because at base it was just four ingredients: flour, water, salt and yeast. 'And yet it's one of the most complex food systems that exist.' Perhaps because of that people attach intense values to it. 'They talk about authentic recipes. But what does authentic even mean? If authentic means old, then I'm here to tell you that old bread is awful. I know, because I made a whole bunch of old breads.'

As to sourdough, 'It's all anybody wants to talk to me about. I think it's down to the mythology around the starter.' There is, he says, a myth that the older the starter, the better. 'It's a cool story. Grandma passes on a starter on your wedding day. But it's not true. If I stored my starter in a different room every month, it would make a different bread. I would call it the finest expression of locavorism because it's the result of what's in the air.' It's not the wild yeast, he says. It's the lactic acid bacteria, which outnumber the yeast by a hundred to one. I ask if he thinks their method – making dozens of different versions of a type of bread – has resulted in the ideal sourdough recipe. 'Yes,' he says. 'I think it has.' The problem with so many of the hip modern sourdoughs, given their moment in the media sun on Instagram, is that they are made with a highly moist dough. This is very difficult to work with for the amateur cook. 'And it has a very open crumb. It's very hard to make sandwiches with it.' I tell him I will be coming soon to the US, and we make arrangements for me to visit the Modernist Cuisine lab. He wouldn't be there, he said – ironically, he'd be visiting London – but members of his team would happily show me their ideal sourdough.

One night a few years ago I stopped breathing. My lungs stopped inflating and deflating and my broad plateau of a chest fell still. I was not dead, not yet at least, but my body was flirting with the idea. It was imitating the outward signs of the end of life.

I don't know which night this was, nor which year. Later, when I finally had a name for it, I would discover that my body could pull off this morbid act of imitation more than seventy times an hour. As I rolled deep into sleep my throat would relax, my airways narrow and my breathing halt. It's called sleep apnoea, and it doesn't just imitate death. It can cause it too. People with untreated sleep apnoea are more prone to have a heart attack, are three times more likely to have a stroke and have three times the risk of premature death. The condition contributed greatly to the death of the actress Carrie Fisher, aged just sixty, in 2016.

At this point I do not have sleep apnoea, because no name has been attached to it yet. I am just a snorer, from a long line of them. When I was a child my mother worked a punishing schedule, so I thought little of it that most evenings when she was at home, she would fall asleep on the sofa and snore, a huge bass rumble that could shake the light fittings. Later, in adulthood, I realised that my parents occasionally slept apart, my father shifting off to the spare room because he could not be bothered to try waking her.

This generation of the family is more democratic. My snoring keeps Pat awake. Sometimes she clears off to the spare bed; sometimes I go. We share the disruption. The impact of ageing creeps up slowly, like high cloud coming in to fill a once clear sky on a summer's day. These separate sleeping arrangements, the emptying of the marital bed, are an occasional occurrence at first, and then a regular one, and will eventually become a constant. But I don't quite notice until Pat and I acknowledge that this really wasn't the plan, what with being married to each other and all. It really isn't very friendly. I've often read celebrity profiles in which the subjects proudly boast about their extremely civilised separate sleeping arrangements. I've always thought, 'How bloody miserable is that?' Now, by default, we are one of those couples.

Pat tells me that sometimes I appear to stop breathing. Sometimes, she says, my body bucks and jumps as I start breathing again, as if I've suddenly remembered that there's something I should be doing. Perhaps, she says, it might be worth seeking a little medical advice. I point out that apart from the whole separate sleeping thing, I suffer no ill effects. I still work a full-on schedule. I don't pass out at my desk. Okay, I sometimes fall asleep on the sofa in the evenings, two glasses of mediocre Sauvignon Blanc to the bad, but which middle-aged man doesn't do that?

Even so, she says.

I agree to do as I'm told. I make it sound like I'm doing it for Pat, but deep down I know that's not the case. Something is up.

It's one of those sunny San Francisco days when the sunlight has a clear, crystalline quality which makes everything look like it has been outlined in felt-tip pen. I am crossing the city in search of my bread epiphany. As far as I can tell, there is nowhere else to be but here. French bakers first came to San Francisco in the nineteenth century to help feed the prospectors seeking their fortune in the gold rush. They brought with them their own way of making bread, which became synonymous with the city. It's so much a part of San Francisco's culinary culture that in the 1970s, when scientists isolated the strain of natural bacteria responsible for the bread's sour flavour, they called it *Lactobacillus sanfranciscensis*, thinking it was unique to the Bay Area. It wasn't; it later turned up in bread all over the world. But it helped secure San Francisco's extreme sense of superiority as far as bread is concerned.

Sourdough toast menus are a big thing in this city, in cafes staffed by men with sculpted beards, the ceilings criss-crossed with industrial ducting. At a cafe called Outerlands in Ocean Beach I try the $4 slice of toast. It's two inches thick and freighted with butter, cinnamon, sugar and meaning. It is the humblest of foods turned luxury item. There is a distinct sour tang beneath the sugar. A few doors up another place charges me $6 for toast with butter and marmalade, though it is at least two slices. Back in town at The Mill, which was set up by Josey Baker, a victim of nominative determinism if ever there was one, I am charged $6 for a single slice of thick toast piled with their strawberry jam. I like the jam. I like the jam very much. The toast itself is dense and heavy and has a crust that dentists must love for all the potential work it might offer.

Eventually, I make it to Tartine Manufactory on Alabama Street, in the city's Mission district. Right now, this space with its high ceilings and rough-and-ready tables is ground zero in the San Francisco sour-dough movement, a veritable bread Mecca. The original, much smaller Tartine was founded over on Guerrero Street in 2002 by a tall, rangy, laid-back, bearded Texan – in the world of sourdough, beards are prac-tically obligatory – called Chad Robertson. Back in the 1990s he had eaten a life-changing grilled-cheese sandwich, made with bread created by a baker called Richard Bourdon, who was based in the Berkshires of Massachusetts. 'I had never tasted bread like it,' Robertson tells me now, as we sit at a table in his crowded cafe. 'A sandwich on good bread changes everything.'

Plates of his bread are delivered to us. Some are spread with bur-rata – the most immature of cheeses, which is gently sinking into the holes – then laid with peppery rocket and marinated wild mushrooms. Other slices arrive toasted alongside slabs of roasted bone marrow, baked beneath a rust-coloured 'burnt end xo sauce', which sounds like a good food idea, squared. I adore XO sauce, the intensely savoury Chinese condiment made with dried shrimp and sugar. I love burnt ends, the rib tips that darken during the low and slow US BBQ pro-cess. I can't quite work out how these two things have come together, but the result is meaty and sweet and savoury and can be my friend. I scoop out jewels of the blissful XO sauce-smeared hot marrow and dollop it onto the toast. There is crunch and then sour and the encour-agement of something hot and lightly gelatinous.

Robertson freely admits Bourdon had a 'guru-like quality' and that he swiftly asked to become his apprentice. Bourdon agreed. It was with Bourdon that he learnt about the culture of the living 'mother', of the righteous interplay of wild yeasts and lactic bacte-ria. He learnt to make all sorts of breads, but when he eventually opened Tartine it was the sourdough everyone talked about. Why, I ask, between scooping more nuggets of hot bone marrow onto more of the toast, had that particular bread become such a thing in San Francisco? 'I think it's the climate,' he says. 'It's the perfect temper-ature here. Not too hot, mostly cool.' He is watching me eat. I try not to feel too self-conscious, though pure greed is winning out over social awkwardness.

Like Migoya, Robertson is amused by how moist-lipped and emotional people get over the concept of the starter, or 'mother'; how they imbue their bread, or the process of its making, with a living, breathing personality because of the wild yeast. 'A mother dying isn't such a big deal,' he says. 'I can always make another one. All that happens if you maintain it over a longer period is it becomes more predictable.' I ask what his plans for the future are. He has just returned from opening a Tartine in South Korea. In what may come as a shock to those who worship Robertson for his artisan status, he tells me he is setting up a unit in Los Angeles which will increase production by a factor of ten, using robots to get the loaves into the high ovens.

I look up from the toast gripped between my greasy, eager fingers and blink. 'Los Angeles? But I thought you said climate was vital.'

Robertson shrugs. 'Air conditioning.'

A couple of days later, I take a cab out to Bellevue, a bridge-crossing away from Seattle, to the cluttered laboratories that are home to Intellectual Ventures. The space given over to Modernist Cuisine is on the first floor, past the metal skeleton of a dinosaur, built to prove its tail would have whipped faster than the speed of sound. It's just up the stairs from the functioning version of Charles Babbage's difference engine, arguably the world's first computer. Babbage designed it in 1822, but never managed to build one. That didn't happen until the 1980s, when one was built for London's Science Museum. The only other one in the world is here, tucked away down the corridor, commissioned and paid for by Nathan Myhrvold. It must have cost a fortune, which is exactly what Myrhvold has.

The Modernist Cuisine lab is a random-looking collection of benches piled with cooking equipment, both professional and domestic. Along the back wall are stoves, including a wood-fired oven. At the moment they are working on the definitive pizza book. There are piles of other people's pizza recipe books, and in one corner they are trying to photograph tomato sauce bubbling away, though actually recording it on film is tricky; they're experimenting with firing air through it and then capturing the eruption with a superfast shutter speed. This is what they do every day at Modernist Cuisine. They play with their food. They have agreed to break off from pizza research for the morning to show me their bread.

Migoya and Myhrvold have hired restaurant-trained cooks to work here. One of their research and development chefs is a tall, blocky, Asian American guy called Johnny Zhu. He leads me to a glass-fronted, temperature-controlled cupboard which is kept at a steady 55°F. It's where they store their live starters, often known by the French term 'levain'. 'At the top we have a rye sourdough starter,' Zhu says. It has a label bearing the name Ryan Seacrest, the US television host and producer. 'Of course we name them. It's a rye sourdough, so Ryan.' Okay. The one at the bottom is called Sir Yeast a Lot and was started over four years ago using yoghurt.

He takes out the one at the top. It's called Levain James, a play on the name of the American basketball player LeBron James. Zhu takes a portion of the starter and adds flour and water. 'We use a 65 per cent hydration. So to a kilo of flour we add 650ml of water. Chad Robertson does an 85 per cent hydration. That makes his dough much wetter and harder to work with and produces that much more open crumb.' To this he adds diastatic malt powder – 'It speeds up the enzyme reaction.' Now he probes his dough with a pH meter, which records its acidity on a scale from one to seven. 'If it measured one, it would be pure acetic acid,' he says, watching the digital readout climb, like he's taking the bread's temperature. I ask Zhu if he had a baking background before coming here. 'No, I'd never baked anything. But you learn. With each bread in the book we did hundreds of versions.' Our bread has a pH of 4.15. 'Gentle and very pleasant,' he says with a nod.

Not that I'm going to find out. Because naturally enough, here's one they made earlier. Or, to be more exact, three they made earlier. There's a classic sourdough. Alongside it is one made with caramelised farrow grains, which has a sweet-savoury, occasionally crunchy texture. Next to that is a third made with a fungus that grows on corn kernels. To go with the corn-fungus sourdough is a dish of what they call *mole* butter. *Mole* – pronounced 'mol-ay' – refers to the extraordinary Mexican condiment-cum-sauce made by using dozens of herbs and spices and controlled burning to produce deep, rich chocolate and earth tones. Here, they've whipped it into butter and scattered it with toasted pumpkin seeds. I'm touched they've gone to all this trouble, and slightly overwhelmed. The butter is a flavour bomb, a whack around the chops with fats and umami. It's all the very best things, and I dredge through it with lumps of their dark, earthy bread.

I have to draw myself away to try the standard sourdough. It has a tight crumb, which I can see is useful for sandwich-making. It's not as absurdly sour as some of those I tried in San Francisco. It's extremely serviceable and very well made indeed. I am certain it's reliable and that the recipe works. But it doesn't move me. In constructing my last supper I'm not in the business of finding the perfect example of each ingredient for the table. It's about the ones that mean something to me. This loaf of sourdough is probably the product of more nerdy study and consideration than almost any other loaf of bread ever baked. But admiring it is not the same as loving it. Plus, it's being shouted down by the whole *mole* butter thing, which is brilliant but way too rich to be allowed onto my table. It's an ecstatic culinary punch in the teeth. In one of my restaurant reviews I'd joke about it being the sort of thing you'd want to take into a room with a consenting adult, but this butter would distract you from recherché sex-food games. I slather another piece of bread with the butter and think very carefully about all the breads I have ever loved.

*   *   *

It was just after I had eaten the greatest bagel of my life that I was invited to witness the coming of the Messiah. These events weren't related, save that they happened in the same place, and that the experience of the bagel roots me to the memory. This is what the best foods do – they act as a time machine. It was February 1993, and I had been sent to New York to cover the aftermath of the riots that had taken place eighteen months before in Crown Heights, Brooklyn, between the African American community and the Lubavitch Hasidic Jews. A seven-year-old black boy, Gavin Cato, had been killed by a speeding car driven by a Hasidic Jew who had then tried to flee the scene. In the four days of rioting that followed during that hot August, a rabbinical student called Yankel Rosenbaum had been stabbed to death. The pavement where he fell was later chipped away so that the concrete stained with his blood could be buried with him, as was the custom. I had arrived just after the trials of all those accused in both killings had ended in acquittals. It was a fierce political, racial and social mess. My job was to talk to all sides and make sense of it.

I had interviews with the key players booked but I wanted to get a sense of the place, so at dusk on a very cold Sunday afternoon, a few hours after I arrived, I went for a walk around the neighbourhood and found myself outside a spartan coffee shop. I was cold but also hungry. I was jet-lag hungry, hollowed out by the passage through time and space. And there was something else too: a kind of homesickness brought on by familiarity. The Lubavitch are an extremist Hasidic sect. The biblical-style garb – frock coat, wide-brimmed black hats – looked anachronistic even when they first started wearing it in eighteenth-century Belorussia. But many of them are, like me, Ashkenazi Jews from Eastern Europe. The faces around me were so familiar. Everybody I saw on those streets and in this cafe looked like a possible relative. I am a godless Jew. I follow no ritual and I have no time for a deity that is such a picky eater. But that doesn't stop me identifying those who come from where I come from. I was a long way from home, and yet not. In the cafe I ordered a bagel with lox – smoked salmon – and cream cheese. I recall nothing about the filling.

But the bagel! That I remember. The world-famous New York bagel is nothing like those served in Jewish bakeries in London. New York bagels tend to be big and fluffy and quite savoury; I've sometimes wondered whether they are made with boiled dough in the traditional style. Those made to this day in London's East End are much tighter, denser and sweeter. The one I was served in Crown Heights was exactly the same as an East End London bagel. I had always suspected the New York bagel was an aberration, despite the massive Jewish community in New York. Here, to my mind, was the proof.

Of course, that's rubbish. It just so happens that there are two sorts of bagel. Neither is 'right' or, to use the appropriate Yiddish, 'echt'. But one of them rooted me. It was a profound cultural experience, to eat this familiar bagel in this room full of familiar-shaped, jowly faces so very far from home.

Which may explain why, when I was asked if I would like to witness the coming of the Messiah, I said yes. I had left the cafe a little dazed and wandered over to what was now the global headquarters of the Lubavitch, the biggest Hasidic sect in the world. It is a brooding red-brick building, looming over Brooklyn's Eastern Parkway. Frock-coated Lubavitch were gathering for evening prayers. Three of them, young men in their twenties, approached me and asked what I was doing standing there looking at the building. Their Manchester accents threw me. Yes, they said, they were in New York studying. So what was I doing there? I explained I was a journalist.

'A journalist?' said one. 'Would you like to attend the coming of the Messiah?'

'Sorry?'

'The coming of the Messiah. It's tomorrow evening. We have a media facility.'

'The Second Coming is inside this building tomorrow night?' I said, pointing upwards.

'The first. Jesus wasn't a messiah.'

A rookie error.

It transpired that the Lubavitch believed their leader, the nona-genarian Rebbe Menachem Schneerson, to be the Messiah. He just hadn't got around to revealing himself yet. A scholarly interpretation of the scriptures had indicated that the great moment was at hand.

Normally, I would have given the Lubavitch a wide berth. I abhor fundamentalism of all kinds, especially messianic fundamentalism. It just takes itself so terribly seriously. And yet, with my belly full of an utterly Proustian bagel, I said yes. The next evening I came back to Brooklyn and was shown into a vast hall, filled with upwards of a thousand Lubavitch men – a misogynist, segregationist sect such as this had no space for women – crammed into every nook and cranny, standing on benches, hanging from the galleries, cheering and singing that the '*Moshiach*' – the Hebrew for 'Messiah' – 'is coming'.

I am led through the crowd to the media facility, which is three trestle tables pushed together. It affords a good view down the hall to a curtained-off space in the gallery. I introduce myself to the other reporters there: the guy from the *New York Times*, the chap from the *Daily News*. I get out my notebook to mark off a page for notes. This is what reporters do. It is what we are all doing up here on these trestle tables.

Suddenly, I sigh and say, 'Look at us. Professional journalists and we've got our notebooks out to report the coming of the Messiah.'

'Yeah,' says the guy from the *Times*, without looking up from his. 'But if it happens, what a story.'

The Messiah did not reveal himself. They drew back the curtain to reveal the ninety-one-year-old Schneerson, who, it transpired, had not long ago suffered multiple strokes that had left him mute. Apparently, he was deaf and going blind too. He was unlikely to reveal what he'd had for his lunch, let alone that he was the Messiah. The men on either side of him gave a massive Hebraic shrug as if to say, 'Feh, what can you do? Maybe next year.' And they closed the curtain.

* * *

It's time for a confession: I don't eat that much bread. This isn't because I am gluten intolerant. I'm not. I don't just tolerate gluten, I bloody love it. I'm intrigued by the way the protein forms a robust mesh that provides structure to breads and pastas when it's worked. Clever stuff, gluten. Unless you are part of the unfortunate 1 per cent of the population who are coeliac – with an autoimmune reaction to gluten that can cause a raft of unpleasant symptoms – you almost certainly won't have a problem with it either. The evidence of a so-called non-coeliac gluten intolerance is so limited as to leave it firmly in the column marked 'not proven'. Repeated tests have recorded people who claim a gluten intolerance reporting no symptoms when fed the stuff without their knowledge. This would make sense. The Paleo claim that humans did not develop the capacity to digest gluten is based on the idea that evolution is a cul-de-sac: that it stopped the moment we stood upright and developed the intellectual capacity for small talk and carving arrowheads. That isn't how evolution works; it's an ongoing process. We developed the capacity to eat gluten and bovine dairy because they were readily available sources of nutrition. Many Palaeolithic individuals who could not eat these things would have died, leaving only the gluten and dairy eaters in the community to thrive and pass on their genes. That's what 'survival of the fittest' means.

Where has it come from then, this weird, unsubstantiated fretting about bread? It's possible it's an intolerance to something non-gluten-related in wheat, though even if that does exist – and again it's not proven – it will affect far fewer than the number of people who now claim to be gluten intolerant. More likely it's about people seeking control of the world around them through their food choices. It's about announcing their delicate specialness through all the things they cannot do. Food is deeply emotional. We associate it with nurture. That's why I told the story about my mother and the egg and buttered toast in a cup. How better to reach back to the delicacy and specialness of childhood than through food choices?

So why don't I eat that much bread? Because I like it too much. If I start, I'm not quite able to stop. As a man who has struggled with his weight all his life, the one thing I have learnt is that reducing my carbohydrate intake keeps my weight in check. It's as simple as that. Doctors may not necessarily approve of low-carbing as a dietary tactic, but it works for me. And in any case, I'm never carb-free. I don't avoid anything while reviewing. I just rarely eat bread at home. I can go for a couple of weeks without eating any.

But then a loaf of something good arrives and, well, it would be a shame not to. Especially if you have the good butter. Which is why I am enjoying this whole process so much. In deciding to design my last meal on earth I have given myself professional licence to eat all the good stuff.

Though to be fair that also means eating bad stuff too. I'll take the rough with the smooth.

There are two types of people: those who spread butter thickly, right up to the edges of the toast, and those who favour a meagre translucent smear which runs out before the crust. There are some who don't hold with butter at all, who see no use for it in life, but they are not really people at all. Or at least not my sort of people. They can safely be ignored.

I don't have much time for the meagre smearers either. I suppose some might congratulate them on their restraint, but I've always been hard pushed to see restraint as a virtue, and certainly, in the context of a last supper, it has nothing to offer. If ever there was a moment to spread the butter thickly, right to the edge, this is surely it. But what to choose? Again, when I was a child, butter was a thing. My family of five must have got through a block of the stuff a day; we all of us spread it thickly to the edges. Then my mother did some more of her dangerous reading, plundering the pages of the medical journals that gathered in the house like fallen leaves in autumn, and everything changed. She concluded that the saturated fats in butter were Bad. We needed poly-unsaturates, which were Good. So now we ate Flora from a plastic tub that was dressed in shades of yellow and green and covered with heart shapes to shove home the health message. Back then it described itself as 'soft margarine', but eventually they dropped that term. It wasn't a good sales pitch, what with margarine being reliably disgusting. It's just one long foul aftertaste, the residue from a chemistry experiment that should never have been embarked upon. Margarine, an attempt to mimic the emulsion at the heart of butter but substituting vegetable for dairy fat, was one of those inventions which proved the maxim that just because it can be done doesn't mean it should be.

Flora was better than basic, cheap margarine. I don't recall being repulsed by it. Then again, puréed cat would have been better than cheap margarine. The instruction to eat it instead of butter, however, gave the latter the allure of the forbidden, and I've always been a sucker for that. (Quietly, after we'd all left home, my mother also abandoned Flora. A block of butter appeared in the cupboard at my parents' house, on a wooden dish. The health advice, she said, had been wrong. There were good saturated fats and bad ones, and anyway the link between fat and cardiovascular disease was vastly overstated.)

As a student I sought butter out, like a convent student going in pursuit of the carnal, and learnt to spread it even more thickly. Soon you couldn't quite tell whether it was bread and butter or butter with bread as supporting act. I started learning to cook at university and in the years immediately following, and while there was a bottle of olive oil at my side – I was nothing if not cosmopolitan – I knew instinctively that butter was better. Just as you should never cook with a wine you wouldn't drink, why would you use a fat you weren't happy to eat neat? I knew that butter brought deeper, nuttier tones to the table. It is simply a better medium for flavour. A roast chicken, basted in butter, is a more beautiful thing than one that has not been afforded the privilege. I just had to be careful not to let my then girlfriend see exactly how much was going into the roasting tin.

'Oh, that? It's really not that much if you think about how big the chicken is . . .'

In restaurants around the turn of the millennium the quality of the butter served with the bread started to become a thing, not just an afterthought. At the Fat Duck in Bray I was introduced to a hand-made goat's-milk butter, with a pronounced cheesy edge that I wasn't sure I liked. In 2006 self-taught chef Stephen Harris showed me how he whipped up his own butter for the dining room of his pub, the Sportsman, in Seasalter, on the north Kent coast, using cream from local cows. Then he flavoured it with salt made by boiling the sea-water from the shore just out the back. I watched as the fat separated from the buttermilk to produce something deep and ripe and fulfilling. Back then a chef making their own butter was eccentric; now it's common. Words like 'cultured' and 'aged' appear alongside references to 'our' butter. In restaurants that obsessed about the details I came across butters in different geometric shapes to distinguish salted from unsalted, hidden beneath pieces of porcelain manufactured entirely for the purpose. I concluded I couldn't see the point of unsalted butter. Who wants a mouthful of unflavoured fat? Unsalted butter on the table is just butter that hasn't been finished.

I met butters flavoured with seaweed or herbs or chilli or acorns or black garlic or, in one case, with Marmite. These all struck me as noble inventions. But my first love was always the simplest: the thick, yellow, salted variety, balanced carefully between cream and fat. If I was to lay my table with bread, the right sort of butter would have to be next to it.

One early-January day I went in search of the good stuff down the narrow lanes of County Down, Northern Ireland, fringed by green fields just waiting for cows to come and start converting them into something useful. The satnav led me to a modern bungalow high on a hill, just above the fog line. It is home to Allison and Will Abernethy, friendly, stoical people with a slight air of constant surprise. Once upon a time she was a nurse and he was a farmer. Her father was also a farmer, who, from time to time, would take his grandmother's blackened metal butter churn to agricultural shows to demonstrate how butter was made the old way, by hand. One day, in the mid-noughties, he wasn't able to attend a show, so Allison stepped in. She filled the churn with thick cream from cows raised on those local meadows. Then she cranked the handle until she could hear the promising slap, slap, slap of the fats separating out from the slightly sour buttermilk. She washed the butter of its buttermilk and sold off the small amount they had made. It was a good spectator sport. Someone in the crowd told them they should turn it into a business.

So they did. They created a pleasingly old-fashioned, curled block which is lightly salted and the colour of daffodils on a Mother's Day card. 'A little old lady in her nineties came up here and showed me how to use the grooved wooden paddles to turn it into a roll,' Will says, waving them like he was bringing an aircraft into its bay. Demand rose and they had to upgrade from great-granny's 2.5-litre churn to a thirty-five-litre electric churn, though the washing and patting continued by hand. They introduced a smoked butter. 'I thought if you can smoke cheese, why can't you smoke butter?' Will says. 'Though to be honest, I'm not a chef. I didn't have a clue what I was doing.' He shrugs as if to say he still doesn't, which is the closest a nice, honest man can come to lying. They created another butter flecked with purple flakes of dried dulse, a seaweed collected on Northern Ireland's north coast. From making twenty litres of butter a week they have ended up making 1,000 litres, all of it wrapped in greaseproof paper and stamped with a pen-and-ink drawing of the sort of churn that they no longer use. They gave up their day jobs and dedicated themselves full-time to the way of butter. It was picked up by Fortnum & Mason in London and then by Heston Blumenthal's Fat Duck, which had fallen out of love with the cheesy goat's-milk butter they used to use. It won armfuls of awards.

The room where cream is beaten into submission is a featureless white Portakabin. When they started, they used the kitchen of what was once a granny flat for Will's mother, but they needed more space. There's a big picture window in here looking out over the roll and cleave of the hills, but Will prefers to work facing a blank wall. It's less distracting that way. So, I ask, is this really the same butter as Allison's great-grandmother used to make? No, she says. 'In the old days they collected cream from the milking through the week, so inevitably it would begin to ferment. It would give the butter a cheesy, sour edge. There are some butter makers today who are trying to make it like that.' They say it's more traditional and authentic and real. Which it would be if you were living in the nineteenth century. Old is not the same as real or authentic. It's just a function of the available technology. (Someone somewhere should really start filling goat-skin bags with cream, then slinging them over a warm horse and riding out over the gallops for ten miles so it churns without extra effort, this being butter's ancient origin myth. Imagine them shouting, 'You want real? I'll give you real.')

Cheesy butter is not Allison and Will's thing. Abernethy butter is made from fresh pasteurised cream from a farm just up the road. Will demonstrates, using the original churn, cranking the handle vigorously until the cream stops sloshing and slaps against itself. I give it a few turns. This is proper work. At the end of a day's churning your arms would know all about it. He washes the butter, then squeezes it out to reduce the water content to as low as possible. Finally, he shows me how to pat. It's an extremely satisfying business: slapping the butter this way and that to shape it on the bottom patter, then pulling forward so it rolls. It is now so high in fat that it slips away from the wood easily, curling in on itself eagerly. Will nods approvingly. 'That will do,' he says.

Later, we have tea together. There are buxom scones that Allison has baked for us, with slabs of the salted butter. It is deep and creamy, and salty in a way that wakes you up without dominating the flavour. It is one of those moments which quietly forces the world to stop.

There are some people who think that the heating of milk to destroy the pathogens in it – pasteurisation, as the process is called, after its originator, Louis Pasteur – destroys a glorious natural product. Supporters of what's called raw milk, pumped straight from teat to bottle, say it is more nutritious and has health benefits, that it makes people less prone to allergies. I am not one of those people. I do not think Louis Pasteur was a health-and-safety nut. I think he was a brilliant man who has saved millions and millions of lives from a whole range of bacillus infections, including tuberculosis. In 1938 a quarter of all food- and water-related outbreaks of illness in the US were caused by contaminated milk; by 2005 that had dropped to less than 1 per cent. Pasteurisation is good.

Then again, I am looking for butter for my last supper. If I start worrying about violently regurgitating my guts and hacking up blood as a result of a touch of listeria or E. coli O157, I wouldn't be playing the game properly, would I? Hence, when I go shopping for butters for my tasting, among them is a product made from raw, unpasteurised milk. This raw butter, from East Anglia, comes in a round puck, with a forked-over surface, which is contained within a thin wooden container of the sort normally used for soft cheeses. Apparently, they make it from cream that is still warm from the animal, which they then culture by adding various strains of lactic bacteria. I get it out of the fridge to soften alongside all the others. It is a deep yellow, the surface pin-pricked with moisture.

I spread the butter on some white toast I have made for the occasion. I push its softness against the roof of my mouth and then let my tongue fall still. There is a long, pronounced, cheesy end. I let the flavour build. My mouth falls open. It tastes rancid. It tastes gone. It tastes like someone hates me. According to research conducted for the Nordic Food Lab by Dr Johnny Drain, a materials scientist from Oxford University, the flavour molecules which make it taste like this are exactly the same ones that we prize in blue cheese. And yet, when they turn up in butter, they don't always make us happy. In the raw product they do not make me happy. It's not the only one to have this effect. There's a cultured butter I have to order online, for collection a week later over at a market near Tower Bridge. It is bespoke butter, made especially for me. I appreciate the specialness and the care, but it too tastes sour and gone. There's Artisan Bordier Butter, a French brand from Brittany made by Jean-Yves Bordier. It's highly prized among the sort of multi-starred restaurants that supply stools for ladies' handbags. It's worse. There's a back note of bile, like it's part cream, part salt, part vomit. I suppose that saves me the trouble. I push all of those to one side.

There's a Jersey cream butter which is inoffensive, and a whey butter made by the same people who make the famous Keen's Cheddar, which is much more than pleasant.

In the end, though, it comes down to two. There's butter from Netherend Farm, which, the label tells me, using language that only a food producer desperately trying to hark back to the old days would use, is 'betwixt the Severn and Wye' in the west of England. It's a hefty, attractive cylinder in a gold foil wrapper and is smooth and creamy and salty in all the right places.

And then there's the Abernethy. I spread some of it on a piece of toast. I admire the mottled effect where the hand-churned and -patted butter has been shaped. The saltiness does not outstay its welcome. The creaminess is deep and pronounced but stays creamy. I think of stoical Will in his Portakabin, carefully patting out each curl and round of this butter, forever the accidental butter maker, delivered from labouring in the fields and into the dairy.

That's what clinches it. I've watched this butter being made. Hell, I've done it myself. It's a real, living thing. Or at least it is to me.

I have one last stop to make, informed by a piece of information given to me by Chad Robertson in San Francisco. Over the years many people had come to learn the way of sourdough from him, just as he had learnt from Richard Bourdon. One of those who had come to study with him for a few days was a Londoner called Fergus Jackson, who later returned home and launched the Brick House Bakery, in East Dulwich.

One brutally snowy day, shortly after I returned from the US, I took the bus half a dozen stops from my house to the Brick House Bakery's HQ, which I had never before visited. It is located inside a former warehouse. It was bitterly cold outside, but inside was the hiss of the coffee machine and the smell of freshly baked bread. Jackson is a big-shouldered man who quit an unrewarding career in advertising to set up his own bakery. We discussed the emotional nature of sourdough. Words like 'nurture' and 'care' were used. I mentioned that I thought his Country White and Chad Robertson's famed sourdough were quite similar, and he politely demurred. 'Theirs has more of a tang about it.' And I knew he was right. His was a sourdough that knew when enough was enough.

I asked him how he liked to eat it. 'I take a loaf home and cut off the crust end. Then I spread it with thick butter. To me it's like pork crackling. It reminds me why I do what I do.' I knew that I would be taking a loaf home with me that day. And I knew that I would be doing exactly the same with it when I got there. After all, I had a store of really good butter in the fridge.

Buttered cabbage

You have to like the taste of butter to enjoy this. Make sure to use a salted butter that you like on your toast. If it's right for breakfast, it's right for this. It takes about twenty-five minutes from start to finish.

Serves four as a side dish

INGREDIENTS

Half a white cabbage

300ml stock (from cube, either vegetable or chicken, depending on whether you wish to keep it meat-free or not)

50g salted butter (double it if you fancy)

Olive oil

One clove of garlic (optional)

Salt and pepper

Remove the core of the cabbage and slice the rest up. You need to have reasonable-sized leaves a few centimetres across.

Gently heat a tablespoon of the olive oil in a high-sided frying pan.

After a minute or so, add the cabbage and move around to coat with the oil.

Add the butter in two or three pieces. When it's melted, stir the cabbage around to coat.

Pour in 150ml of the stock, mix it all together, then turn the heat down so the liquid is on a gentle bubble. Don't move the cabbage around. The liquid will thicken.

When it has reduced down to a thick syrup, add another 150ml of the stock, stir and leave it to bubble away again. You want the leaves at the bottom to caramelise slightly in the reducing buttery liquor. At this point you can add slices of garlic to the broth, if you want to.

When the liquor has thickened again, the cabbage will be done. Add a grind of black pepper.

(Tip: a generous teaspoon of sesame oil will shift it a few thousand miles to the east.)

The Playlist

Charles Spence, professor of experimental psychology at Oxford University and one of the world's leading experts on the way external factors impact upon food experiences, once explained to me how mood music could impact upon a dinner party. Play fast, jaunty tunes, he said, and people will eat more quickly, which is handy if you don't like your guests. You can subtly encourage them to clear their plates and go. Songs which are slow and languorous will have the opposite effect. Lots of high notes will accentuate acidity; rounded bass notes will big up the softer flavours. If I were devious and rigorous, I would now carefully engineer a playlist for this last supper of mine which would show off every dish to its best advantage, but I'm not that man. Instead, my music choices are, like the food, going to tell a story. The fact is that somewhere along the way, I became an accidental musician. I never intended to earn part of my living playing the piano. I didn't think it was possible. That was for other, more talented people. Or at least for people who had bothered to learn their scales when they were nine years old, which I didn't. But lives never stick to the foolishly imagined plan. Each step in my journey has been marked by a particular piece of music. Here, then, is my playlist, one song at a time.

▶ 1. 'Ain't Misbehavin'', Fats Waller (1929)

It is the autumn of 1979. I am thirteen years old and I am in the living room of the family home in Harrow, north-west London, listening to an album that my parents have brought home from their first trip together to New York. 'We went out and bought it in the interval,' my mother says excitedly, passing me the double-album fold-out sleeve, with its art deco imagery in shades of amber

and brown, through which run lines of piano keys. In the middle
are illustrations of five African American performers: bowler hats
on the men, plunging necklines on the women, now too close to
the parody of the Negro minstrel, but then understood to be fine.
They are all toothy grins and wide eyes. What I do not know yet
is that the music I am about to hear will consume thousands upon
thousands of hours of my life. It will ignite in me an ambition
which is utterly unachievable. No matter. Failing will bring me huge
amounts of pleasure.

The album is the cast recording of a show called *Ain't
Misbehavin'*, which opened off Broadway in 1978, before
transferring to Broadway proper. It is a compilation of songs, mostly
by the great stride pianist Thomas 'Fats' Waller – his mother's '285
pounds of jam, jive and everythin'', as he is heard to say right at
the start in a scratchy recording. And then there he is playing the
opening bars of the title track. Slowly, as we come to what I will
eventually know is the middle eight, the voices of the modern cast
come in, followed by the piano-playing of Luther Henderson, the
show's original musical director and one of the few people qualified
to take over from Fats on Waller's own music.

At this point I have been learning classical piano, with muted
enthusiasm, for a couple of years and am a few grades in. It turns out
that dainty pieces of music with names like 'Walking in the Garden'
do not do it for me. This sound changes everything. Stride piano,
which owes some of its sound to the syncopations of ragtime and
the rest to the blues, involves the left hand slipping between bass
notes and chords, while the right provides the tune. It's a function
of poverty. If you can't afford a whole band – and in the bars and
brothels of New Orleans and Chicago money was always too tight –
then the piano must be the band. Here are Fats and Henderson doing
just that: being everything. I did not know the piano could sound
like this, could be so full of joy and rhythm. This is the sound I now
want to make. As the tune comes to an end, I get up and go into the

next room, where lurks our knackered Collard & Collard baby grand piano. I sit down on the bench and stare at the keys, baffled. It is the start. I will be spending an awful lot of my time sitting here, baffled.

Oysters

It has to begin with oysters, because all the best meals do. I'm supposed to add qualifiers here. I'm supposed to add caveats about all the great meals that don't begin with oysters; but my heart isn't in it. Oysters are the greatest of curtain-raisers. They are the edible equivalent of Jule Styne's overture to *Gypsy*, which is the greatest overture of all time. And no, I don't care if you have no interest in musical theatre. The analogy works. If a meal starts with the ritual of raw oysters on the half shell, everything that follows will be fine.

I can't be sure when I ate my first one, but for the sake of memoir we will make it sometime in the spring of 1976, because that's the occasion I am most certain of. I was ten years old and spending a day out with my mother. Once a year, always on a Tuesday in the school holidays, Claire would treat each of us three siblings as an only child. She would take us on her weekly tour of the various newspaper and magazine offices she would visit to submit copy and expenses, pick up post and gossip. She was giving us a glimpse of the adult world. That morning I had already been to the offices of the *Sun* on Bouvier Street, just off Fleet Street, which still had ten years to run as the home of national newspaper journalism. It was a huge, open-plan space of controlled chaos that smelt of ink and oil and fags; hacks smoked themselves to death in here. Later, their colleagues could wander down the street to St Bride's, the journalists' church, for the memorial service, followed by an afternoon boozing in Ye Olde Cheshire Cheese, an ancient pub held together by spilt beer and expense accounts. Journalism was a compact business in those days.

The newsroom rattled to the batter of typewriters and laughter that turned into hacking coughs, and later in the day it would rumble to the turn of the presses in the basement. Ashtrays overflowed, paper gathered in drifts and men in three-piece suits showed an interest in me. Perhaps I could see myself coming to work in a place like this one day, they would say, with a crooked grin. Perhaps I could. They asked Claire if she had anything especially salacious for her problem page. She would roll her eyes at them.

From there we went to the south side of Covent Garden and Rules, London's oldest restaurant. It is located on Maiden Lane, which acquired its name courtesy of the prostitutes who cruised it a century before. Rules, an outrageous confection of brass rail, mahogany bar, red velvet and terrible Victorian art, first opened in 1798 and has somehow managed not to become prisoner to its own history, despite being armpit-deep in the stuff. To this day I still send people there, when asked to recommend somewhere that has all the good British food and none of the bad British food. Famously, it has its own game shoot, from where much of the meat for a section of the menu headed 'Furred and Feathered' is supplied. We sat side by side on a red velvet banquette for two, my mother and I. Claire was asked by a white-jacketed waiter who evidently knew her if she would like oysters to start. He said it as if it were a rhetorical question, the words a mere matter of politeness for a woman who knew the right way to begin.

Yes, that would be the thing to do on this special day, and have you met my son?

The spindly, circular frame is brought to the table still empty, awaiting its moment. There is a white plate alongside, holding a small dish of pink vinegar with, in its depths, a fine dice of shallots. With that is a small bottle bearing the legend 'Tabasco'. It looks terrifying, like something to be administered rather than eaten. There is a quarter of a lemon tied up in a muslin shroud that is closed off with a ribbon.

Now there is another waiter, with a tray bearing small plates and forks.

'Will sir be eating oysters too?'

Claire looks at me. My call, but I know what is expected. My family has a simple rule: you cannot say you do not like something if you have never tried it. And even then, frankly, being weird about food is frowned upon. Other kids do that. Other kids are picky, fearful, high-maintenance eaters, the sort who will grow up to have intolerances and look for the tick boxes marked 'dietary requirements'. But not us. Not the Rayners. In an essay I wrote once about the joys of the stinkiest of foods, I identified in my love of them a genuine form of machismo. I was a fat child with weak ankles and fallen arches who was terrible at running. I was awful at climbing trees, and please don't ask me to skim a stone across that lake – it will fall in with a plop, much as I will. But at the table I would leapfrog all the kids my age and older by eating the exotic and the pungent and the wobbling and the intense. I would become a man. So naturally enough, yes, I will be eating the oysters.

The metal platter arrives, piled high with crushed ice and on it the teardrop-shaped oysters, silvery and ancient, the outside of their shells hewn from the depths, the inside as polished and glistening as the polished metal surrounding them.

There is a curious gap in my memory here, because of eating them I recall nothing. I do remember being given a sip of Claire's glass of chilled white wine. 'It's called Sancerre. Take a sniff. It smells like cat's piss.' This was something I knew a little bit about because cleaning the litter tray was my job. She was right. It did.

What stayed with me of the oysters was the aching, adult glamour of it all, the sense that any meal which began in this way – with so many accessories and so much attention to detail, and so many pressed and ironed people coming to the table – had to be taken seriously. Much later, as a student, trying to impress a woman who kindly told me she adored me, but only as a friend and, no, she didn't want to do that, I ordered oysters in a London restaurant because I understood myself to be someone who ate them, even though I hadn't eaten them since that time with my mother. I also did so because I thought it would impress her. I remember the invigorating shock of eating them, of the brine, like consuming the sea. No, like being a part of the crashing surf. It was an elemental experience, one that focused me on the moment. No, she wasn't going to go to bed with me. But it turned out I adored oysters. The night was chalked up as a good one.

Do I need to point out after telling these stories that mine was a childhood of great privilege? It was for the most part gilded and sun-lit. I like to intone the great Rita Rudner gag: 'Mine was a standard middle-class Jewish upbringing. We were exceptionally wealthy.' But it was a childhood of privilege lived under the shadow of my parents' impoverished childhoods. We knew they both had nothing once, that their childhoods had been gloomy and tarnished. My father, Des, was never massively comfortable in restaurants. I don't think he ever lost the brooding sense that he was in some way an interloper. My mother was different. The move from nursing to freelance journalism to newspaper columnist gave Claire access to a world she craved, and it was, in turn, part of my inheritance.

Long before I earned my living by writing about eating out, long before I even got a sniff of the job or spotted that you could make a living that way, she instilled in me a love of restaurants. It was not simply the sweet simplicity of the deal – they bring you a list of dishes that sound nice, you choose a few, they bring them to you, and you don't have to do the washing-up – it was the dynamic of the environment. So many of the conventions of normal life are left outside the restaurant door. There is an unavoidable intimacy to eating together which allows for things to happen. At restaurant tables things have happened to me. They've not always been good things, but they've happened.

It is the spring of 1992, and I have been sent to Munich by the British edition of *Cosmopolitan* magazine. Normally, I write what they call 'emotionals' for them – columns about sex from the male point of view; why men are jealous of women's orgasms, and so on – but they also like to use me as the news reporter I have become. I am here to get some 'colour' for a piece on the rise of the far right across Europe. The British revisionist historian David Irving is on trial here for making a speech in one of the city's *bierkellers* denying the Holocaust, and I have come to attend court. I am also to file a news piece for the *Guardian*. The room is crowded. There are the judges, young Germans in their thirties who seem determined not to allow the sins of their parents' and grandparents' generations go unchallenged. There are anti-fascist campaigners. There are the David Irving groupies: a man with steel-grey hair in full Bavarian dress, the light-green tweed of his jacket edged in forest-green leather; a young woman with finely plaited blonde hair wearing a dirndl, playing the parody of the Aryan dream. Irving himself, in the dock, appears to have learnt his declarative speaking style and arm gestures from watching too much Hitler archive. He repeatedly sweeps his black fringe back from his eyes and frowns.

Like the best courtrooms, it's a terrific drama. But I'm focused less on the process than on the thin twenty-six-year-old blond man at the back of the room. His name is Ewald Althans, and he is described as a marketing man. His product: Nazism. Althans is assisting Irving with his case, while also awaiting trial on charges of belonging to a banned Nazi organisation, to add to previous convictions for wearing Nazi uniforms. Althans is quite the conviction marketing man.

As the morning session comes to an end, he nods to me across the room. We have arranged to have lunch together, at the same *bierkeller* where Irving made the speech for which, later in the day, he will be convicted. (My *Guardian* report, written longhand into a notebook, then dictated to copytakers while lying on my hotel bed, will gift me my first front-page byline. Thank you, David Irving.) Outside the hostelry, there is late-spring sunshine and the smell of verdant blooms. Inside, the dining room is a space of dark varnished wood and gloom. There is something brooding about it, but the brooding may be mine.

The solidly built waitress wears her own take on a dirndl and does not smile. The lack of hospitality feels appropriate. After all, I don't especially want to be here. My wife and parents had encouraged me not to come. Eighteen members of my extended family were murdered in the Holocaust. Why would I want to have lunch with a man who thought their deaths were at best a lie, and at worst a good idea? I told them it was a good story.

We order extremely Teutonic platefuls of roasted meats with mashed potato, and I embark on my interview. It's easier to hate your enemy when he is faceless; he can take on whatever form you like. The reality will always be painfully banal. I had come to Munich to meet a Nazi; what I found was someone who looked like a management trainee. I felt strangely empty. This Nazi looked so ordinary.

We talked generally at first, meandering around Althans's vision of a new Germany. He said he believed that it was human nature to be racist. Only through segregation could the white race survive. Everyone else would have to go. Government would be by dictatorship. We forked away at our food. Democracy, he said, did not work. I asked him his position on the Jews. 'Are you Jewish?' he asked. I nodded. 'I thought so,' he said. 'You have the looks. I can always talk to Jews. You like to argue, to discuss. Too often people close their ears when they talk to me.'

He said he considered the Jews to be coloured people. He had already said that all coloured people brought problems to German society and would have to leave. The Jews would have to go too. 'They have to decide whether they want to be Germans or Jews. They cannot be both. They create inflation by their business practices. If I could control international banking systems and had imperialist ambitions, I'm sure I'd do the same.'

I asked where he thought the Jews should go. He said sharply that he did not care. They could go wherever they liked. It was one of the few occasions when he lost his cool. Most of the time he made his opinions sound so ordinary. This, he was trying to say, was not the rebel yell of extremism but pure common sense. If he had ranted and screamed and kicked, I would have known what I was dealing with. But Althans was far too clever. Like Irving, he said he believed the Holocaust had not taken place, that it had been invented by a conspiracy of Jewish film-makers in Hollywood determined to smear Germany.

How, I asked, could Althans account for the missing members of my family? Who had killed them, if not the Nazis? They could, he said, have died of disease. 'That was a terrible thing,' Althans said coolly, 'but it is not a Holocaust.' We finished our lunch quickly after that. I paid the bill, and later, after Irving had been convicted and handed a five-figure fine, and I had written the news story reporting it, I went to another *bierkeller* in central Munich. I ordered roasted pork knuckle and got very drunk.

It is early in 1999, and I am having lunch with the editor of the *Observer's* magazine supplement in one of the host of new restaurants that have opened not far from the newspaper's office in London's Farringdon. We're in a place on a corner site that used to be a pub and is now a curious brasserie mash-up serving an approximation of Caribbean food. There is no reason for the lunch other than that it is my turn to have a bit of quality time with Sheryl Garratt, who made her name as the editor of style bible *The Face*. I am a jobbing writer for her, as I have been for the whole paper for the past three years, filing general features and standing in for columnists when they are away. Sheryl has had me writing everything from the fashion column – why big-arsed men should never wear pleated trousers – to travel pieces.

And so we gossip. She tells me that our restaurant critic, Kate Flett, is stepping down. 'She's off to be the TV critic.'

I pause, my cutlery held in mid-air. I can't even look at her as the thought flits across my mind.

'Well, that's a job you can't apply for.'

'No,' she agrees.

'I mean, if you advertised for a new restaurant critic, you'd have a massive queue.'

'You would.'

'But I'd like to do it.'

Over the years I have been asked one question repeatedly: how do you become a restaurant critic? I got asked the question so often I eventually wrote a letter, stored away on my hard drive, that I could email back to anybody who asked. It explains that it is a writing job, not an eating job. You have to learn how to write, how to shape a story, and then perhaps at some point in the future you might just get a chance to write about restaurants rather than other things, but only if one of the very few openings comes up. Until that exact moment at that restaurant table in Farringdon when Sheryl mentioned Kate was moving on, it had never occurred to me that I might become a restaurant critic. I loved restaurants. I spent my own money in expensive ones. I collected menus and read reviews of others I hadn't visited. As the editor of the student newspaper at Leeds University, I had produced a whole edition dedicated to food, including a page of reviews written by my staff of meals that had been comped by restaurants eager for the coverage. My first-ever review, of a venerable Italian called Manfred's, was in there. But that was me indulging a whim. Not for a moment had I thought such a gig might be mine, even when, a year before, they had asked me to stand in for Kate because she was away. (I reviewed a restaurant in a faux country house, not far from my home in south London. I quite liked it.)

'I'd like to do it.'

'Really?'

'Yes . . .' And I told her about a life lived through restaurants: about my mother taking me to eat oysters when I was ten; how my wife and I had spent £267 – a large sum now, an astronomical sum in the early 1990s for a man of barely twenty-five – just to find out what Marco Pierre White's Michelin three-star restaurant at the Hyde Park Hotel was like; I babbled on about my collection of *Good Food Guides*. I laid it on thick. I did not express an opinion on the food we were eating – she was paying.

Two weeks later, Sheryl told me she had good and bad news. The good news was she wanted me to be the new restaurant critic. The bad news was the paper's editor, a dynamic, brilliant, often infuriating newspaperman called Roger Alton, did not. I was one of the paper's news-focus writers, charged with producing major features on the story of the week. It was a tricky job, delivering 2,500 words of fresh reporting, colourfully written through, on a tight deadline. Not many of us did it. Roger said, 'If you start writing about restaurants, you'll disappear into writing about food.' He was absolutely right. That was why I wanted the gig so badly. It wasn't just because of my love of restaurants or my sheer excitable, borderline pathological greed. I was exhausted by well over a decade of being a generalist, of changing subject day after day. I wanted a specialism. I needed a specialism.

Roger had a different idea. He wanted our highly regarded chief political columnist, Andrew Rawnsley, to do the job because he took an awful lot of people out to lunch. He was very good at the lunching, apparently; he did it with uncommon vigour and commitment. It would be the perfect way to double up on expenses. There were problems with this: Andrew would never be able to reveal the identity of his companions because they were all off-the-record sources from the highest ranks of politics; and he'd never go anywhere more than a mile away from Westminster.

Oh, and there was one other problem: Andrew really didn't want to be the restaurant critic.

Roger suggested a compromise: a job share. We agreed. Andrew wrote one review. I wrote ten. Andrew wrote another review. I wrote another ten. Andrew announced he was going on sabbatical to write a book. Later, he would tell me that while he could write a political column on anything – and he really could; his column remains unmissable and he has multiple awards to prove it – he felt he'd said all he

59

had to say on restaurants in those two columns. At the end of that first year I was shortlisted for an award for my restaurant writing. It was a brilliant stroke of luck. Awards are lovely. Everybody loves a prize. But the real point of them in journalism is this: even just a nomination for an award is enough to guarantee the bosses can't sack you. I was the *Observer*'s restaurant critic. All I had to do was keep being the restaurant critic.

But now it's 2018, another shamelessly blue-skied morning in San Francisco, and I am off to eat oysters for breakfast. I know where to go. A decade before, I had been taken on a food tour of the city, which included a stop at the Swan Oyster Depot, a landmark and as good a place as any in which to gain an understanding of the mystery of the oyster. It opened a block away from its current location on Polk Street in the late nineteenth century, but burnt down in the city's fire of 1906. It reopened in this location in 1912. In 1946 it was bought from the original owners by Salvatore Sancimino, and today it is operated by his sons and their offspring, all of them thick-armed men in aprons who talk in italics. What goes on here is never fancy. It's a very straightforward business.

That's the point of the Swan Oyster Depot, a rough-and-ready cafe with a long marble bar. In London, oysters now come with crisp linen and a price tag. The Dickensian story of oysters as poor people's food is just a folk memory. Once upon a time, the US was producing two billion oysters a year, and they too were for everybody. Those days have gone, but in appearances at least the Swan still echoes that earlier utilitarian time, of working people eating oysters to fuel their way through a day of hard labour, courtesy of pure protein. The prices at the Swan these days tell a different story. A garishly drawn sign, painted onto planks of wood, then hooked up onto the wall, like this is some beach shack that can be packed away at the end of the season, announces that a mixed dozen will set you back $32.

'Why did we start eating oysters?' I ask Tom Sancimino across the marble counter. 'Look at them,' I say, waving at the pile of rock-like objects stacked up in their compartments against the white tiled wall. 'Who would look at those and think, "Food!"?'

'It must have been somebody who was very hungry,' he says, without looking up.

The Swan Oyster Depot is a narrow strip of a space, which does not encourage lingering. On the customer's side of the counter there is just enough room for the eighteen stools, and clearance to squeeze behind them when you leave. It's not much better on the other side, where the seafood is stowed. There is a small cold store at the back. The place doesn't open until 10.30 a.m., but at 8 a.m. it's already busy. They are preparing the day's outside catering orders, a rush of men marching up and down the corridor of a restaurant, unloading boxes of stock, with ice and sacks of oysters carried from van to front door on shoulders. In a back room a woman is breaking down crabs. Here, in the front, one of the nephews is getting the clam chowder going, $5 a bowl. I ask what goes in it. He shrugs. 'Clams, cream, onions.' What more do I need to know? Ask a stupid question.

Already a queue is beginning to build outside. There will be a queue all day.

They serve ten to twelve sacks of oysters a day, and all of them come from the west coast. 'We used to have Gulf oysters from down in the south,' Tom says. 'But . . .' – he shakes his head sadly – '. . . they don't travel. The Pacific waters are cold, which is great for oysters, especially at this time of year.' He puts together a selection for me: Kumamotos, which he says will be creamy; Miyagis or Pacifics, which will be briny; and a couple of Oles, short for Olympians. He works the blade swiftly, cracking the hinge at the back to get the oyster open, then flashing it around the meat to release it from the shell but letting it stay there, ready for me to pour into my mouth. He positions them with the narrow tips to the centre, at even intervals, as if marking out a clock face around the ice-filled platter.

It's a craft, opening oysters. A TV producer once came up with the brilliant idea that I should shuck some oysters live on air for the BBC's peak-time *One Show*, for which I was the food reporter. When I arrived, they presented me with the specimens they had got hold of. They were massive things, the size of a baby's head. I should have cracked the hinge before we went live, but I felt that would be cheating.

I said to the producer, 'There are three possibilities: I get the oysters open; I don't get the oysters open and spend five minutes of airtime struggling with a recalcitrant bivalve; or I stab myself in the hand.'

He nodded slowly. 'Whatever happens, it's great television.'

I didn't get them open.

Tom has done the business. He shoves the tray towards me with a nod. 'Eat.'

The Kumamotos and the Miyagis are exactly as he described. The revelation, though, is the Oles. They are tiny. They are thumbnail-sized, though the meat fills the whole shell. It's intense and rich and almost overwhelming. It's both creamy and briny. I try a little of their 'cocktail sauce' – tomato sauce bashed up with horseradish – but I decide I prefer them plain. I wonder about trying to get enough Olympians from the west coast of America to my dinner table in south London. I like the image of promising oysters to my guests and then presenting them with the tiniest examples they have ever seen. But logistically, flying oysters all that way seems absurd. That's not a story I could sell. In any case, I'm starting to think about a different kind of oyster, from a lot further south.

Let's deal swiftly with a question around oysters. Some would call it the key question. The only things you ever swallow without chewing are those things you didn't really want to have in your mouth in the first place. Medicine you swallow. A raw oyster you chew. It's not just about the cold and the wet. It's not just about the taste of something salty and the sea, as it slips from lip to gullet. It's about a whole bunch of other things that are deeper and richer and more profound than that. Yes, it's a bit fishy. It lives in the bloody sea, where the fish live. It's meant to be fishy. But that's to see the oyster in only one dimension. Stewed oysters are a massive hit of umami, a mother lode of savouriness. Hence oyster sauce. A great raw oyster delivers some of that too.

A few years ago, I suggested in a column that no woman should ever take as a lover someone who didn't have a taste for oysters and sea urchins. I said it would limit the options, and many women, both gay and straight, wrote to me to agree. To eat a cold, fresh, raw oyster is to make a connection with what it is to be human. If you have no idea what I mean, then, really, I despair. Move on to the next chapter. It's about snails.

The Grand Isle is an ambitiously named strip of land just seven miles long and half a mile wide a couple of hours' drive south of New Orleans. For a few years the nineteenth-century pirate Jean Lafitte had his headquarters here, where he managed to accumulate more ships than the US Navy. Now it is a drowsy community of a little over a thousand souls which makes its money from the seafood business, or what's left of it following the *Deepwater Horizon* oil rig explosion and associated spill of 2010. One of those souls is Jules Melancon, a fifty-nine-year-old Cajun with big meaty hands and creased skin the colour of a polished wooden table, whose family has been harvesting Gulf oysters for generations.

About twenty years ago, I was sent to New Orleans on a press tour to write a travel piece. I drank bourbon I didn't quite have a taste for, weaved my way from bar to bar across the French Quarter and woke each morning with a marching band of a hangover. One evening we were taken to the Acme Oyster Bar, where I was served oysters the likes of which I did not know existed. They were pale and creamy and deep-flavoured. They were invigorating, like all the best oysters, but they were also encouraging. My dark secret was that sometimes even I found an overly briny oyster a little challenging, like getting into the sea can be challenging. I loved having eaten one of those, rather than the process of doing so.

These Gulf oysters were entirely different. Later, I would eat oysters in London and talk about the ones I had eaten once in New Orleans. It must have been very annoying.

Now, two decades later, I have come back to Louisiana and I am being driven down the bayou and over the concrete causeways, on stilts dug deep into the marshy land, to meet Jules Melancon, who I have been told produces the very best Gulf oysters. As I flew in at dusk the evening before, I looked down from the plane and got a sense of how Louisiana had been shaped by its relationship with the water. This is land that is both here and not here, a smudged place broken by rivulets and rivers and wider expanses of water, constantly in negotiation with the elements.

My guide is a Louisianan called Jim Gresson, who was born in Lafayette seventy years ago but made his fortune in restaurants and seafood wholesale up in Houston, Texas. He's a tall, big-shouldered man who is determined to cheerlead for the oysters he adores.

'Growing up Cajun, a big meal was the only kind of entertainment,' he tells me on the drive, his car's big fat wheels bouncing slightly as they bump over the places where the road's concrete slabs join. The sky is a pale, sun-drenched blue and a glare flashes off the shiny bonnet. 'I was a kid when I first tried an oyster. It was always exciting to me to try them, to see what was inside. We'd eat them off the folded-down back of a pick-up truck, like it was an oyster bar.'

A decade ago, Jim noticed that the oysters coming from the east coast were more consistent and were being sold at a premium to those coming from the Gulf. The difference: they were cultivating them on the east coast, while in the Gulf they were all wild. Cultivating them in cages – common practice all over the world – was illegal in the Gulf. Back then, with the aftermath of Hurricane Katrina still dominating the industry, Jules Melancon was thinking of packing it in. He just didn't think he had the volume any more.

Jim convinced him there was a future, if he moved into cultivation. He offered to help finance the initiative. 'I told him not to worry about sales, that I'd deal with that. I said I could sell anything he could produce.' There was a small hiatus while they got the law changed to allow cages into the Gulf, but soon they were up and running.

Now Jules has 550 cages in shallow water and is supplying his oysters into some of New Orleans's best restaurants. But we are going to try them here, at source, right off the water. We hop from lowland to lowland, via grey concrete bridges built to facilitate the maintenance of the oil refineries converting crude from the fields out at sea. As we traverse the last causeway and make landfall at our destination, we pass a sign that reads: 'Jesus Christ Reigns Over Grand Isle'. The Lord may reign, but here you have to make your own arrangements to deal with what nature will throw at you. Most of the buildings are up on stilts, for when storm surges bring the sea in over the levee. Jim's house is a solid, brown wood building which, in the old Louisiana argot, he refers to as 'the Camp'. It is February, but it's hot. The temperatures are nudging into the high 80s, and a heavy haze is hanging over the waters of the Gulf that we can see from the deck at the back of Jim's house.

'I just need to put out my flag so people know I'm in residence.' Soon the Stars and Stripes are fluttering in the breeze.

We have called Jules en route, and he rolls up in his own pickup just a few minutes behind us, pulling into the shady area beneath the house. There is a heavy old ceramic sink here, perfect for oyster shucking. Jules opens a cold bag.

'I got some big ones in here,' he says.

Jim says, 'How big?'

'Two year.'

Jim nods, approvingly. I'm confused. I'm used to native oysters, of the sort I eat in London, taking around four years to reach an eatable size. Even the cheaper rocks or Pacifics take two years to get there. I can't quite see what could be so interesting about a two-year-old oyster.

He finds what he's looking for.

Christ alive. It's almost a foot long.

I say, 'That's vast.'

Jim says, 'Wait till you see what's inside.'

Here, caged in the warm waters of the Gulf, this is how they grow. 'The water is our greatest resource,' Jim says, as Jules sets to work. With one this big, Jules says, you can't go in via the hinge. You just have to go in under the shell. 'Probably gonna break it, to be honest,' he says. Though the first one comes off intact.

Later, I post a picture of what's hiding in there on Twitter, with the message, 'Fancy an oyster?' The responses are, 'No!' and 'Woah!' and 'That's verging on indecent.' One person replies, 'They get any bigger we can start keeping them as pets.' Another says, 'Pretty sure that's a facehugger from *Alien*.'

A third says, 'Is that your spleen?'

I get their point. It's huge. Vast. Not 'It's big, but there might be a bigger one over there' big. The beige meat all but fills the shell and looks like the bulbous sole of a flip-flop. And it's all ripe muscle. I shudder quietly. I'm with big, hard-handed men. Proper men who have worked at sea. I've tried not to be embarrassed about my soft hands. I know I have not been shaped by hard labour. But the least I'm meant to be able to do is eat. That's my job. But this . . .

I ask if it's possible for it to be cut into smaller pieces, and they laugh, cheerfully. Jules takes a blade to the oyster, slices it in two and gives me the smaller part. It is, to be fair, everything I'd hoped: rich and meaty, creamy with the bright, soothing hit of the sea. Happily, he now opens some of the yearlings. These are what I came for, the very best of the Gulf. Pearlescent, and glorious. We stand in the shade of the house and eat freshly shucked oysters, with the smell of the sea just beyond the levee behind us coming over on the breeze. In the UK, I'm used to oysters being put through filtration tanks for at least forty-eight hours before being served. Here, they don't bother.

'No need,' Jules says, as he opens another. 'I eat them straight out the water.'

Jules passes Jim a plastic box filled with pre-shucked oyster meat from more of the two-year-olds. We go up to the house, where Jim has fitted a restaurant-standard kitchen into the back of his heavy wooden shack by the sea. We are joined by a local shrimp processor, a diehard Cajun called Dean Philip Blanchard, who has brought a bag of raw shrimp to be boiled up. While Jim cooks, the men talk about the challenges of dealing with the authorities.

'I got told I was in trouble with one lady,' Dean says.

Jules says, 'Why? What d'you do?'

'I called her a nigger.' He grins. I blink. 'But she called me a coon first, so it was okay.'

I try to stifle my deep intake of breath.

Jules turns to me and says, 'What's the best-selling beer in Britain?' I identify a way to defuse a situation which is, to be fair, only uncomfortable for me.

'Really sorry,' I say, 'but you've got the wrong Jew. I don't drink beer.' I think to myself, 'That will do.'

Dean says, 'You're a Jew?'

I nod nonchalantly, as if to suggest I mentioned it for no reason at all. 'Jew-ish. I'm not practising.'

'My grandfather always said, "Dean, never sell to the Jews." I said, "But, Grandpa, we are always selling to the Jews." He said, "No. They're buying from us. We got something they want."' He tells a story about how, when he was a young man, he was a 'hothead', and when some damn Jew held out on paying his $40,000 bill, he decided 'to get a machine gun and go up there and kill the son of a bitch'. He got as far as South Carolina, where he was stopped by the local police for speeding.

67

'The police officer, he looks in the back and sees the machine gun. He says, "What's that for?" So I tell him I'm going to New York to shoot the son of a bitch who owes me all the money. And he went, "Okay," and waved me on my way.' As long as he was planning to murder someone in a different state, South Carolina's finest really didn't care. They laugh. I nod, with my mouth slightly slack, which could be taken as a smile by some people and as an expression of utter disbelief by others. I say, 'And did you . . .?'

'Nah, he paid.'

I try to tell myself it is a come-one-come-all ecumenical sort of racism. This Cajun is cheerfully bigoted against everybody.

Behind the counter Jim has been boiling up a pot of what he'd call grease. The huge oyster meats are dredged in cornmeal and dropped in there. He serves me an oyster po' boy: six of the deep-fried oysters in a white bun, garnished with mayo punched up with Tabasco and a few slices of tomato to make me think I'm being healthy.

When I've finished eating I call it 'the impossible sandwich'. Surely no restaurant could serve this? It would cost too much. Each of these huge oysters would be a fair few bucks apiece.

'In a restaurant you'd have to charge maybe $40,' I say.

Jim nods. 'Maybe.'

I may have eaten better sandwiches, but not many, and I can't think of another while this one is in my hands. Partly, it's about the blunt appeal of the deep-fried, of something crisped quickly in hot bubbling oil, against the softness of the sugary white bread. But what's so compelling is the way the fierce heat has made the oysters more themselves. Underneath the crisped overcoat they are deep and sweet, and full of high umami notes. I find myself reaching for words and phrases – 'ethereal' and 'angel's kisses' and 'luscious' – which I know will make me hate myself in the morning.

I tell the men what I was told in San Francisco: that Gulf oysters don't travel well.

Jules says, 'That's not the problem. We just haven't got the volume no more.' He tells me how freshwater diversions have killed the reefs. That Katrina destroyed some of the fleet. And then came *Deepwater Horizon*. Dean says, 'Oh yeah. BP screwed this whole area up. They asphalted the bottom of the Gulf of Mexico.' In the aftermath of the spill, fishermen were asked to spot oil floating on the surface. When they did so, Dean tells me, BP came along and sprayed it with a chemical that made it sink to the bottom of the ocean. There used to be eight shrimp-processing companies on Grand Isle, but now there's just one. His.

'We used to ship oysters to the north-east,' says Jim. 'Not any more. Now we only have enough oysters for the bars round here.'

I get the full story the next day, when I drop by P & J Oysters in New Orleans. The company, run by generations of the Sunseri family, has been trading in oysters since 1876 and is the oldest of its kind in the US. It used to send product all over the country from the nearby Southern Railhead, but those days are gone. Today it is staging an event for the biggest donors to the Culinary Institute of America, the country's most prestigious and venerable cooking school. It's part of a series of happenings created to make the deepest of pockets feel most loved by the Institute. They are located in a tidy, open-fronted warehouse on the edge of the famed French Quarter, not far from where the railhead used to be. It has been cleared out to make space for a stand of freshly shucked oysters, another where you can get deep-fried oyster sandwiches and a third dispensing tumblers of Maker's Mark bourbon to these retired titans of industry, with their chinos and their interest in the 'culinary arts'. There are speeches. They are all about family business and legacy, and soft, sweet bread rolls filled with deep-fried oysters.

When the speeches are done, I get a darker story from Al Sunseri, president of the company. 'BP made the oyster farmers multimillionaires,' he tells me. 'But it also changed the business, because they don't have to work any more.' Many of them are of Croatian descent, he says, and have bought houses in Croatia with the compensation. 'Our business is down 75 per cent,' Sunseri says. 'We've been through wars and hurricanes, but nothing has affected us like BP.'

I ask him what his company will do. He says, 'We're not going to be a volume business any more. We're going to become something else. I'm thinking of turning this space into a restaurant.'

I can see the logic. New Orleans loves its oysters. It was here, in 1899, that Oysters Rockefeller was invented. Jules Alciatore, son of the founder of the venerable restaurant Antoine's, was looking for a dish to replace the snails that his customers came to him for, because of a shortage. He decided to put the topping of breadcrumbs, parsley, butter and other herbs that they used with their snails onto oysters instead and then bake them. In a glorious piece of marketing spin, he named it after oil tycoon John D. Rockefeller, the wealthiest man in America, because it was so rich. In turn, rival restaurant Arnaud's created Oysters Bienville, topped with shrimp, mushrooms, green onions and various herbs. They sold so well that Arnaud's also came up with Oysters Suzette (topped with bacon and pimento), Oysters Kathryn (artichoke hearts, garlic, Parmesan) and Oysters Ohan (aubergine and andouille sausage).

All of these have their place, but my heart is still with the raw oyster. I ask Al Sunseri what he thinks the appeal of them is. 'It's really the only animal you eat while it's still alive,' he says. 'Some people don't want to know that, but it's true.'

A food that dies as you eat it. To be eaten as you think about dying. How could I hold my last supper without oysters?

But which ones? Back in London, I start hunting for someone who can supply oysters to match those from the Gulf of Mexico. I browse the Web and stare at pictures of newly shucked specimens, like some shellfish perv with a pronounced bivalve fetish. Perhaps that's what I am now. Perhaps it's not natural to be this interested in them.

Eventually, I stumble across a company called Rooney Fish, in Kilkeel, Northern Ireland. Their Pacifics are the only oysters to have won three stars in the Great Taste Awards, an annual ranking of over 12,000 British food products. Only 165 received three stars in 2017. Rooney's were the only oysters. I owe it to myself to find out if they are all that.

Andrew Rooney, who now runs the company, is less than responsive by email but eventually says he is happy for me to come and see him. It's a ninety-minute drive south-east from Belfast, and then a twist through an industrial estate to the complex of large sheds that now houses the company, which was originally started by Andrew's father John. The son is a stocky, balding, bearded man in his forties who looks like he'd be quite happy out on a fishing boat. These days, he says, he's mostly behind his desk. He shows me into his quietly chaotic, scuffed office, with its view of the packing sheds.

Historically, the company has dealt in crabs, langoustines and whelks. They only started farming oysters over in Carlingford Lough in 2014, because supplies of some of the other shellfish they dealt in were dwindling. 'We needed to do something to produce product,' he says. 'We needed something we could control.' He has a lot of employees who depend on him for work. Oysters seemed the way to go.

'I went to France and met some very helpful people. People are very forthcoming in the oyster business. I was quite shocked.' They told him how to run the cages, how to shake them and turn them. He got leases on over eighteen hectares of the lough and set up 6,000 'trestles' – stands raised off the seabed for the cages – in nice straight lines. He shows us photographs of his trestles at low tide. 'I'm a bit OCD on my straight lines,' he says.

Their first harvest was in 2017, and immediately they were winning awards. He shows me more pictures, this time of opened oysters. They look glorious. Unlike most of those in Britain, where the creamy-coloured muscle is about a third of the meat, these are muscle right up to the edge. They are Gulf-esque in their creaminess. I ask him how he's achieved this. 'It's about not putting too many in the cage at the start,' he says. 'And turning them in the right way and working the tides. The water in the lough is good and cold.' He talks about the winds coming in over the mountains that fringe the waters, about a happy accident of geography.

I am excited now. I say, 'It would be great to try some.'

'Oh, no. I'm sorry. I don't have any.'

'But . . .'

'We don't have another tide for a week or so. We can't reach them at the moment.'

The most recent harvest has gone to France. They love them in France, apparently. Rooney send their brown crabs to China, their whelks to Korea and their oysters to France.

'Who sells your oysters in London?'

'Nobody,' he says. 'We don't sell to London.'

He'd like to, he says. But he hasn't quite got round to it. He's been meaning to. He just hasn't. I leave empty-handed, unoystered. Unfed.

I am stone-cold certain I have found the right ones.

I just need to come up with a way to get them to my table.

Hot and sour oyster dressing

I could have come up with some long, complicated recipe involving cooked oysters. They really can be a marvellous thing. Throw a couple of raw oysters into a beef and ale pie or a Lancashire hotpot, and they will give you a huge depth of flavour and a slap of umami. Deep-fried battered oysters are a joy. But those ideas are for others to explain; my heart wouldn't be in it. Instead, this is a simple dressing for raw oysters, based on two very specific condiments, one of which will require some effort to find. Dashi vinegar is extraordinary stuff: rich, deep and smoky, with an acidity low enough that it can be used as the base for cool, limpid broths, which are glorious with raw fish. As for the green Tabasco, well, it's obvious what that does.

INGREDIENTS

50ml Tosazu dashi vinegar

1tsp Tabasco Green Jalapeño Sauce

Mix them together in a small bowl. Apply to raw oysters with a teaspoon just before eating.

▶ 2. 'Ghost Town', the Specials (1981)

Music is a time machine, and few songs take me to a particular moment in time more than this one: the rumbling vibrato of the organ, the attack of the horns and then the driving reggae beat of one of British pop's most searing pieces of social commentary. By the early 1980s I had already decided that I wanted to be a journalist and had taken to watching the news obsessively. Political arguments filled the dinner table, or at least they did between my mother and me, though there wasn't much we disagreed about. Margaret Thatcher was a brutal, uncaring witch who was doing terrible things to the country. This wasn't an opinion acquired from the news. Claire saw it daily in her postbag, in the agonised letters from destitute parents who had no idea how they were going to feed their kids or keep a roof over their heads. Jerry Dammers wrote 'Ghost Town' as a reaction to the riots of 1980 in Bristol and Brixton (where I would eventually end up living), but just as the single was released in June 1981, the streets of Britain burnt once more. Riots, ignited by the damage done to Britain's inner cities and the prospects for the young by Thatcher's economic reforms, broke out across the country. It didn't matter where 'this town' was, it was 'becoming like a ghost town'. Courtesy of the Specials, those riots had a soundtrack, and it was one you could sing along to.

Later, I would realise there was something else that drew me to this tune. I've long suspected that our musical reference points are shaped by our parents' earliest musical choices. My parents were obsessed by music hall, the entertainments of the urban working classes from which they had come. They were fascinated by the likes of Flanagan and Allen and Max Wall, by Marie Lloyd and Will Fyffe. They were members of the Players' Theatre, a last bastion of music hall, located in a railway arch in London's Charing Cross. It wasn't exactly pastiche. It had opened in the 1930s, when the music halls were still going strong; even in the 1970s some of the older performers there had played the last of the music halls that died out after the Second World War. But by the time I went there was no doubt it was an act of remembrance. It had the air of a life-support machine, maintaining the social commentary of songs like 'If It Wasn't for the 'Ouses In Between', about the gorgeous view of the world the poor could have but for all the terraced houses that got in the way. It was about audience participation and shared choruses and the lot of the huddled poor.

The best of late-twentieth-century English pop – the Kinks, Ian Dury and the Blockheads, Madness – drew on that music-hall tradition and its ribald approach to social commentary. 'Ghost Town' by the Specials did exactly that. Naturally, I learnt to play it on the piano. I learnt to play it very badly.

Snails

Looking back, I see now that snails were my gateway food. They were the compulsive item that got me into the whole damn incessantly hungry business. They pre-dated oysters and offal and were a long way ahead of salted anchovies and stinky cheeses. They were an early marker for where my interests were to lie. As with the oysters, it was the accessories that got me into them. I do so love an accessory.

In the early 1970s, as my mother's career took off, my parents opened an account at a restaurant on Panton Street, near Piccadilly Circus, called Stone's Chophouse. It was first launched as a coffee house in 1812 by a Mr William Stone, but soon widened its repertoire. Throughout the nineteenth century it was, by turns, the height of fashion and the lowest dive for the brawling classes, before regaining a certain class in the twentieth century, though only if you were a man. Women weren't admitted until 1921, a full three years after some of them had got the vote. By the 1970s it was a grand place under the ownership of the Savoy Hotel Group, with wall drapes the colour of shimmering amber and a menu of things white-jacketed waiters could set fire to tableside. Snails were among them. My mother encouraged me. She said they were my kind of thing. Claire had my measure.

They came with a paraffin burner, the guttering flame causing the garlicky butter in the dimpled tray to bubble and fizz so that you could fry your bread in it. First, though, you had to master the tongs. You had to work out that once the snail was held inside the bowl at the end, you had to keep your grip light. The temptation was to squeeze while digging in with the fork. But if you did that, you risked opening the tongs and flicking the snail halfway across the room. The Rayners liked attention, but it had to be the right sort of attention. Family lore says that I got it first time, that I was a natural. Given my failure at other boyish pursuits, I wore this as a badge of honour. I worked out quickly that you had to upend the shell to release any extra garlicky butter, that it was okay to probe them with your tongue for the crusty bits of parsley and garlic. Or at least nobody told me off. This was dinner as adventure. Eating snails showed commitment and an unwillingness to be perturbed.

Later, we would eat them at home. Those snails came in a tin, which was at the bottom of a clear plastic tube filled with the shells. Your job was to reintroduce the one to the other, then backfill the shells with hunks of green-flecked garlic butter. It was dinner-party food, to be eaten using the tongs we had at home. They lived in the drawer of the over-varnished Welsh dresser in the kitchen, alongside the yellow plastic corn-cob holders and cheap plastic chopsticks I hadn't yet mastered.

All families have their own stories and legends. The key one about me, the one which defined me in the eyes of the rest of the family, involves snails. I have told it before (in my book *The Man Who Ate the World*), but in this context it has to be told again. I was in Switzerland on a school skiing trip, in the process of discovering that, perhaps unsurprisingly for a ten-year-old boy with weak ankles and fat thighs that rubbed together, I was lousy at skiing. I was already certain that I had damaged one of my knees for life, I couldn't master carrying the skis over my shoulders, hated the hotel, which smelt of mothballs, and in particular despised the food. It smelt of boiled cabbage and disdain. I was homesick.

One day, on the stumbled walk back from the slopes I noticed an old wooden hotel. There was a menu pinned up outside. I had a look. The only word I immediately understood was 'escargots'. It speaks volumes for my gilded, privileged, overfed childhood that this was the word which made me pine the most.

That evening, after eating the mediocre dinner at the hotel I skidded and slid down the snow-packed lane back to the other hotel. I got myself a table and ordered the snails – '*Eas-car-go sill-vooo-play*' – from the bemused waiter. They came on a fearsome burner, a giant of a thing, which had the lakes of melted dairy bubbling within seconds. My toast became crisp and my cheeks warm, and for the thirty minutes I was there I forgot about the misery of the slopes and falling over and my physical incompetence. I came back the next night, and the night after that. By that third night I was a master of the burner. I knew how to pull the snails from their shell deftly and at such an angle as to save the mother lode of garlic butter within. I knew how to fry the toast to crisp and then move it off to the edge of the platter so it didn't incinerate and become bitter. I cranked the burner up again and again.

Naturally enough, the whole thing ignited. Bright orange flames roared upwards a foot or more from the surface of the top plate. I was in an ancient hotel, built entirely of wood, watching flames leap into the air. The hotel had survived centuries of the elements up here in the mountains. Would it survive an evening with me?

The episode ended quickly. The waiter appeared noiselessly at my side, flung open the window to my left, lifted the whole flaming contraption up and threw it out into the snow. I asked for the bill. He agreed this was a good idea.

This might have put some people off snails. Not me. It drew me to them, not least because the fried garlic toast had been spectacular in the moments before ignition, that perfect combination of crisp and oily and salty. Plus, it was the sort of story any greedy person wants told about them. It made me sound buccaneering and committed. I would risk burning down buildings in pursuit of my dinner.

If ever there was a food that deserved to be a part of this last meal of mine, it was snails. Wrapped up in them were memories of parental approval, of bravery and appetite and derring-do. Plus, I really, really liked eating them. I just had to find the right ones.

I am sitting in the consulting room of a nice consultant physician called Brian Kent, who is part of the team at the sleep clinic of Guy's

Hospital, just south of London Bridge. I have already had a consultation with an ear, nose and throat specialist who has shone lights down my gullet to see whether I have any structural issues which might be causing the snoring. It's nice of him to look, but even if he finds anything worth operating on, there is no way I'm going under the knife. I have two friends who had chronic snoring problems. Both have undergone the procedure to slice open and stretch the soft tissue at the back of the throat to tighten it up. Both of them have described it to me as the most unpleasant and painful experience of their lives, one which lasted not just hours or days, but weeks. Pat and I have agreed that no matter what the situation, I am not undergoing surgery.

Instead, on a previous visit, the sleep clinic gave me a recording device to wear overnight. It involved attaching electrodes to my chest to measure my heartbeat, a small cuff on my fingertip to measure oxygen uptake, a couple of tubes up my nose to record my breathing and a device strapped elsewhere on my chest to recognise what position I was sleeping in. Dr Kent, a tall, thin chap who has made it clear he reads my restaurant reviews, gives the impression that my case is interesting, though it may just be a highly developed bedside manner. Each time I have attended the various clinics I have been given a sheet and asked to score my drowsiness during the day. I am asked how likely I am to doze off, on a score from one to three, while travelling in a car, talking to someone, watching TV and so on. For most of these, I score low. Watching TV gets a two. That is quite likely, but anecdotally I know most of my middle-aged mates do it. I have yet to meet anybody so dull that simply talking to them renders me unconscious. That gets a zero. My overall score is on the slightly high side of normal.

Dr Kent has the results from my overnight sleep test.

'You're an interesting subject.'

'Lord save us from being boring.'

'Well, indeed.' He picks up a fragile sheet of paper, marked with a graph. 'Looking at this, we can see that you have positional sleep apnoea.

When you sleep on your side, you are completely normal: very little in the way of snoring and fewer than ten episodes of sleep apnoea, which is standard for the population. But when you sleep on your back . . .'

'Yes?'

'. . . you are catastrophic. An average of seventy-two episodes an hour.'

I stop breathing more than once a minute? The problem is, I spend at least half the night on my back. By this point I have done a little research into sleep apnoea, have understood the way it mimics death. I have joked about me occasionally pegging out in the night. But seventy-two times an hour? That doesn't leave much space in which to mimic being alive.

Naturally, I have looked at causes. Extra weight is an obvious and unavoidable one, and I am a fully paid-up member of the club. But there is also the simple business of being a man aged over forty. It's more common in men, and more common the older you are. There can also be a genetic predisposition to such things, and I am certain now that my mother had untreated sleep apnoea. A neck measurement of seventeen inches or more is an indicator, and mine is exactly seventeen, which is probably where it should be for a man of my build and height. I can keep working to lose weight. I can get down in the trenches and fight the great war that will probably never end, but it's unlikely to alter things greatly.

Then again, Dr Kent says, I am also a curious case because I don't appear to be reporting major side effects. My blood pressure is absolutely fine. My heart rate is even better than fine, pumping along in the fifties. This, I tell him proudly, is a genetic inheritance from my mother. She told me we all have athletic hearts, which, given my hatred of team sports, is hilarious. We discuss my drowsiness, which is not a major issue.

'If you were a truck driver, we might be required to have a serious conversation,' he says to me. 'But as you're a restaurant critic . . .' He doesn't need to finish the sentence. Me falling asleep in a bowl of sensitively roasted beetroot is hardly a hazard to anyone. I ask him for advice.

He shrugs. There is a device to treat positional apnoea called a NightBalance. You wear it, and whenever it senses you are on your back it buzzes so you know to turn over. But it hasn't been approved for use by the NHS.

He says, 'Honestly, I'm minded to suggest we don't treat it at all.'

I like this idea. I like this idea very much. Yes, I may have sleep apnoea, but it is of a sort that is not worth treating. I am a mild case. I am not yet that old or that dead. Guy's Hospital, being near London Bridge, is also close to Borough Market, the gloriously overstuffed repository of killer ingredients from all over the world. I celebrate my lack of deadness by going across and buying a bunch of asparagus, a pack of cooking chorizo and a loaf of sourdough. I go to the German food stall there and stock up on bratwurst, including the ones made with cheese. I do love a cheesy bratwurst.

This is a good day.

A damp spring evening, and my Uber is being driven in tight circles around Châtelet-Les Halles in central Paris. Like Uber drivers the world over, Rigaud – the app immediately puts you on first-name terms – doesn't appear massively knowledgeable about his patch. He's at the mercy of the satnav and getting tetchy as the route, etched electronically in blue across the screen, keeps changing without actually getting us there. Eventually, as it looks like we're about to start a third loop, we bail. I am too excited to spend another ten minutes sitting in this damn Toyota Prius, watching the same Parisian mansion blocks and red awnings pass me by. There are snails in my future, and I don't want to wait for them any longer than necessary. I have done my homework. I know I am going to the right place.

I am an old hand at restaurant research. I don't regard finding the right venue as a chore; I see it as part of the anticipation of the meal to come and, therefore, of the meal itself, a means by which to extend the pleasure. You start thinking about the joy of a particular dish. You browse menus, try to ascertain from the wording (usually written by someone who went into catering specifically to avoid having to write ever again) whether it is the edible wonder you are dreaming of. You seek out recommendations. In this case, I emailed Michel Roux Jr, chef patron of London's Le Gavroche, a temple to classicism. If anybody would know where to go for the best snails in Paris, it was him.

'The ones at Allard in Paris are excellent,' he replied. 'I had some a few months ago, lots of good-quality butter, cooked through and just the right amount of garlic.'

I looked up Allard. It's one of those old-school bistros in Saint-Germain-des-Prés. It first opened in 1932 and changed hands a few times before being bought by superstar chef Alain Ducasse. He's made a habit of saving old-school bistros and then doing absolutely nothing controversial with them. Paris is brilliant at taking its restaurant clichés seriously, of venerating them and wallowing in them. Looking at the Allard website I could see it was indeed one of those glorious, honey-toned clichés: red velvet banquettes, a little brass rail here and there, floral wallpaper and a menu full of foie gras, endive salad, Challandais duck with olives and, praise be, escargots. Yours for 22€ the dozen. I booked a table for dinner.

Then I got the fear. Michel Roux Jr knows his stuff. He's Anglo-French, did his military service with the catering operation of the Élysée Palace. He literally trained to protect the French republic from aggressors by knocking up hollandaise sauce and clarifying stocks and making persillade. If anybody was going to know where to get good food, it had to be him. Didn't it?

I started doubting myself, and him.

I returned to doing my research. I looked at food blogs, written by people who just love the smell of a comped meal in the evening. I read overheated travel pieces on Paris which bathed in all the bad clichés and used the word 'romance' in a manner that suggested they'd never experienced any. One afternoon I even typed the words 'escargot', 'Paris' and 'TripAdvisor' into Google, and immediately hated myself. TripAdvisor is an echo chamber for the sound of grinding axes; it's where criticism goes to die. Afterwards I deleted my search history so that nobody would find out what I'd done.

Not that it really mattered. All of my labours had pointed me at the same place: L'Escargot Montorgueil, on rue Montorgueil. It opened exactly a century before Allard, in 1832. It had the French word for snail in its title. It had a dedicated snail menu. Naturally enough, you could have them with garlic butter, but also with truffles or foie gras. You could have them with blue cheese or something described as 'curry' in the staggeringly arrogant French way that turns the entirety of the food from the Indian subcontinent into one appalling, astringent, over-roasted spice mix. I would not let this trouble me. I was going to Paris for snails specifically because they were a classic of the belligerent French repertoire; to criticise a Parisian restaurant that was serving them for displaying the usual snobbery and ignorance towards other culinary traditions would be like slagging off the chief rabbi for being a bit too Jewish.

I cancelled the Allard booking. I sorted out a hotel room, a Eurostar ticket and a companion in Paris, a guide who operates food tours, and rebooked for L'Escargot Montorgueil. It is located on a road that is now pedestrianised, which is what had given our driver's satnav a nervous breakdown. Still, it wasn't hard to find. It has a huge bloody sculpture of a snail above the door, a big undulating thing in polished metal. We pushed our way inside. The dining area was made up of multiple rooms. The banquettes were the familiar deep velvet red. There was polished brass rail and dark wood and the air was heavy with the tang of garlic, just cooked down from raw. So far, so good.

It was as we were led towards our table that I started to have my doubts.

I have been to famous French restaurants that attract tourists before. I have been to Bofinger, the brasserie just off the Bastille, with its groaning oyster stand outside and intricate stained-glass dome over the dining room; or the bistro Chez Georges in the 2nd arrondissement, where they bring the soused herring pot to you and tell you to take as much as you would like. Naturally enough, you hear voices in those places that aren't French: a few Americans perhaps, or maybe an Australian. There's always a Japanese couple or two. We all admire each other for having had the good taste to find our way here when others didn't. But it's also obvious that most of the tables are occupied by locals. The giveaway is usually a dapper gentleman of middle years, eating alone with a glass of red wine, a newspaper and an invisible sign that reads: 'Go away; I have no need of your company'.

L'Escargot Montorgueil was not like that. Almost every diner was Asian, either Chinese or Japanese. The only French I could hear being spoken was among the waiters. Still, all of these other customers seemed to be enjoying themselves. A glut of tourists was not necessarily a bad thing, and I was also a tourist. What mattered was the food. That was why I had made the effort to get here. A dozen Burgundy snails in garlic butter was 34 euros, twelve more than at Allard. But hey, this was *the* place. I ordered half a dozen with garlic butter and half a dozen with truffle butter, followed by a 1kg côte de boeuf and chips.

They brought spring-loaded tongs. They brought tiny forks, the better to reach inside the shells. They brought napkins, the better to clean up the mess I was preparing to make. They brought toast.

Hang on.

What is this?

A small basket had been shoved onto the table, containing batons of white bread toasted only on one side. They were cold. I frowned, picked up one of the miserable pieces of cotton-wool bread and turned it this way and that in my hands. I tried to imagine who would think this was a good idea.

Then the main event arrived, and it turned out the bread was an irrelevance. Usually, you need it to mop away at the foaming sea of herb-ballasted butter. It's a part of the joy. But these dimpled metal trays, holding the six filled snail shells, were completely butterless. The clean metal still shined under the lights. As for the snails themselves, they were dry. Snails work as a vehicle for other flavours. They have their own flavour, something deep, nutty and lightly bitter, but it's subtle. They don't just go well with garlic butter; they need it. There needs to be enough to smear your cheeks and get behind your ears. These appeared to have been introduced to the butter dish in the kitchen, but only formally, like a duchess being introduced to a charity worker. They were dry, wizened, unfortunate. As to the ones made with truffle butter, they might as well just have had the word 'truffle' shouted at them aggressively, for all the difference it made. They tasted of truffle not at all.

Years ago, long before I became a reviewer of restaurants, before food became my subject, I made much of my living as a reporter covering murders and the evil that people do. I sat in courtrooms, listened to evidence and recorded jury verdicts. Outside those courtrooms I gave witness. I was there to make sure the world knew in detail what had happened. Suddenly, in this restaurant, faced by this calamity, this expression of mediocrity and laziness in a dimpled tray, I concluded my experience as a reporter was perfectly suited to the moment. I could be the one to record the calamity.

Until I was fourteen I thought I was going to be an actor. My father, Des, had been one. Although he got bored of being hungry and eventually left the theatre for a career in fashion PR, many of his friends were still actors. As a result, whenever we went to the theatre, we usually 'went back' to say hello to whichever cast member was a friend of my father's (or of my mother's, who was good at collecting famous people). By the time I was ten I had been backstage at every major West End theatre. I had drunk Coke with Tommy Steele in the star dressing room at the Palladium – it had its own pinball machine – and been allowed inside the Tardis used as a prop for a stage adaptation of *Doctor Who*. It turned out it was just a wooden box.

This, combined with a tendency to show off and an ability not to forget lines during a primary school panto, convinced me that I too was destined to be an actor. Then, when I was fourteen, I auditioned for the secondary school play and made a discovery: I was rubbish. It turned out that there was more to acting than remembering lines and showing off. So now I looked to my mother and concluded that she was a far better role model. I would be a journalist instead. Every morning four newspapers came into the house and were divided up among us – probably a ruse by my mother to avoid having to talk to us over breakfast. I became absorbed by a column in the *Daily Mail* from America of what used to be called 'miscellany': random, light, amusing stories which individually didn't amount to much, but which cumulatively created a gripping portrait of the country. It appeared every weekday and was written by a journalist called Dermot Purgavie. Just his name was terrific. Purr-gah-vee. I concluded that being Dermot Purgavie looked like fun. You got to find out things and tell people about them. Plus, all the journalists I had met with my mother seemed interesting, like they were only seconds away from having to go and attend something important. I was told that some of them carried their passport with them at all times, just in case. That sounded like a life.

At sixteen, I applied to Leeds University, partly because I liked the sound of the politics course, but mostly because it had what was then the largest student newspaper in the country. Eight thousand copies of *Leeds Student* were printed, covering all the colleges in the city, and it had a readership estimated at 25,000. Most importantly, you had to be elected by a cross-campus vote to the editor's chair, which was a full-time job with a salary paid by the students' union. It was probably as a function of the gross sense of entitlement gifted by an expensive public-school education that I decided I would go to Leeds, work my way up the paper and get myself elected. That way nobody could accuse me of having got where I was in journalism just because my mother was a well-known journalist. It was an absurd, over-reaching, ludicrously arrogant plan. It was also exactly what happened. My first job in journalism was as editor of *Leeds Student* from 1987 to 1988. It made no difference to people accusing me of having got my job through nepotism. It still goes on, even now, despite the fact that she died in 2010, though why having a mother who was an expert on premature ejaculation should have got me a job on *MasterChef* I shall never know.

It took me twenty years to come up with that line.

At the end of my *Leeds Student* editorship, still greasy with entitlement I concluded I didn't have the patience to go on a journalism training course. I reckoned I knew what I needed to know. Arrogance springs eternal. At first it seemed I was right. In the late 1980s the national press had decided that if they could grab readers while they were still students, they might have them for life. All of the then broadsheets started publishing student supplements of one sort or another. If you were a journalist who appeared to know anything at all about what students were interested in, they wanted you. There were only about half a dozen full-time student newspaper editors in Britain, and we were all approached by the nationals. My first paid piece, an observational 'My Week' column, appeared in the *Independent*'s summer-term student supplement in 1988. The byline was a calling card. That summer I worked for most of the student supplements, from the *Telegraph* to *Time Out* and back to the *Independent*. Eventually, I landed at the *Observer*, which was soon to launch Britain's first tabloid newspaper supplement, a London-only lifestyle and arts magazine called *Section 5*, funded by the late-1980s boom in property advertising. I was taken on to research and write property pieces.

At the launch party the editor, an old features hand called Nick Wapshott, who had recruited me, asked what I thought of the new supplement. I was still just twenty-one, but I had already made it onto the nationals so, patently, I knew absolutely everything there was to know about journalism. I said, 'It's great, but it's got the worst diary column I've ever read.' It was a grand statement, but it wasn't wrong. The writer, a journalist twenty years my senior, was using the space to witter on about people he had met at launch parties and whether the latest washed-up 1970s band he'd been to see play were any good. He was literally writing a diary; which is to say, his own. The column needed stories.

The editor said, 'Actually, I agree.' Two weeks later, Wapshott sacked the diary writer and gave the job to me. 'Go see my secretary. She'll give you all my party invites. Go to all of them, and don't forget to collect the taxi receipts.' I fed myself from those parties. Life was a parade of platters filled with goujons of plaice and flutes of free booze. At one launch I met a diary-column old hand, who said, 'Welcome to journalism. It's a champagne lifestyle on beer money.' He wasn't wrong.

My first column, published in September 1988, included a story revealing the identity of the media advisor to Prince Charles (it was Wilf Stevenson, then the director of the British Film Institute), something about Malcolm McLaren judging a vogueing competition in New York and a cracking tale about how the Museum of the Moving Image was looking for a company to transport the five-metre-high model of King Kong from the 1976 movie to London for free. However smug about it I may have been, it wasn't exactly Woodward and Bernstein. I was horribly inexperienced and shouldn't have been given the job. Still, at least they were stories.

Four months later, Wapshott decided to publish an American edition of *Section 5* to coincide with the inauguration of George Bush Sr as president. He told me I could go to the US if I could wangle a free flight. I phoned Virgin Atlantic, who had only just started their service to New York. Because I had no shame and no morals, I offered them a credit on the page in return for the flight.

'Okay,' they said. 'And we'll upgrade you.' It seemed of a piece with the way things were going that I should fly to New York for the first time in their equivalent of first class. Giving them that credit wasn't hard. Once airborne I slipped back into economy. I found two nuns in full habit. Nuns flying Virgin wrote itself. Further behind them was Lemmy from Motörhead; in a smart ruse to drum up publicity Virgin had offered to fly any bona fide pop star for free, and Lemmy qualified.

I asked him why he was going to New York.

He growled, 'I'm going to a party.'

'Oh yes?'

'Yeah, it's Joey Ramone's. Wanna come?'

I did go. In reality, it was a gig in a filthy old theatre down in the Meatpacking District, where they played roaring metal and burnt an effigy of Ronald Reagan on stage. The next night I blagged my way into the premiere of a spoof blaxploitation movie. There I met a press photographer who took pity on me. He told me about a party the next night for a new movie called *Tap*, starring Sammy Davis Jr, about generations of tap dancers. I turned up at the Peninsula Hotel to discover it wasn't, as I imagined, some press junket but the wrap party for cast and crew. They let me in anyway. I stood in the ballroom of the midtown hotel and watched as veteran tapper Sandman Sims and the younger Gregory Hines took to the floor and started tapping against each other, cheered on by the team who had made the movie. They were followed by the then fourteen-year-old Savion Glover. Then Sammy pushed his way through, knees lightly bent, those skinny fingers of his clawing at the air as if he were about to get airborne. Somehow I had managed to gatecrash one of the greatest tap-offs the city had seen in decades. For a boy raised on the Arthur Freed MGM musicals, who had idolised Fred Astaire and Gene Kelly and who had even taken tap-dancing lessons as a delusional clumsy ten-year-old, this was bliss.

Afterwards I was cornered by a PR woman, who said, 'I assume you're here because you're interviewing Sammy tomorrow.'

It was time for some more Olympic-standard blagging. I said, 'Yes. Remind me when and where.'

The next day I went back to the hotel and joined what's called a 'round table': groups of journalists corralled into sets of rooms, through which the stars then circulate to be interviewed. I hogged the interview, squeezed Sammy Davis Jr for every last quote. We talked blackness and the appropriation by the very white Broadway musical of African American dance traditions. At the end, clocking I was the only British journalist in the room, he asked me when I had got into town.

I said, 'About three days ago.'

He nodded slowly. He knew *Tap*'s press screening schedule. It had been the week before. 'Then you haven't seen the movie.'

I was busted. 'No, but I'm very much looking forward to it.'

He reached up and clapped me on the shoulder. 'Chutzpah,' he said, and left the room.

At the end of my week I lay on my hotel bed – I had booked into the Algonquin; it was the only New York hotel I'd heard of because my parents stayed there – and dictated my column to copytakers. Afterwards I was transferred to the magazine's deputy editor. He told me that Nick Wapshott, the man who had employed me, had quit to become political editor. I knew immediately my time was up. My filed copy was full of names that were misspelt, sometimes in multiple ways. I would mangle grammar. My reporting would occasionally be dreadfully inaccurate. Each press night, as we worked to finish that week's edition, I would sit next to the staggeringly patient chief subeditor as she reworked my copy and, quite reasonably, shouted at me. If my mentor and protector was now gone, the *Observer*'s patience would soon run out. I had to go too. I flew home overnight, went straight to the office from the airport and quit. The new editor accepted my resignation with what felt like indecent haste. In truth, I was relieved. I suspected that, given my ignorance of libel law, it was merely luck that I had dodged being sued. I also feared that my ludicrously fast start in the business had been some fluke. If I really was made for journalism, if I had a future, I had to quit, go freelance and see if I could make it all over again.

While I was working out my notice, a journalist friend told me that the arts editor of the *Guardian* was interested in me. I phoned him up.

His name was Roger Alton and he barked at me. He would continue to bark at me for the twenty years that I would end up working for him.

'I hear you like my column in the *Observer*,' I said.

He said, 'Yeah. What do you want to do?'

I panicked. 'Er . . . well, I've got an interview with Sammy Davis Jr.'

'One thousand eight hundred words. Tuesday.' He hung up. He often did that.

At the time, the *Guardian*'s cinema pages appeared on Fridays in the paper's second broadsheet section. My interview with Sammy ran the Friday after my last *Observer* column. It was the whole front page of the second section. I bought multiple copies of the paper and stared at my name on a newspaper supplement's front page.

Everything was going to be okay.

There are other ways to eat snails, apart from stuffed into their shells with garlic butter. While on holiday in northern Spain one summer a few years ago, there was a thunderstorm. Within an hour of the rain stopping the lanes were filled with people clutching plastic carrier bags and picking at the hedgerows. It turned out they were foraging for the small local snails. I later tried them at a huge restaurant on the main road towards Girona called Can Barris, which first opened in 1949, where they served them in trays of fifty, 100 or even 250. They were baked under a spiky paste of tomatoes, garlic, olive oil and herbs. Whole family groups would order hundreds and then sit around digging at them with wooden toothpicks and sucking at the crusted shells and chucking the empties onto a central plate. I liked them very much, enjoyed the intense, meditative eating process, akin to picking the kernels out of salted pistachio shells. But they felt like a lesser experience than the classic French preparation.

Naturally, when Heston Blumenthal announced he had come up with a dish called snail porridge at the Fat Duck, I had to try it. As is often the case, he was playing with language. In truth, it was a risotto, with the rice replaced by oats. So, yes, it could be called porridge, but it was closer to a polenta. The oats were used as a vehicle for an intense persillade: all the joyful pleasures of salty butter, garlic and, to give it an outrageous green colour, handfuls of blitzed flat-leaf parsley. On top of this were the shell-free snails, with a little acidulated fennel. It wasn't so much a new dish as a reworking of the flavours of the classic snails in the shell with garlic butter, presented in a different form. I liked it for all the wistful memories it brought back, but it lacked the tongs.

I have had garlic sautéed snails as a topping for steak and in little tarts, and as part of a canapé. But none of these has replaced the full experience I was looking for in Paris.

The morning after my meal at L'Escargot Montorgueil I had arranged to meet and interview the head chef, a big-shouldered twenty-seven-year-old called Tom LeFevre. Through an interpreter he confirmed that 80 per cent of their clientele were from abroad and that 60 per cent of those were either Chinese or Japanese. 'They come to France specifically to try these dishes, so they come to us.' He told me they shifted 2,000 snails a day, all imported from Romania or Hungary. 'The species of snail from Burgundy are protected, so we get them from Eastern Europe instead. They come in live and are blanched in stock by our supplier before being sent on to us.'

I asked him if he felt the weight of history on his shoulders. 'In this place, yes. Snails are emblematic. It's like an onion soup. I would like to serve them out the shell more, but here you can't do that.' He said he had a brilliant idea. 'I want to do a snail burger.'

'As in chopped-up snails? Like a steak haché?'

He nodded vigorously. 'But they wouldn't let me do it here.' Then he said, 'Now then, you should try some snails.'

I said, 'It's okay. I came last night.'

His face fell. 'You've already eaten here?'

'Yes.'

'How was it?'

'Fine,' I said, pursing my lips. He sloped back into his kitchen.

Then I did what I should always have done. I followed Michel Roux Jr's recommendation and bagged an early-lunch table at Allard. It was everything I wanted a Parisian bistro to be, as were the snails. Butter overflowed hotly from the shells. There was a good strong baguette to mop up with. I felt the fire and light of garlic on my breath. Afterwards I ate a lardons salad with big, crisp pieces of belly pork and bronzed croutons and a bright vinegary dressing that stripped the dairy fats from my tongue. It was all those clichés taken seriously.

I was happy, but I was not content. They'd been good, these snails in their glossy shells, but they hadn't been great. They hadn't been the best. I had a suspicion I knew where to get great ones from. It was a plan that I knew would make every Parisian chef worth their demi-glace roll their eyes. Still, I realised what I had to do.

L'Escargot on Greek Street in London's Soho is not quite as old as its namesake in Paris, but it pre-dates Allard. The original was opened in 1896 by M. Georges Gaudin as Le Bienvenue, at the bottom of the same street, but moved to its present location in a tottering townhouse in 1927. At that point its name changed to include that of the dish for which it was most famous. Now it was L'Escargot Bienvenue, a celebration of the fact that it claimed to be the first restaurant in Britain to serve snails. If you ignored the Romans, who doubtless had hostelries serving them during their four-century rule, then this probably was the case. For many years the snails came from a farm in the basement, though now the space is occupied by the kitchen.

Today, L'Escargot is a cosy set of interlocking rooms, hung with some serious modern art. The tables are thickly clothed, the glassware shines and the menu takes French clichés more seriously than the French do. It includes a lobster bisque with a depth of flavour that suggests it has been cooking down since M. Gaudin first sparked up the gas in the 1920s. There is Tournedos Rossini, fully garnished, coq au vin and a crème brûlée.

And there are snails. I order half a dozen for £16. And they are perfect. As in a complete and utter joy. The snail-filled shells come on a searingly hot cast-iron platter and are bathed in a foaming pea-green sea of garlic butter, hinged somewhere between liquid and solid. It is what bread was invented for. I mop and mop again and mop some more. I pull the snails from their shells and dredge them through the sauce, and find myself thinking back on all the good snail experiences: at Stone's as a kid, and in Switzerland on my 'fire-starter' holiday, and at many other French bistros that were nearly but not quite. It felt like each of them was leading up to this all-consuming snail experience. I have written glibly over the years about how too much of my emotional well-being is rooted in the quality of my lunch. I have tried to use it as a self-deprecating joke. But sitting here, bathing in the molten garlic butter of the gods, I begin to wonder if this were indeed so. Was there something excessive about the happiness this gave me?

And then another thought occurred to me, a slightly darker one. If these were the best snails I had ever eaten – and they really were – then how was I going to replicate this at home for this grand life-framing meal I was planning?

At which point it struck me that I hadn't thought any of this through at all. Was I actually going to be serving this grandstanding meal at home? And if I was, would I be the one cooking it? Did that make any sense? Surely that would turn my last supper into my long chore? I rubbed at the cast iron with my bread, let the herby garlic butter get under my nails and all over my fingertips. I had focused on the ingredients, but I hadn't made a plan. I needed one. And it had to be good.

Escargots Parmentier

Any dish with the word 'Parmentier' in the title celebrates the life and work of Antoine-Augustin Parmentier, an eighteenth-century pharmacist who celebrated and promoted the potato as a food source throughout Europe. Any French Parmentier dish therefore involves potatoes in one form or another, though usually mashed or boiled. I do think snails should be in their shells, but this delivers all of the flavours in a rather tidier form. It's also outrageously rich, but I can't apologise for that. Canned snails are relatively easy to get, though sometimes turn up in tins containing five or six dozen. Rest assured, they freeze. And no, I'm not giving you a recipe for mashed potato. I'm assuming you know how to make that. If you don't, go look it up.

Serves two greedy people as a starter

INGREDIENTS

Eighteen snails

80g good-quality salted butter, softened

Two large cloves of garlic, crushed

2tbsp chopped flat-leaf parsley

Two medium potatoes, mashed (make with salted butter and season as normal)

2tbsp breadcrumbs (Japanese panko are best, but any will do)

Extra butter

Drain the snails on kitchen paper so they are reasonably dry. Then cut each one in half.

Mash the butter with the garlic and parsley.

Mix the snails in with the butter evenly, then spread across the bottom of a small oval dish. Place in the freezer to chill for an hour or two.

Make the mash and chill that too.

Heat the oven to 220°C.

Cover the chilled snail–butter mix with the mash, score the surface and sprinkle with a thick layer of the breadcrumbs. Dot with extra butter.

Bake in the oven for around thirty minutes, until the topping is golden brown.

Serve by digging the spoon right to the bottom to get both garlicky, buttery snails and mash.

Have a lie down before the main course.

▶ 3. 'Love Cats', the Cure (1983)

I tried very hard to be a proper teenager, with a serious and appropriate interest in the indie charts. I claimed to like Bauhaus and Joy Division, and could talk knowledgeably about all four sides of *London Calling* by the Clash. I bleached various bits of my hair with an old toothbrush and a bottle of peroxide, and gave up on the piano and bought synths in an attempt to sound like the Human League. Eventually, I managed to acquire what almost looked like a stack – a Juno-6 polyphonic job; an SH-101, which you could wear round your neck like a guitar if you didn't mind looking like a dick; and a rudimentary drum machine which sounded like it was worked by hamsters on wheels – and pretended I was Howard Jones. (If only I'd kept those instruments. They became extremely valuable collector's items.)

But my heart wasn't in it. I would always perk up at the sight of a band with a brass section, and I loved a lush string arrangement. (For the record, 'Our House' by Madness had it all.) All those Sunday afternoons sitting in front of the telly with my parents watching the MGM musicals had left their mark on me. I was waiting for the moment when I could admit that, really, what I wanted to listen to was jazz. Interestingly, the early 1980s weren't a bad time for this. Sade, Working Week and Everything but the Girl weren't just jazz-inflected, they were jazz. But admitting you liked them was tricky and could be divisive. Sade's 'Smooth Operator' was a terrific song, but it was also for a particular kind of suburban north London soul boy with a Ford Capri and a taste for Bacardi. That wasn't me.

'Love Cats', with its brilliant walking bass line, was the swing tune it was okay to adore. The Cure had already laid out their stall with the post-punk of 'Charlotte Sometimes' and 'Killing an Arab'. That 'Love Cats' was actually a sweet, frothy song with a hint of Looney Tunes about it didn't matter. It was the Cure. It was jazzy. And liking it was cool.

Booze

My first-ever alcoholic drink was, objectively, disgusting. It was created for me by my mother one evening during the early stages of a dinner party, when I was nine years old. The worst thing about it is, Claire was trying to be a good parent. She was trying to be kind. Into a small, tight-waisted liqueur glass she poured a measure of advocaat, the bright-yellow Dutch concoction made with eggs, sugar and brandy, which is, depending upon your point of view, either a soothing boozy custard or as close to alcoholic phlegm as makes no difference. Into this she poured a depth charge of cherry brandy, its deep-red colour expanding out of the yellow against the glass and settling in whorls and spirals on the surface. This she called blood and pus, and I took her word for it. She had been a nurse. She knew about these things.

It's obvious, isn't it, that she knew little about drinking. Nor did my father know any better. Des and Claire were part of a generation of Jews born in London's East End who regarded drinking as something the others did. Tumblers of whisky before dinner and cognacs after were for the non-Jews. The Jews did cake. They got high on sugar and arguing. I do not recall my parents ever going to a pub for a drink. Lunch maybe, and only then in one of those country pubs that did its very best to disguise its true nature by the careful use of tablecloths and waiter service. But never for a pint. They had a drinks trolley. What did you expect? We lived in the suburbs, for heaven's sake. It was stacked with cut-glass decanters filled with whisky, sherry and gin, for they understood there might be social obligations, that offering a drink was part of the contract. The contents were so rarely touched that over time the darker spirits tended to lose their colour due to the sunlight through the windows, next to which the trolley was parked. There was a bottle of sherry on there too, a sweet Bristol Cream. Claire would have a glass of that, but only once a week. If they served wine at a dinner party, it would be a blunt, overly effervescent German sparkling that they bought by the caseload because it was a bargain. They kept it mostly for the huge lunch parties they liked to throw, and they would always offer to dilute it with orange juice. As a kid it seemed odd to me that anyone would choose to drink the sparkling stuff neat, because proper, sophisticated people would surely always choose Buck's Fizz? Also, it was nasty without the orange juice.

I cannot recall ever seeing my parents drunk, and yet when I was nine, and often afterwards, my mother would pour me that blood and pus. Alcohol could only become an issue, she said with an authority that could not be challenged, if it was shrouded in the adult mystery of the forbidden. Far better to get me used to it early by offering me a drunken version of pudding, the sort of alcoholic drink I would never again encounter.

Not that she needed to worry. When the time came, I put my back into it.

When I was ten years old, my family moved house and I moved school, to somewhere a forty-minute coach ride away from home. This meant that for two years I had no friends. It wasn't that I was unpopular or smelt; I simply didn't know anyone who would either like or dislike me. When I was twelve, my parents sent me to a summer camp run by the youth section of the Reform synagogue movement, to which we belonged, despite my mother's deep suspicion of organised religion. She really must have been desperate to send me there. The local synagogue – indeed, any place of worship – was too great a source of prejudice, of bigotry and judgement of the sort that caused so many of the people who wrote to her so much pain. 'I hate the idea of sin,' she once told a television interviewer. She was hardly going to have much time for a form of worship that couldn't exist without some concept of sin.

My dad was less dogmatic. I think he was hedging his bets on the whole God business. 'You only regret what you don't do,' he said, as if he'd weighed the evidence. We would be members of the local synagogue, so that my brother and I could get bar mitzvahed at thirteen. Think of the party, he would say. There would be salmon with hollandaise sauce, with blintzes to follow. Later, there would be pastries. Many, many pastries. Think of the fountain pens. It would be an orgy of leather wallets and encyclopaedias and envelopes filled with cash. But there were other benefits of synagogue membership. Hence, when trying to find me friends, they chose the summer camp: 200 Jewish kids aged twelve to sixteen accommodated in a minor British public school miles from anywhere, with a full programme of adventure activities, sports and pointed lectures on the Holocaust. Because what's a summer holiday without getting to watch the Richard Dimbleby report on the liberation of Belsen?

It worked. I returned home with a profound sense of unease and a tight circle of just 130 friends scattered all over London who would wander the city in a pack every Saturday night.

When, in 1981, a few of them announced they were going on a tour of Israel with the same Jewish youth group, I asked if I could go too, despite having no particular interest in either Israel in particular or Zionism in general. I was certain that Harrow and Kenton were my homeland, and that I would be miserable living in a desert state. I've never been that convinced by sand. It's unreliable. But as a holiday it could be a laugh, and it was. We climbed to the top of Masada at dawn to watch the sun rise over the Negev. We bobbed high in the Dead Sea, as was obligatory. We camped in the Sinai while somebody played 'The Sound of Silence' very badly on a guitar. We worked as plum-pickers on a kibbutz. We tried to snog each other. Some of us failed. I failed.

One Friday night we stayed at a hotel on the shores of Lake Galilee that smelt of stewed vegetables. That's where I discovered there was a different kind of drinking, far removed from blood and pus. I got drunk for the first time. By which I mean properly drunk, so that the flat ground pitched and the clicking of my tongue against the roof of my mouth became a proof of life. It was on a bottle of Israeli brandy. Just those two words together sound wrong. What the hell was anyone in Israel doing making brandy? Up to then the only Israeli alcoholic drink I'd tried was Palwin No. 9, a red wine with the texture and flavour profile of cough medicine, but none of the efficacy. Nobody drank it because they liked it; they drank it at Passover, because ritual demanded that they should. Israeli brandy tasted like it had been made by the paramilitary wing of the Palwin company as a warning to others. All I recall is the harshness of the burn and the conviction that I just had to push on through, that this is what you did on the cusp of adulthood. It made the playing of 'The Sound of Silence' on the guitar better. Of the night I remember not much, save that a crowd of us sat by the lakeshore so we could hear the waters lapping and our voices bouncing about the emptiness.

The next morning came. That I remember. I remember the pneumatic drill inside my head, which I quickly identified as a hangover, to be endured amid the Israeli summer heat, and alone. This was not something you referred to a responsible adult. Their job would be to disapprove, and I didn't need that on top of the pain. I remember the scramble for the shade of a tree outside and the smell of hot pine needles and the hope that soon it would stop.

That's the thing: my memories of drunken nights are all hazy, a blurred film running too fast through the gate. But hangovers, those I remember. There was the one a year or so later, during a Jewish youth group tour of Europe by coach. We had stopped in Florence and had many rooms in a cheap hotel overlooking the cathedral. Ours hosted a party. I know I mixed Cointreau and Asti Spumante, by which I mean I put them in the same glass repeatedly and emptied the glass repeatedly, so that I felt the booze work its way up my body from knees to chest, until I rolled off a bed and landed on my face. I found myself still there the next morning, cheek down on the cooling marble, as dawn broke through the open shutters. My head hurt.

There was the hangover that I incurred at university trying to make a student radio show about the Otley Run, a pub crawl from one end of Leeds to the other through twenty different venues. I recorded myself getting drunk on half-pints of cider at each stop. I drank ten pints of cider and then . . . nothing. But oh, the hangover.

There was the one the day after a New Year's Eve when I drank Moscow mules.

There was the amazing one I managed to inflict on myself at a Muslim wedding, albeit a secular Muslim wedding.

There were the ones that followed the champagne parties thrown in the early 1990s by friends of mine who were wine writers. Four of them would get together and call in a bottle of vintage and non-vintage from thirty or more champagne houses. They would open the lot during a Saturday afternoon, tasting and spitting out no more than the top 100cl. Then they would fill a bath with ice and invite us all round to finish the job. The bar was the bathroom of a semi-detached in Colliers Wood. We drank until we couldn't, knowing by then what the consequences would be. The next day we would swear that we would never do this again. We always did.

Let's stop there for a moment and review the evidence. The alcoholic drinks I have referenced have been mostly awful: advocaat and cherry brandy, Israeli brandy, Cointreau and Asti Spumante. Champagne gets a mention, but instead of being the luxurious icon of the good life, I've reduced it to the status of slattern, sprawled in the bath in massive volume. Champagne is meant to be precise and refined. I've made it fat and cumbersome.

The fact is this: I've never been a very good drinker. I don't mean that I'm a lousy drunk. I think I'm a great drunk, which is to say I'll never be your or anyone else's problem. I don't get shouty or uninhibited. I don't try to put my underpants on my head or stick my tongue into anybody I shouldn't. You can wave me out of the door alone at the end of an evening and know that I'll make it home without being arrested. And I'll know exactly when the time to leave will be. I'll go from 'jolly' to 'had enough' in a shallow breath.

I also hate being around people who are completely lost in the bottom of a bottle. Inebriated people make me anxious and uneasy, as if something very bad is about to happen which will result in a mess that I will be required to clean up. Also, compared to some who make their living around food and drink, my capacity for booze is limited. I know people who can swap from white to red, from cocktails to digestif and back again without pause. I am not that person, and I am disappointed in myself for it. At some point in my thirties a phrase came into my head, probably when I was recovering from the night before, and it was this: I hate hangovers more than I like being drunk.

I haven't been able to escape this thought. It can't be unthought. It isn't just that hangovers are awful, though they are. It's just that, as time passes, it seems to take less to bring them on, and more effort to get rid of them. They are one of those physical afflictions that come with a side order of shame and self-loathing. It comes down to one word: control. I fear losing it. And that fear comes from one evening, late in my first term at Leeds University. Naturally, it involved eating something, in a bad way.

It is December 1984. My friend John and I have each just polished off a mushroom Cup-a-Soup, and we are waiting for the effects to kick in. Not the usual low-level nausea and sense of self-disgust that comes with eating something so grim and pallid. Or at least not just that. These Cup-a-Soups were laced with handfuls of magic mushrooms, obtained from a friend, and I was now vibrating with cheerful expectation. I had already watched, intrigued, as the wizened woody strands had inflated as the boiling water hit them; imagined this to be the first of many transformations I would witness tonight, courtesy of the beautiful hallucinations that lay ahead of me. This wasn't guesswork.

I had taken magic mushrooms twice before and hugely enjoyed the experience. There was a lightness to the psilocybin high, and a vividness to the images which I seemed able to control. I regarded magic mushrooms as an utterly benign drug.

Partly this was because, by then, I considered myself a master of narcotics. I had smoked my first joint aged thirteen, and enjoyed the experience so much I was soon buying my own dope from a rat-like man who lived in a North Harrow squat that smelt of cat's piss and the lizard tank in the corner and damp. Very quickly, I knew the difference between Red Leb and opiated black. I could roll a three-skin joint and knew how to cup my hands around the base of a clay 'chillum' pipe and suck the smoke deep.

I knew exactly what I was doing because, at home, there was a great resource. My mother took her work as an agony aunt and health-advice columnist for a national newspaper very seriously. One whole shelf of her office was filled with box files containing papers from medical journals. There was 'A' for Anxiety and Agoraphobia, 'B' for Bloating and 'N' for Narcotics. Before I tried any new drug I consulted the box file. (When a small amount of opium became available in my corner of north London I did my research: apart from addiction, one of the main issues was male impotence while under the influence. I was sixteen. No one wanted to shag me. It wasn't an issue. I found it just sent me to sleep and chalked it up as dull.)

Now I am in a friend's attic room on the edge of the university's campus, and the mushrooms have kicked in. There are others here who are only smoking dope. Everything is hilarious. Everything is light and good. I mentally congratulate myself on upping the dose from the time before. I had found some larger mushrooms in the little plastic bag and, though I had been told they could be much more potent than the others, had thrown them in anyway. More. Bigger. Better. Given my elation and my enjoyment of kaleidoscopic lights and the way my hand swooped and dived whenever I lifted it in front of my face, there was no doubt that this had been a terrific decision. Well done me.

An hour in and I am lying on a beanbag. John comes and stands over me. He says, 'How are you feeling?'

'Fine. Great.'

He says, 'I don't know who I am.'

'What do you mean?'

'I'm . . .' He pauses for so long I think he has forgotten I'm there. Then he says, '. . . lost.'

The night spirals out of control after that. He begins to panic, and so do I. A thick lump of anxiety rises in my chest. My throat begins to swell. I am fighting for breath. I stand and walk in circles, bashing my sides with my arms to remind myself that I am alive. John grabs onto another friend for support. He will be babysat through the entire night. But that's not my way. I don't want anyone near me. I rush out. I need to be away. I need to be alone. It is raining outside and the ground is made of molten gold under the sodium lamplight. I walk faster and faster but come to a halt on a bridge over the inner-city motorway. I stare at the cars, at the blistered rush of head- and tail-lights, at stripes of white and red. I think about jumping off into the crash and spray of the traffic. It will be a quicker way to die than this slow, toxic end. Because I am now certain: I have poisoned myself.

I make it back to my student flat, position a bucket by my bed and manage a terrible, haunted, hallucinatory sleep. I wake to a cold grey dawn, surprised at my apparent aliveness.

It's the last time I take recreational narcotics of any kind. From then on, I also avoid mushroom Cup-a-Soup. Every cloud . . .

My doubts about booze do not make me happy. I want to be the kind of man who has a taste for a particular kind of single malt, but until recently I wasn't even sure what a single malt was. I favour vodka over gin because the latter tastes too much of hedgerows and self-importance. In other words, I like vodka precisely because it is not terribly interesting or complex.

I positively hate Negronis and, indeed, bitters of all kinds. An Aperol Spritz doesn't sound like a drink; to me it sounds like a warning. In this I accept I may have failed to reach adulthood. Liking bitter alcoholic drinks is what grown-ups do. They cup them lovingly and find the bitterness invigorating. I just find myself looking deep into the glass and thinking, 'Who did this to my drink?' A bitter cocktail feels to me like a punishment for a crime I have yet to commit. For years, in my late teens and early twenties, I drank huge amounts of vodka and lime. I think I was creating my own alcopop: something sweet and beguiling and childish enough to enable me to neck it so I could get to the point where I wanted to be. But also, courtesy of the vodka, it made me adult enough to be out in grown-up society. I was thrilled on my first trip to New York as a journalist aged twenty-two to discover that this drink had a name.

'You mean a gimlet?' said the white-haired man in the white jacket, in charge of the legendary (now closed) Blue Bar of the Algonquin Hotel, once a resting place for proper wits and drinkers like Dorothy Parker and Robert Benchley.

'If vodka with lime is called a gimlet,' I said, 'then, yes, a gimlet.' He asked me what vodka I wanted. I panicked. I didn't have a clue. What did I know about vodka? Nobody had ever asked me before. I waved airily at the bottles staring back at me reproachfully from behind him. 'That one,' I said, indicating the bottle with the red, gold and white label.

'The Stolichnaya?' he said. 'Good choice.' Ha! Lucky choice.

It's odd. I can tell you in excruciating, tedious detail why the smoked salmon from the Port of Lancaster smokehouse is better than that from Forman & Son of London (it's all about the texture and the depth of the cure). I can tell you that the salt beef at Monty's Deli, on London's Hoxton Street, wins over that at the Brass Rail, inside Selfridges, on account of the fat. I can distinguish one butter from another, and pinpoint the exact cafe for Cantonese roast duck in London's Chinatown, despite it being available in three dozen different restaurants within a radius of 150 metres. (It's the Four Seasons on Gerrard Street, the one on the left. The glaze is darker. The fat is better rendered.) But I just can't quite find it in myself to show the same interest in wine. I like wine very much. I can tell when it's corked or just crap. But beyond a basic standard I am, secretly, one big shrug. Naturally, this drives wine enthusiasts insane. They disapprove. They think I am not showing anywhere near enough respect for a vital part of the restaurant experience. By which they really mean: what they regard as *the* vital part of the experience. And they hate me even more when I tell them that twenty years as a restaurant critic – twenty years of corresponding with readers – has convinced me that on the whole the readers agree with me. Generally, the people who complain about my lack of wine coverage are the ones who make their living in some way from the wine business, either as a wine merchant, sommelier or writer.

My particular approach to wine is a boon to the editors of the *Observer*, who have never had to question an excessive bar bill on the expenses claim submitted for my reviews. I am a committed orderer of the second-cheapest bottle on the list, even though critics like to tell me this is not where the greatest value will be found. So sorry, but you've got the wrong Jew. I barely know one winery from another, and have no idea which bank of which river is meant to excite me. I can say things like 'I don't like over-oaked Chardonnays' because I don't. If I wanted to suck on a log with my dinner, I would. We know I can reference the cat's-piss tang of Sancerre. I know I hate those absurd Californian Cabernet Sauvignons which are 14.5 per cent alcohol. To me they look like a headache waiting to happen. You can't drink enough of one of those to pass a whole evening. For the most part you'll find me circulating around familiar, untaxing grapes and regions like Albariño or Gavi di Gavi if it's white, and Pinot Noir or Gamay if it's red. In ordering these things, in running my finger down the list in search of them, I am trying to hide a lack of knowledge, which in turn hides something much more shocking: a lack of interest.

That said, my interest in wine is practically obsessive compared to my interest in beer. I have literally none. I don't like it. I regard it as a waste of drinking time, a victory of volume and froth over taste. For many years I was embarrassed about this. I was a man. A man is supposed to drink beer, multiple pints of the stuff downed in one. Ergo, if I didn't like beer, I wasn't much of a man. I made peace with this when I turned forty. It struck me that this was the age at which I should stop apologising for myself. At the age of forty I decided that there were loads of things I was no longer going to apologise for. I would no longer apologise for my love of musicals. Jazz hands all the bloody way. I would no longer apologise for the fact that I would never see another production of *Hamlet* for as long as I live (once you work out he's got a few acute mental health issues which demand an intervention, the rest of the play is just a waste of your time). I would no longer be apologising for preferring a chilled glass of rosé over beer at any time of the year.

My own peculiar tastes aside, booze does have its uses for a journalist. Just as with restaurants, things happen in bars and pubs. Alcohol moves things along. Nowhere did this become more obvious to me than in a beaten-up Essex pub one grey lunchtime in 1991.

It's when I hear the mutterings of 'CID, CID . . .' from the drinkers around me that I realise what I've got myself into. I look up from the notebook that I have only just withdrawn from my pocket. Now a silence falls in the saloon bar. The half-dozen other patrons of this scuffed and tired Essex pub stare back at me. I try to smile, nonchalantly, as if it's the best joke I've heard all day.

'Not police,' I say, holding the notebook aloft. 'Writer.' I think this is a better word to use in here than 'journalist', and it seems I may be right. They look back at me, utterly baffled.

It had seemed such a good wheeze when I suggested the piece to my editor. A friend who worked for the BBC in Essex had told me about a pub in the dock town of Tilbury, on the northern shore of the Thames estuary, where it opens out for the biggest of container ships. The Ship, Paul told me, was the hardest, most violent pub in Essex. The place went through landlords at the rate of one every few weeks. Someone had once ridden a horse through the saloon bar, not in a sexy 1970s Studio 54 sort of way, more in a 'get out of my fucking way I've got a fucking horse' sort of a way. He told me the police liked it to stay open because it meant they knew where all the local drug dealers, burglars and fences were. Hence, when it burnt down – somebody set fire to the curtains with a cigarette lighter – it was back open within weeks.

In my callow, youthful way, I loved this story of poverty, crime and casual violence. I said to Paul, 'Essex is the hardest county in Britain. If the Ship is the hardest pub in Essex, it must be the hardest pub in the country.' He shrugged. 'I can see that.' An idea began to form. Once, Tilbury had been a vibrant bustling place, made rich on global trade through the docks. Much of that trade had moved elsewhere, mostly to Rotterdam, across the North Sea. Britain was now part of a European trading zone and it no longer mattered how goods from around the world entered the country. The Dutch port had won out. In these early years of the 1990s the debate on a federalist Europe, which eventually led to the tragedy of Brexit over a quarter of a century later, had started gathering steam. In those days I was totally freelance. My entire income depended on my ability to come up with story after story. I could see a cracking story in the Ship.

I went to see the editors of the British edition of *Esquire*, which had not yet even launched. In the US *Esquire* was known as a home for muscular, macho, immersive reporting. The king of New Journalism, Tom Wolfe, had made his name there in the 1960s and '70s. Reporters like George Plimpton and Jimmy Breslin, who disappeared into the subjects they wrote about, who gave a voice to ordinary life on the streets, were regarded by my peer group of young feature writers on the make as people to whom we should aspire. We were soft-handed, university-educated, middle-class kids who wanted to prove we were somehow authentic by documenting the stories of those at the bottom end of society. The idea of giving voice to the marginalised was noble; too often, though, it came across as a kind of self-important poverty porn.

The new British *Esquire* was well up for it. How about I go and spend three days at the Ship in Tilbury and ask the punters what they think about the debate on Europe? Sure. One thousand eight hundred words, please.

It was everything I had hoped for, and less. Which is to say, this was where the dream of England had run into the sea. It was a grey expanse left behind by the economic boom of the 1980s, the brooding, silent skeletons of the cranes at the docks, their heads seemingly bowed, standing sentry over social decline. The Ship was where the forgotten took refuge. There was John, 'a greying man in tired brown nylon trousers whose only shot of colour came from the blood vessels marking their weary path across his cheeks'. He was nursing a pint with his one good hand. He'd put the other through a wood saw but, because he didn't have the guard on, had received no compensation. I bought him a drink. 'There are really tough fights here. Knives and stuff,' he told me. Eagerly, I took notes. 'The prostitutes come here and they cause fights. Men bring their wives, and the seamen start talking to them because they think they're on the game. The men don't like that.'

There's Ray, just out of prison, who's got 'LOVE' tattooed on the knuckles of one hand and nothing on the other. 'Ray's a bit of a novelty in this part of the world,' I wrote. 'Most of the men who decide to write on their knuckles get HATE down first, then forget about the rest.' I documented the racism, both casual and vehement, and on the third day gained access to the so-called Public Bar. The public bars of pubs, the real ones, had always mystified me. Their name made them sound welcoming, but in truth they were a mark of the way pubs had widened their appeal in the nineteenth century. Saloon bars, with their cushioned benches, ornate mirrors and polished brass, were for Victorian England's newly emerging middle classes. The public bar, spartan and basic, was where the working classes went.

The public bar at the Ship was a constant lock-in. You only got access by knocking on the door. If they liked you, they'd let you in. It was home to a couple of dozen local lads in their late teens and early twenties, with names like Daz and Sha, Ginger and Gino, who ruled the pool table, kept out strangers and dealt dope to each other. I got in because Sandra, the landlady, vouched for me. 'What we want', says Daz to me, 'is 75 per cent local labour at the docks. And a golf course . . . And forget Europe. I don't care what currency we have as long as it's got a picture of the fucking Queen on the back. We don't want no German emperor on our coins, do we?' Later, they try to cut up a piece of dope, but nobody has a knife. 'Bit unusual this,' Daz tells me. 'Usually we come armed.' They try to break it up by biting down on the lump of hash, but their teeth are not up to the job. Another marker of poverty. After three days at the Ship, I left, when one of the Public Bar lads pulled a knife on me.

The piece appeared in the second edition of British *Esquire*, in May 1991, alongside gritty black-and-white photographs of pallid-skinned lads, their knuckles encrusted with sovereign rings. For the headline, they took inspiration from the popular Carlsberg beer ads, then playing on a loop on TV: 'The Ship, Probably the Hardest Pub in the World'.

Two days after publication, a story appeared on page 3 of the *Sun*, next to that day's pair of breasts. Taking its cue from the headline that I hadn't written, it declared that the Ship had been named the most violent pub in Britain, then recounted the details of my story. It was picked up across the media. Later that day, the pub started getting calls from other pubs in Essex. In less than polite terms the callers informed the landlady that the Ship was not in any way the hardest or most violent pub in Essex. Theirs was. What's more, they were all coming down to prove it. The police were alerted, who informed the brewery, who closed the Ship down. It never reopened as a pub. Within a few years it was a pound shop.

Journalists are meant to be proud of outcomes like this. My story had become a talking point. Action had been taken. But I felt terribly guilty. In those days Tilbury gave the impression of being a dead town, and I'd helped to kick the corpse. The jobless there had little enough to do as it was. Now, thanks to the furore caused by my story, they had even less.

It's a few months later, and I am sitting at another bar, a sleek, sexy, downlit one in Amsterdam. I am nursing a vodka and lime when the barman asks me whether I would like the services of a prostitute.

I take a swig of my drink and hold it in my mouth for a moment, until I can start to feel the alcoholic burn. I say, 'Interesting thought, let me check,' and I pull a die from my pocket. To numbers 1, 3 and 5 I allocate the answer 'yes'; to numbers 2, 4 and 6 I allocate 'no'. I roll the die, watch it bounce and stutter on the bar. A five. I stare at it for a moment, then look back at the young barman, who is watching me, quizzically. 'Yes,' I say, scooping up the die and returning it to my jacket pocket, 'it seems I would like a girl for the evening.'

This time it had been *Esquire's* idea. My editor had left a message on my answer machine. 'Ever read *The Dice Man?*' he said. 'If not, get hold of a copy, start reading and call me.' *The Dice Man* was a cult novel by George Cockcroft, writing under the name Luke Rhinehart, first published in 1971. It tells the story of a psychotherapist who decides to break away from the tyranny of personality by delegating any choices he has to make to a pair of dice. New options present themselves every day; the ones we choose are dictated by the kind of person we are. Using the dice would open the player up to experiences that might otherwise have passed them by. The novel was very much in keeping with the 1960s and '70s vogue for self-exploration. It was published in sixty countries, went on to sell millions and was regularly hailed as one of the defining books of the twentieth century.

The *Esquire* editors thought it would be great if I lived my life by the dice for a couple of days. Together we agreed I should go to Amsterdam because, with its liberal drug and prostitution laws, there were greater opportunities for me to wander off my normal path. I agreed, but with two conditions: I wouldn't have sex with anyone and I wouldn't do hard drugs.

At first, the dice smiled warmly upon me. I could have been forced to hitch-hike my way to Amsterdam and then sleep rough or have to blag a night on a stranger's sofa. Instead, they told me to fly there and stay at the Pulitzer, the most expensive hotel in town. (Later, I would be forced into the city's cheapest backpackers' hostel and be required to get all my hair cut off.) That first evening the dice told me to go to the bar of the hotel, where I sat rolling myself a mixture of gin and tonic, tomato juice and Scotch, one after the other. The dice made me mix my drinks. Hence, by the time the young barman leaned across and asked if I needed a girl, I was already sloshed.

Rocco questioned my decision-making process. 'You gamble with everything in your life? That could be dangerous.' I agreed it could and invited him to roll himself a drink. He got gin and bitter lemon. He told me he hated gin and bitter lemon. I told him I didn't care, that he had to drink it. The dice had decided. He did as he was told, then made a phone call. Twenty minutes later, a limo pulled up at the back door. It drove me around Amsterdam's darkened streets, along roads that were unfamiliar despite my regular trips to the city over the years. Eventually, it drew up at an anonymous doorway marked only by a brass plaque with the word 'Chatterley's' embossed upon it and the logo of a snail. At the door a white-haired man of late middle years separated me from 350 guilders (a little north of £100), gave me a laminated card stamped with the snail logo I'd seen outside and ushered me into a sparsely populated bar area. The room was ringed by soft, low, black banquettes, occupied here and there by bored-looking women wearing underwear, stockings and perhaps a see-through top, as if to suggest there was something that might need taking off later. Apart from them and the barman, there was only one other person in there, and by the look of his white suit and black shirt I had him marked down as staff or, at the very least, an interested party. Set into the wall behind the bar were a couple of TV screens, which played out the same 1980s porn, all big, lacquered hair and lip gloss. I took a stool, ordered a vodka and lime and tried not to watch the vigorous blow job being played out in front of me. This wasn't prudishness on my part. I just wasn't used to watching porn in a public place, in the company of strangers. What is the protocol for viewing fellatio in a bar? I had no idea.

Quickly, I was joined by two women in their pants. They whispered to me from both sides in soft, accented English about what sort of fun I might be looking for. I downed my drink and told them I was a writer, that I was just here to 'watch'. It sounded wrong as I said it. Normal men came to a brothel for sex. Only total pervs came for something else. Ergo, I was a perv. One of the women got up and wandered off. She wanted none of whatever weirdness I was there for. The other tried again: surely I wanted to see what the rest of the club had to offer? She nodded towards a set of stairs. Again, I declined, and ordered another vodka. I was drunk enough to have forgotten to roll the dice. I was also a long way out of my depth.

She sat back and looked at me, as if some form of restart was necessary. She stuck out her hand, formally. 'Natalie,' she said.

I introduced myself. We shook.

She said, 'When you came in you were given a card, yes?' I agreed. Yes, that had happened.

'Okay. My job here is to get card off you, and then when I give card back to the manager I get paid.'

'Ah, I see.'

'I'm not sitting here dressed like this for health reasons.'

'Yes, because that would be odd.'

'So why don't you come upstairs with me and have a bath. They have nice baths here.'

Which is how I ended up taking all my clothes off with a Dutch hooker I had only just met and getting into a big, foamy, oval-shaped bath with her. She had been so polite and so logical about the idea that I concluded refusing would have been rude.

She said, 'You are really a writer?' Artificially scented steam rose about us.

I nodded, apologetically. I explained about *The Dice Man* and the article based upon it that I was writing.

'This could be dangerous.'

I looked around. 'It seems to be working out okay. The great thing is, both of us are being paid to take this bath.'

She laughed. 'This is true. This is the easiest job I have done in a while.' And suddenly, in my vodka-boosted, lime-cordial-drenched way, I felt like I was doing good.

One evening I run into a friend on a Tube station platform. Rich Avery and I are friends in a very twenty-first-century manner, which is to say, until this moment we have never met. He is an actor and was in a National Theatre production of *War Horse*, adapted from the Michael Morpurgo book of the same name. His part required him to sit on the front of the stage and sketch, as if drawing the battlefields of First World War France. Deep into the run he had taken to sketching something related to what he could see in the audience. One night I was in that audience, and he later tweeted me a drawing of a jay (the bird). He's a terrific actor; Impressionist artist, not so much. We became Twitter friends, encouraged by the fact we lived close to each other in south London.

Now, all of a sudden, we are shaking hands on a Tube platform. He told me he had been intending to get in touch.

'Do you like wine?' he said. 'It's an odd question given your job, but . . .'

I said it wasn't an odd question at all, that I had been writing about my relationship with booze, and mostly it was about hangovers and control issues. I told him I was no longer sure what my view was.

He told me he was planning a supper in memory of his late father. 'He was rather serious about his wine. I was going to open some special bottles that meant something to him, tell some stories, and I wondered whether you'd like to come.'

We were only together on that platform for four minutes, waiting for the rush of air signalling the arrival of our trains, but in that time we hatched a plan. I told him I was planning my last supper, that I was finding the whole booze thing baffling. 'I think being around people with a deep emotional connection to wine could be very useful.' I asked if I could not only attend the dinner, but take notes. I offered to cook. Later, we decided to stage the dinner at my house, given the food would be coming out of my oven.

The morning after our Tube platform meeting I did a bit of googling. Rich's father wasn't just rather serious about wine; for many people in Britain he *was* wine. His name was John Avery and, until his death in 2012, he was the latest generation of his family to run Avery's of Bristol, one of Britain's great wine merchants, originally founded in 1793. John was responsible for introducing serious wines from California and Australia to the UK. He was the first to import the now world-famous Penfolds Grange from Australia, and later did the same with wines from New Zealand. It was John Avery who coined the phrase 'New World' for the product of the US and Australasia, for a tasting in the mid-1960s.

A few years after his death, there had been a major sale of his personal collection at Christie's, but a kernel of that collection remained. All the wines we would be drinking would come from John Avery's cellar. To stop it being random, Rich asked us for our birth years.

'If you ask me my age,' Rich later told me, 'I have to think about it. I know my vintage. I'm 1971. Working out my age is a different matter.' All of his siblings knew their vintages. Their family was deeply steeped in wine.

Rich gave me only two rules. I was not to enquire after the value of the bottles we would be drinking. 'It's not about value with these bottles,' he said. 'They're just representative of my dad's life. And no overly spicy food.'

Both of these made sense.

I built a menu. Some oysters to kick off with, perhaps the ones from Andrew Rooney in Northern Ireland that I hadn't yet been able to try. I called a meat producer friend based not far away from Rooney to see if he might be able to slip some in a box alongside a consignment of other pork products, for me to try out for another part of my final meal. Next up, my take on a tagliata. It usually involves sliced steak over a rocket salad, but the word means a 'cut', especially made with a single blow, and can be applied equally to fish. I'd come up with a version using seared scallops and sea bass. (The recipe, such as it is, can be found at the end of this chapter.) For the main, a shoulder of lamb braised in red wine and non-piquant chorizo, with butter-braised cabbage and hasselback potatoes (sliced almost through, then roasted in butter so they open up like a slinky). That would stand up to any grand red wine. There would be a cheese course that Rich's sister Mimi, the next generation of Averys to join the business, would bring. To finish there would be an upside down pavlova: a red-fruit salad of raspberries and strawberries, topped by whipped cream, finished with broken meringue.

That sounded like dinner to me.

Naturally enough, on the day of the event the Post Office announced they had mislaid my food package from Northern Ireland. It was languishing somewhere in Coventry. I've been to Coventry. It is no place for what I had been told are some of the world's best oysters. It seemed I was not destined to try Andrew Rooney's fabled product. I began to think of them as being literally legendary, in that people only told stories of them, but they never proved themselves to be real.

Nevertheless, one warm spring evening we gathered in my back garden. Rich came with his partner Larissa, the 'favourite daughter-in-law'. There was Mimi and her other half, plus Matthew Hemmings, a Master of Wine, a title held by fewer than 400 people worldwide, and described by Rich as 'Dad's final ultimate Jedi protégé'. There was Rich's friend Jeremy, an Australian wine writer, my wife Pat and my eldest, Eddie, who was then eighteen years old.

Eddie looked at the array of bottles and said, 'All of these wines are older than me. I find this disturbing.'

I told him it was less disturbing than the fact that, at eighteen, he was about to get to drink wines that most people would never experience.

We began with a champagne commissioned by John Avery in 1989, to be laid down for four years and released for the company's 200th anniversary in 1993. 'We're drinking it on the company's 225th anniversary,' Mimi said. She pointed out what she said were the 'brioche' tones. It was indeed sweeter and deeper than any champagne I had tried before. But perhaps I was enjoying it more because I knew its story? Mimi said it was possible, and that there was nothing wrong with that.

Over the fish tagliata we were to drink a bottle of Tyrrell's Vat 47 1980 Chardonnay, in honour of Matthew's birth year. Vat 47 is the most prestigious wine of a prestigious winery. Many winemakers have them, a particular version of their wine that they prize over all others. There is no rhyme nor reason to the labelling. For Tyrrell's it was Vat 47. We looked at the bottle suspiciously. The liquid was a good inch and a half down the neck from where it should be, loitering like an off-the-shoulder dress. This could mean that it had leaked out, and if wine had leaked out, air could have got sucked in, meaning it would be oxidised. We pulled the cork. It snapped.

'That's a good sign,' Jeremy said. 'It means the cork was tight.'

And it was. This was nothing like the bright, light Chardonnays of France that I was used to, like a crisp Chablis. It was soft and mellow and deep.

'It's a perfect example of the wines that Dad pioneered from Australia,' Rich said. He told a story about how, in the very early 1970s, Penfolds, then an obscure winery, won a competition run by the great French gastronomic guide *Gault & Millau*. The win would make their name across Europe. The company's management were startled because they weren't aware they had even entered. 'Dad owned up that he had entered them. To say thank you, they gave him three cases of their 1971.'

Next, over the lamb, Rich indulges in a blind tasting: two bottles of red, both wrapped in silver foil so we can't see the labels. 'I don't want to know which is best,' he says. 'I just want to know which you like.' Opinion splits across the wines, with the majority favouring the first. They are both deep and powerful but with a soft, gentle finish that goes on and on. They aren't brusque and tannic. They go down very easily. I know they are more complex than any I have tried before.

He pulls the foil off the first. We let out a little gasp. It's a bottle of the 1971 Penfolds Grange. 'It's basically regarded as the best red wine ever to have come out of Australia,' Rich says. He is not casual or offhand about this. The bottle is to be taken seriously. A major tasting in 2015 also judged it the best wine of the 1970s. 'I loved telling you that story about the *Gault & Millau* competition knowing this was coming along.'

Drinking it was also an extremely rare pleasure. 'These days a 1971 Penfolds is regarded as an asset,' Matthew said. 'Most bottles of this stuff cross the world, being traded. Nobody actually drinks them. Whereas this one went from Penfolds to John's cellar to here. And we're drinking it not because of value but because it represented who John was.'

And the other bottle? It was a 1971 Petrus, a Pomerol from Bordeaux generally regarded as the greatest red wine in the world. 1971 wasn't the greatest of Petrus vintages, but as Matthew said, it had travelled less than more serious vintages, so was probably in better nick. 'What's more, just as my dad was the first to bring Penfolds into Britain, my grandfather Ronald was the first to import Petrus,' Rich said. We sip and stare at our glasses and think of men long gone who knew brilliance when they tasted it.

We drink on. To mark my birth year, 1966, there is another Pomerol: a bottle of La Pointe, another huge red. 'Yours was a terrific year,' Matthew says, and my chest swells at my happy accident of birth, as if it somehow made me a better person. As we head into dessert there's a 1982 Rieussec, a Sauterne the colour of distilled gold. The label is smudged and blackened. 'My mum put some toast on, then forgot about it and went upstairs,' says Rich. 'She set fire to the kitchen.'

The bottles, which were out in the kitchen, were only outwardly singed. The Sauterne is all peaches and raisins and sighs and thank-yous. We sip. Now deep in the bottom of our glasses, we give thanks for the fire that did not carry off the surviving Avery parent.

There is one last bottle, the oldest served. It is a 1963 port, specifically blended by John Avery from ports made by the great makers, Taylor's, Fonseca and Sandeman. It would be ungallant to say whose birth year it was, because Pat would be livid. As he pours it, Rich says, 'And this will be the glass we will blame for the hangover tomorrow.' It is May, but Christmas has arrived in my kitchen. It's here in this glass in front of me. It is raisins and plums and spice and spun sugar.

The atmosphere here tonight has been intense, almost nerdy. Throughout, Mimi has scribbled tasting notes into a little notebook. Matthew has spun each wine about in his glass and stared. He has sniffed before coming anywhere close to sipping them. Ordinarily, I might have found this obsessiveness dreary – 'Enough with the analysis already. Let's drink.'

But it hasn't been like that. It's been like eavesdropping on another family's culture. Rich may have chosen a life as an actor, but he seems as deep into the language of wine as his sister. In reality, though, this hasn't been about wine at all. It's been about the impact that one man, John Avery, made on the world and the narratives associated with him.

When I come to my last supper I know what to do or, more to the point, what not to do. I don't need to choose big-ticket bottles of wine. I don't need to be flash and spendy, or at least not necessarily. I need something much more thoughtful than that. I need drinkable stories.

Scallop and sea bass tagliata

I don't regard this as a recipe. It's not even a method. It's more of an idea: 'Why don't you do this, with these nice things?'

Serves four

INGREDIENTS

A couple of big bunches of rocket

A bunch of watercress

Four spring onions

Ten small radishes

Olive oil

White wine vinegar

Sea salt and table salt

Eight king scallops

Four skin-on sea bass fillets

Salted butter

(To scale this up allow two scallops and one sea bass fillet per person)

Finely chop the spring onions and slice the radishes and put in the bottom of a salad bowl. Add three tablespoons of olive oil and a tablespoon of white wine vinegar (less if it's a particularly sharp vinegar). Add a good pinch or two of sea salt, to taste.

Throw in the rocket and watercress and mix to dress the leaves. They should be well coated with the dressing.

Spread the leaves out on a good-sized platter.

Slice each of the scallops horizontally into two discs. If they're especially large, make it three. If the roe is still attached, take that off, then make sure to remove the dense piece of muscle that attached it to the scallop. Discard that but keep the roes.

Slice each sea bass fillet into four or five, depending on size.

Season the scallops and sea bass with the table salt.

Heat a cast-iron frying pan until it just starts smoking. Add a tablespoon of olive oil. After thirty seconds add a large knob of butter.

Fry the sea bass fillets skin side down for a couple of minutes, basting the flesh with the hot oil/butter. Turn them over for thirty seconds, then take them out and place all over the salad, skin side down.

Place the scallops in the pan, in a circle, remembering where you started. By the time you have completed the circle it's time to turn them over. Remove and scatter over the salad with the sea bass.

Fry the roes for no more than a minute. Add those. Spoon over the buttery juices from the pan and serve.

▶ 4. 'Night and Day', Cole Porter (1932)

You never forget your first, and 'Night and Day' was mine. It was the first jazz standard, the first tune from the Great American Songbook, that I learnt to play. And it happened because of rampant technology and my inability to cope with it.

Until the mid-1980s synthesisers with grand names like the Prophet-5 and the Jupiter-8 were built around analogue synthesis. This was pretty straightforward, even if you were an idiot, which I was. With just a few knobs and sliders you could create squelchy bass sounds or sharp brass noises, the promising call of industrial pop. In my north London bedroom, circa 1982, I recreated the hard-edged sound of Sheffield. It was fun and creative. In 1983 Yamaha ruined it all by releasing the DX7, based around frequency modulation (FM) synthesis. It was so complicated nobody knew how to do it. Literally no one. I knew lots of musicians, and not one could explain it to me. The keyboard was nevertheless hugely popular, because the pre-programmed sounds were so huge and multidimensional. Everybody used them. Those tubular bells at the start of 'Do They Know It's Christmas?' Pure DX7. You'll hear them everywhere in the pop of the period.

But if I couldn't make my own sounds, I was no longer interested, and so I turned back to the piano. For years I struggled on by myself, on a small Japanese upright the colour of a 1970s velour sofa, using what little knowledge my three grades had given to me to interpret the chords printed on my sheet music. But eventually, in my early twenties, I found my way to a gifted blues pianist called Louis Vause, who had a brilliant line in hats, a talent for personal calamity and an even better one for blues licks and runs. He showed me how to use my happily sizable hands to span a tenth with my left. He introduced me to the mysteries of the 2–5–1 chord progression, and a shape in the right hand which produces lots of lovely augmented chords. I won't bore you with the details, but it was my gateway to jazz harmony.

What's more, I quickly spotted that the 2–5–1 progression lay right at the heart of 'Night and Day', written by Cole Porter for the 1932 stage musical *Gay Divorce*, Fred Astaire's last on Broadway. Like Porter's lyric, there is an unforced elegance to the music. It is brilliant precisely because it is so simple. It can tinkle. It can swing. It can be huge or tiny. I watched, slightly startled, as these thudding hands of mine formed shapes on the keys that made the music I had been looking for. It was a bloody long way off being Fats Waller or Oscar Peterson, but they might just have recognised it as a faint echo of an idea of jazz. Within it was the sound of every sophisticated cocktail bar I had ever imagined myself in, of every classy restaurant where the steaks are served black and blue and the piano player fills the gaps in the conversation. Every jazz pianist needs a repertoire. I didn't have one.

But I did have 'Night and Day'.

Pig

At the far end of Mark Hayward's farm, not far from the Suffolk coast, is a broad, well-appointed shed. It is the place where sex, death and appetite meet. The shed is home to the sixteen grunting, snuffling boars upon which Mark's entire pig business is based; huge animals, with wiry coats of reddy-brown hair, harrumphing and sighing their way around their pens. They are here to produce semen to inseminate sows, whose offspring are then to be fattened and sent to slaughter to feed pig-headed pig-heads like me.

'This was our first boar,' Mark says, standing before a pen deep with pristine, golden hay, into which the animal has burrowed. His snout rests on the surface like the prow of a yacht.

Attached to the front of the pen is a nameplate. It reads: 'Colin'.

I say the name out loud: 'Colin'.

It makes him sound like a small-town accountant rather than a lump of maleness prized for his semen.

Mark agrees. 'Bit ordinary for a big male boar, isn't it? So after we got Colin we changed the way we named them.' He points across the shed. 'We called the next one Brave Heart. Over there is Gorbachev, that one's called Prince Buster and then there's Genghis Khan.'

'That's a bit more like it,' I say. We fall silent for a moment and listen to the huffing and rustling and snorting of Genghis, Gorby, Brave Heart and Colin, these prized testicles on legs.

The pig business that Mark runs with his brother is called Dingley Dell, a name borrowed from a half-remembered children's nursery rhyme. For all the pastoral overtones, there is nothing especially cute about it; Dingley Dell is a very serious enterprise indeed. It is like no other pig farm in Britain. 'I know of one other farm in the world doing what we're doing, and it's in Korea,' Mark says. 'Other than that, it's just us.'

Mark has a thesis: that the pork business in Britain is in decline because of the post-war emphasis on breeding out the fat. British pigs are just too lean, their meat just so much dense protein. Because fat is where the flavour is, too much British pork tastes of very little. 'If the experience of eating pork was nearer that of eating lamb or beef, we could sell it for more,' he says. 'But it isn't.' His father ran a standard pig farm for decades, but in the late 1980s and '90s the market 'turned to shit'. Various poor animal welfare practices were banned in Britain. Traditionally, mothering sows were kept in stalls so small there was no room to move around. The sows were also tethered – literally tied down to the floor – so they couldn't roll over in the tight space and accidentally kill their piglets while they were suckling. Tethering and tight stalls were outlawed in Britain in 1999, a ban that was not introduced across the rest of Europe until 2013.

It meant British pork was better raised but more expensive. The retailers didn't care about tethered sows, only price. 'They were importing pork from Europe, where welfare standards were lower. Quickly, the industry halved. Businesses were lost and people committed suicide.'

Mark didn't want to be part of an industry like that. He decided to produce a premium product. The mass pig industry was subject to price fluctuations according to market supply and demand. 'We decided we'd set what for us was a viable price, and people could either take it or leave it. We decided we would make it about welfare, taste and sustainability.' To encourage bees they set aside acres of their land for wild flowers. They expanded the outside pens their pigs lived in. Then they started breeding not just for the outer body fat, but for the marbling deep in the muscle. They worked with a genetics company to get the breed right, gave their boars and sows CT scans to measure the intramuscular fat and used a scoring system to come up with the ideal ratio of males to females. 'It's all very well if your animal has had a lovely life, but if it tastes like shit, it tastes like shit.' The key, Mark concluded, was those genetics, combined with some very clever marketing, and ageing.

We know a lot about the ageing of beef, the way friendly bacteria break down muscle fibre to tenderise the meat when it's kept at a cool, controlled temperature. 'I saw aged pork being sold by a retail butcher in Belgium five years ago,' Mark says. 'I'd never heard of it before.' He decided to try it here. It took his brother Martin two years to work out that between twelve and fourteen days was the perfect length of time to age their pork. It reduced the moisture content and intensified the flavour. They started marketing their pork rib-eye as 'aged'.

Except it wasn't rib-eye, at least not in the way we know of it as related to beef. A beef rib-eye is really a piece of muscle from close by the rib, with a thick seam of fat – an eye – running through it. What Dingley Dell was marketing as rib-eye was indeed a thick cut steak, but it actually came from around the shoulder. 'We concluded that to really market pork, we needed to come up with a whole bunch of different cuts.' In recent years Spanish pig producers had started marketing a cut from their free-range, acorn-fed, naturally fat-marbled Ibérico pigs into Britain. They called it a *pluma*. It's from the shoulder. Dingley Dell decided to start marketing their own *pluma*, and then their own 'rib-eye'. Chefs were encouraged to serve it seared outside but knicker-pink within, as if it were beef. Fear of meat-borne diseases like trichinosis from roundworm had long encouraged people to cook pork thoroughly, even though such diseases are generally a thing of the past.

Back at his farmhouse, Mark sparks up his barbecue and throws a thick piece of '*pluma*' onto the grill until it is seared, then he moves it away from direct heat for a few minutes. Finally, he takes it off and wraps it in foil to rest. He knows how best to cook the meat he rears. He has invited dozens of high-end restaurant chefs up here to the farm to try his meat like this. When we get to eat it, I quickly conclude he is right: this is a different way to eat pork. I associate the meat with crisp, crackled skin and fat which has a lower melting point than that of beef, and so sits in a comfortable place between liquid and solid for longer. This is entirely different. It really is much closer to eating a marbled piece of beef. It's brilliant. I find myself muttering words like 'game-changer' and 'revelatory' under my breath. I quickly become a one-man cliché machine.

It's a defence mechanism, because something is bothering me. This pork is great. It's better than great. But it's not the pork I know. When I took the train out to Suffolk, it was with the assumption that I was heading off to try the perfect centrepiece for this last supper of mine; that I was, in effect, taking a shortcut to the endgame. But I now know that I am wrong. This marbled, bespoke, deeply flavoured pork isn't right. It's novel, and I am not looking for novelty. I am looking for the best kind of familiar.

This pork is just too good.

I return to London and, as I always do when I need to think, head to Chinatown. I have many reasons to love restaurants: you pay someone to cook food, and they bring it to you and then do the washing-up afterwards. But there's something else: they encourage disclosure. If you want to work out what type of person someone is, take them to lunch. Watch what they order. Watch how they eat. Encourage them towards comfort foods, to those dishes that root them: the stews and soups and cakes which remind them profoundly of nurture. Watch their guard not so much drop as tumble. I am suspicious of the phrase 'cooking with love'. It is the sloganising of the greetings card, cynically deployed. Please, cook with technique and taste and leave the love at home. But you can definitely feed with love, or access memories of love with food.

I am greedy for so many things, not just the good butter or oysters or snails or pork, but also the vital information: an understanding of what it is that makes someone tick. You did what? With whom? And how did that make you feel? There is a thrill in getting someone to spill their emotional guts across the snowfield of a linen tablecloth. This is a grandiose way of saying I adore gossip.

The intriguing thing is that you can do this with yourself too. I like to eat alone partly because it makes me focus. It helps me to interrogate myself. So I went to the Four Seasons on London's Gerrard Street. (Naturally, I chose the one on the left, at number 12. Who knows what the one on the right is like. Why they should have two branches side by side like this, unlinked even by an internal archway, is a mystery, but not one I ever intend to investigate.) They sat me in the corner just behind the bar, as they always do, and brought me a menu they knew I wouldn't look at. I picked at the little dish of chopped green chillies in sugar syrup, ordered the roast Cantonese duck, with its dark lacquered skin, and a plate of green beans dry-fried with minced pork and chilli, and no rice. 'I'll have rice if I'm still hungry at the end,' I told the waiter, parroting what I was once told was the Chinese custom. I poured myself a cup of steaming, crystal-clear jasmine tea and asked myself a question.

'Just what is it about you and pork?'

I could stick with aesthetics, and that would be convincing enough. I could say that the skin crackles better than any other, and it does. From time to time I am asked to name a guilty pleasure, and I always respond that if I started feeling guilty about my food choices, where would I stop? It would be a dam-burst of shame. But I have to acknowledge that I do sometimes feel guilty, or at the very least a little embarrassed, about my pronounced pork-scratching habit. I prefer to trough a packet unwitnessed, finally digging my fingertips into the corners of the bag for the last salty, grease-softened crumbs before disposing of the evidence. I can argue that for a man who has found a diet relatively low in carbohydrate to be a good way to manage weight, the pork scratching is a great friend. Check the nutritional advice:

Carbohydrate: 0 per cent. Hello, friend.

But that doesn't get over the fact that they are still skin and fat that have been deep-fried and then tossed in a cardiologist's pay day's worth of salt. (I once shot a short television film in a pork-scratching factory in the West Midlands. I recall the slipperiness of the floor, where boiled-down pig had become ingrained, and the way the lard under the skin dissolved into the bubbling oil, only to then be re-absorbed into the crackling as it cooked. I also discovered that I have my limits. I can eat no more than six small packets in a day before starting to feel nauseous. This was a revelation.)

I can talk about the way pork makes the best charcuterie because of the lower melting point of that fat and its relatively neutral flavour compared to that of beef or lamb. I have read academic papers and nodded along to the theory that as well as the five tastes we know about – sweet, salt, bitter, sour, umami – there is a sixth, which is that of fat (oleogustus, to give it its scientific name). Anyone who has eaten low-fat products regularly will know that there is something missing; it's like a rainbow with one of the colours removed. The search is still ongoing for the flavour receptors on the tongue for fat, but there is lit-tle doubt that they will be found, and when that happens, I am stone-cold certain I will turn out to have the mother lode. Mouth-coating oiliness makes me happy. Hence a taste for pig. For whatever Mark Hayward says about the leanness of the modern pig, it's all relative. Pigs are still the fattest animals in the farmyard.

I can celebrate the way a pig's foot, carefully deployed in a soup or stew, will both thicken and deepen it. I can sigh over the way the meat takes a cure which leads inexorably to bacon. Everything tastes better with bacon. I once was asked to come up with a new flavour of marshmallow for another television film. I suggested smoky bacon. We fried the rashers to crisp, ground them down into fragments and mixed them in with the gelatine-set meringue. They were brilliant, an amplified version of the best sweet-cured Canadian rasher.

Back at the Four Seasons, I pick up another piece of roast duck. I have asked for it bone-in, partly because I think it tastes better when the bone is still attached, partly because I think you get more that way, and partly because I think it makes me seem more serious. Only light-weights ask for the hard work to be done for them. I try to hold the cleavered piece with chopsticks, but eventually give up and use my hands. I am much happier doing it this way. The attempted use of chop-sticks was an affectation. They bring me a few packets of wet wipes.

I eat and focus on the duck in my greasy fingers. I conclude there's something else about my love of pig, beyond the aesthetics of taste. I have long rolled my eyes at the Jewish god's eating habits, the pro-hibitions not just on pork, but any seafood without scales – farewell lobster, goodbye clams – and the esoterica of mixing milk and meat. The god of the Jews regards cheeseburgers as an abomination. That's always felt a bit niche and arbitrary, just as not enjoying gardening or folk music would feel arbitrary. And perhaps it is. In one analy-sis, rules like this were created simply to give the Jews a group iden-tity once they had been thrown out of Palestine after the fall of the Second Temple in AD 70. I've long claimed that I don't need a group identity, or at least not that group identity. But it's more complicated than that, because in truth I adore having an identity. In what even I acknowledge is a weird bit of reverse thinking, I like identifying as a pork-eating Jew. It forces people who haven't thought seriously enough about the subject to understand that Jewishness is an identity which goes beyond a bunch of blunt dietary laws. Understand that I am both Jewish and eat pork because there is no God, and you under-stand a few very basic things about me.

It's extremely self-regarding, this pork-eating Jew thing, but that's okay, because what is a last supper if not about the self? The thing is, I'm no closer to nailing which way pig should reveal itself in this great meal of mine. I sit there, unselfconsciously chewing on a duck bone, and watch the waiters pass by with platters of crispy belly pork and char siu, which is a worrying deep red, and salt-and-pepper spare ribs. I use chopsticks to pick up some of the green beans, and then dredge them through the minced pork like they're the scoop of a forklift.

That's when it comes to me. I'm just going to have to try pork in as many different, striking preparations as I can. I owe it to myself and to the dinner. This is serious stuff. I need to put my back into it. I shove the mess of green beans into my mouth, close my duck-smeared lips and grin happily. Oh, the pork fun I am going to have. Self-justification is a wonderful thing.

Sometimes I eat alone just because I'm hungry and need to eat. Sometimes I eat alone because I need time to think. Sometimes I eat alone to reward myself. It is a cold February afternoon and I am in my hotel room at the Holiday Inn, Birmingham, preparing to do just that. There is a printed guide to the city in the room because this is pre-Internet. I am running my finger down the restaurant listings. Today the choice would be wide and varied. Today Birmingham has a sushi place run by a Polish chef. And it's really good. But this is 1994, and Britain's second city is still the place that appetite forgot. I can't name a single place worth visiting, so all I have are these listings. I find an Italian with a name like Il Concerto or De Franco's or Da Generica Italiano, which doubtless does dreadful, destructive things to the Italian culinary tradition. I phone them up.

'Can you manage a table for one this evening, please?' I am un-embarrassed about making this request. I may be calling a restaurant in Birmingham in the dog days of the twentieth century, but they should be able to deal with the prospect of a solo diner.

There's a sigh from the end of the line. Then a man with a Birmingham accent says, 'No, mate. Fully booked.' He hangs up. I stare at the phone. It's a Monday. In February. How the hell can they be fully booked? Was there something wrong with the way I spoke?

I go back to the listings. I am determined to find somewhere good to eat, because I've damn well earned it. Today I have pulled off a serious journalistic coup.

I had been working for weeks on a complicated story about gun-running by Ulster loyalists into Northern Ireland. The story involved a man called Frank Portinari, who worked as an infant school care-taker in north London, but who, in his spare time, was also the London head of the Ulster Defence Association. In Northern Ireland it was banned as a terrorist organisation for the Unionist cause, though it remained legal in London. Portinari's associate in this story was a thick-necked Londoner called Eddie Whicker, who was known to be a leading figure in an organisation called Combat 18, a violent far right movement which had claimed responsibility for arson attacks on various properties belonging to people on the left. The '18' in the name represented the first and eighth letters of the alphabet, or 'A' and 'H', Adolf Hitler's initials.

A few months before, Portinari had been arrested in a Birmingham pub car park while handing over a blue holdall containing a bunch of guns to known UDA men. He was charged and eventually convicted, but given a remarkably short sentence. The day before Portinari was arrested, Whicker, trailed by intelligence officers working on a tip-off, had taken the same blue holdall to the same Birmingham car park, though, for some reason, there was no handover. He too was arrested and charged, but his charges were dropped because no one had searched the holdall at the time. Because the contents remained unknown, the charge of gun-running couldn't be proved.

As well as telling the story, my job was to prove a link between the UDA and the avowedly racist Combat 18. I had asked for a meeting with Portinari's solicitor, who was in Birmingham because the arrest had been made there. He would have been appointed on the cab-rank principle that he was the next available solicitor. Which was interesting, because the man who had been appointed as the legal representative of Frank Portinari, a known associate of far-right racists, turned out to be black.

I said to him, 'Legally, because of client confidentiality, you can't tell me anything about Mr Portinari's case, can you?'

He agreed this was so.

'But there's nothing to stop you talking to me about his former co-defendant, Eddie Whicker.'

'Nothing at all,' he said, and he smiled broadly. He was happy to do anything that might make life difficult for an avowed racist. 'Would you like to see some photographs?'

He pushed a file over the desk towards me. It contained pictures of Portinari and Whicker posing together with revolvers and proudly holding semi-automatic shotguns and rifles, while wearing Unionist sashes. It was pictorial evidence of collusion between the UDA and Combat 18. What's more, because Portinari had pleaded guilty and Whicker had never been tried, these images had not been presented to the court. The solicitor let me take copies away. It was what we still liked to call a 'scoop'. (Later, my reporting on this story would see me named in a book about the intelligence services as a stooge for MI5. Presumably, the only explanation for me getting the story right was that all the information had been fed to me by my intelligence service handlers. Whoever they were. It was both hilarious and profoundly irritating, because it was one of those bizarre claims that are very hard to refute, apart from by shouting, 'No, I got hold of those pictures by using my initiative.')

So I have a real scoop and I deserve a good dinner by myself. But the first place was fully booked. I try another. Also fully booked. I try a third. The same.

In desperation, I ring an American burger joint that even the listings mag can't rouse itself to be that enthusiastic about.

The man at the end of the phone responds, 'A table for one? On Valentine's night? Tough break.'

At no point had I looked at the calendar. I was alone in Birmingham on Valentine's Day, trying to book a table for one in a restaurant. I was suddenly the very definition of a loser. I call downstairs to the Holiday Inn's restaurant. 'Yes, sir, we can indeed manage a table for one.' Because who in their right mind would take their beloved to a Holiday Inn for Valentine's night? Eating alone is a brilliant thing: a table, a chair, a plate of good food, a glass of wine and something to read. It is a profoundly adult experience. But you have to be in the minority, not part of a herd of travelling salesmen caught out on the road overnight. Otherwise it's just plain sad. They offer me a copy of GQ to read as I walk through the door. I take it. I hate myself.

* * *

I am standing in the kitchen of a Chinese restaurant in Paddington, west London, watching a man, sitting down on his haunches, crisp up a whole piglet. This is a special order which I have paid for in advance. My £185 has got me an animal about three feet long. It has been opened out. The viscera have been removed, along with most of the key bones. The whole piglet, including the head, is now flat, so that the two halves of the bottom jaw are pointing forward, a little like tusks. It was first boiled to soften up the skin, then seasoned and hung to dry overnight. It was roasted in the oven for three hours before this final bit of the process, the arduous business of turning it by hand over glowing coals to crisp the smooth piglet skin. The kitchen at Pearl Liang is an extremely modern affair, full of shiny chrome ovens and worktops. But here at the back I am watching cooking done the old way.

I head back to join my friends at the table, who are waiting for the main event. They are the right people for the job. Most of them are panellists on *The Kitchen Cabinet*, a food panel show I present for BBC Radio 4. We travel the country answering pointed questions from live audiences about food and cooking: 'What can I do with a glut of rhubarb?' 'How can I convert my husband to the joys of offal?' 'What's the point of celery?' And so on. Each of the panellists has their specialism. Annie Gray is a food historian. Zoe Laughlin is a materials expert. Tim Anderson majors in the food of Japan. Barry Smith is a professor of philosophy with an acute interest in the senses, which means he knows his wine. But their main superpower is a complete obsession with their dinner; the hour we record for the show is merely the bit of the endless conversation they have about food which happened to take place in front of the microphones. So far this evening we have cleared a platter of cold meats, including gossamer-thin slices of fatty pig's trotter to be dipped in a vinegar sauce. There have been crunchy strands of jellyfish, crimson arrowheads of surf clam, and beef, long braised in five-spice and allowed to cool. There have been Sichuan-spiced curls of deep-fried squid and pieces of beef sirloin swimming in a hot bath of chilli oil and Sichuan peppercorns. There have been bowls of mapo tofu, the cubes of silky, slippery bean curd drenched in a sauce of chillies and ground pork.

And now here comes the piglet. It is delivered to the table with ceremony, as if it were a princely newborn. It is surrounded by hand-tied bouquets of finely sliced spring onions and laid on a bed of lettuce leaves and a julienne of carrot. This is not yet for eating. This is a ceremonial presentation for looking at and photographing if we so wish, which we do. Back in the kitchen the skin was a dull greyish pink; now it has the golden-brown colour and shine of a toffee apple. At one end are its snub snout and the dead slits where its eyes would once have been; at the other is the curl of a tail. There are ears, and though the tiny trotters have been removed, its legs are intact. It is without doubt a pig. Or at least once was a pig.

I watch it head back to the kitchen to be prepared for eating.

I say, 'So help me. What's the moral position on eating it?'

'If you aren't prepared to kill it, you shouldn't eat it,' Barry says.

Tim shakes his head. 'I don't think you have to do the killing. I just think you should be prepared to see the animal killed.' Barry nods. 'That's fair. You should be willing to see it happen.' It's a view with which I have sympathy. I once spent two days working in an abattoir to the north of Leeds, precisely to understand what meat-eating meant, even though I already knew. I worked the pig kill line, pulling the carcasses through a hot-water bath just moments after their throats had been slit. I worked on the sheep line too, helping to drag off their skins. It didn't put me off eating meat at all. I ate it for dinner both nights. But it did leave me wondering whether, to gain a carnivore's licence, you ought to be willing to do as I had done.

I remind Annie that she had once told me it was better to eat pork from well-cared-for animals than to stop eating it altogether and abnegate responsibility for their welfare. 'Yup, I still think that.'

Tim says, 'The way I see it, if you raise an animal for food humanely and then kill it humanely, it will have had a better life than if it had been raised in the wild and ended its life being mauled by a predator.' There is more nodding around the table.

Then Zoe says, 'Eating meat is immoral.' We frown at her: she has been nose-down in the chilled trotter and the sirloin in chilli oil. 'No, really, eating meat is immoral – but it's an immorality I can handle. I'm hypocritical, but I've fully embraced my hypocrisy.'

I sit back in my chair. All the immorality I can handle. All the hypocrisy that's fit to be lived with. I wonder whether I have just found my religion. I have spent most of my adult life writing for left–liberal newspapers, forever agonising over whether my personal behaviour matches up to what I write about and whether what I write about will satisfy a readership drenched in agonies over the injustices of modern life. I have written in detail about the environmental impact of meat-eating, talked about the need to reduce consumption, detailed poor animal welfare and argued about the imperative for its improvement. I have tried not to be a mad, goggle-eyed fanatic, a kind of food-culture Taliban, proposing standards that the majority could never hope to meet, but still, I've covered the waterfront. Back in the pre-Internet days there was only the occasional reader's letter to question me. Even then, they were easily dismissed. How obsessive would you have to be to find a piece of paper, sit down, write a letter, put it in an envelope, stick a stamp on it and then get it into a postbox? The very business of sending a letter to a newspaper made the writer ignorable.

In the age of the Web, however, the entire world is there to tell you that you're a two-faced, hypocritical, lazy tosser, and doing so requires no effort at all. Twitter fizzes with abuse; the comment sections beneath my articles are one long, drawn-out, critical Armageddon, a place where all hope and ambition to be a slightly better person, to do a little less worse than you did before, goes to die. We live our lives amid an electronic shitstorm of name-calling and virtue-signalling and

Internet-shaming. Finding a way through it is a nightmare. But my friend Zoe Laughlin, director of the Institute of Making at University College London, and a woman with a fabulous cyclone of hair, of a sort that small children could get lost in, has nailed it: live a life of immorality that you can handle. Make peace with your hypocrisy.

This fits perfectly with the task at hand, which is to say, the invitation to design a last supper, which, in truth, is all about a meal that represents the true self, free from consequences and recriminations the next day. Look, it's not as if I got them to slaughter and skin a baby panda for my dining pleasure. I'm not François Mitterrand, with his songbirds drowned in brandy. I've not ordered up kitten fricassee or puppy in black bean sauce. If I had, the very process of eating such dishes, each chopsticked morsel, would have been awful in real time. This, the eating of a pig, even a small one with its ears, tail and trotters intact, is essentially quotidian. It sits within the bounds of the ordinary, and I can deal with that.

Talking of which, that piglet is coming back.

The skin has been scored with a very sharp knife into generous squares, which come away easily from the pale flesh underneath. We have dishes of sticky hoisin, with a deep liquorice and aniseed end, and small doughy, steamed pancakes to smear it on. As with crispy duck, we are to put a piece of skin into the sauced pancake and fold it over. Each bite is the softness of the pancake followed by the brittle, satisfying snap of the crisped skin. Quickly, we peel the piglet down. They take it away once more for further chopping, and return it to us broken into manageable pieces of meat. The little legs are there to be taken in hand, and the head is still in place for those who want to have a crack at an ear or a tusk of jaw. At the end there is a little heap of meat left for the kitchen to enjoy, which I am told is good manners. We have done justice to the piglet.

Four of us share a cab home. Night-time London spins by us, all ribbons of tail-light and the sudden insult of car horn, as we head south. Naturally, having talked in advance about how it would be, and then discussed during the eating how it is, we now fall to talking about how it was. As the one who paid for the whole damn thing, it falls to me to say what I suspect everyone else is thinking:

'It was nice and all that but . . . it was no Peking duck.'

The others agree. 'The skin was crisp, but not like duck skin,' says one.

'The meat was too young to actually taste of anything,' says another.

'I think it was more of a status-symbol dish,' I say. Many cultures have those. For the British it is a roast rib of beef, which, in a statement of the obvious, cannot be eaten unless you can first afford to buy it. The expense is rewarded by something that looks dramatic and can taste fabulous too.

This cab ride should be a despondent moment. A sizeable amount of money was dropped on a single food item that was found to be lacking. Happily, it's one of the benefits of a life spent writing about meals in restaurants: the duds come with the territory. I always travel hopefully but accept that arrival may not be all that. It is a marker of my dreadful life that I am inured to disappointing piglets.

A few days after we had reduced the suckling pig to a heap of bones at Pearl Liang, I phoned my friend Tim Anderson, the Japanese food expert. Tim grew up in Racine, Wisconsin, a state which likes to boast that it is the frozen-custard capital of the world, a title which may well be fought over. Wisconsin is famous for cranberries, corn, cheese and kringles, a kind of Nordic pretzel which can be both sweet and salty. It is a hearty, extremely Midwestern place. The Andersons have a family cookbook, a collation of recipes passed down from one matriarch to another. Even by Tim's assessment, it is dominated by dishes which involve the introduction of one canned good to another, generally followed by the application of orange cheese.

When Tim was fifteen, he discovered *Iron Chef*, a fizzing, gladiatorial, extreme cooking TV show from Japan. It was his introduction to Japanese food and cookery. It was love at first sight. He studied Japanese history at Occidental College in LA, and in his early twenties moved to Japan for two years, where he immersed himself further in the food. He moved to London with his British-born wife and made his living managing a bar, but continued cooking with a nerdy, intense enthusiasm. In 2011 he became the youngest-ever winner of British *MasterChef*, with an eccentric, Japanese-inflected menu. He's gone on to write cookbooks, work as a panellist on my radio show and open his own take on a ramen shop called Nanban, not far from my home in Brixton, south London. In keeping with the Japanese love of appropriating ideas from different cultures, Tim isn't slavish in his attempt to create a Tokyo-familiar experience. He certainly sweats over the essentials. His tonkotsu broth, made by simmering pig parts for twelve hours, is a gloriously creamy thing, rich in lip-smacking collagen and porcine loveliness. It's a noble end for the bits of pig that don't necessarily get the love they deserve. But Tim's also not afraid to make, say, a curry goat ramen as a nod to the Afro-Caribbean culture of the neighbourhood his restaurant calls home. (It's an intense affair, full of all-spice and the massive hit of Scotch bonnet chillies.)

I knew Tim was exactly the man for the job I had in mind. I told him what I wanted. He said, 'Give me time. I'll write a menu.'

Eventually, this would require him to obtain one pig's head, three pig's trotters, one kilo each of pig heart and liver, a kilo of aged pork collar, half a kilo of pancetta, two *'presa'* – the shoulder cut from Ibérico pigs – three large bone-in pork chops, various bones and tails, plus three pig's stomachs. The latter was tricky. He had to get them frozen from a Chinese supermarket, where they are labelled in Chinese but apparently come from British pigs. Few non-Chinese people in Britain have an interest in pig stomachs, it seems. Those people did not include the group I assembled to eat Tim's shopping list.

Pork is now the most popular meat in Japan; they eat almost as much of the stuff as they do beef and chicken combined, though it wasn't always this way. The eating of meat rose and fell in popularity over the centuries, depending upon who was running the country. The Buddhists of the eighth century regarded meat-eating as distasteful, as did the Samurai, who ruled from the twelfth to the fourteenth centuries. Later, the warlords of Satsuma fell back in love with meat, and pork in particular. Herds of pigs were sent out with their armies as a kind of walking larder. When Japan started studying Western development during the Meiji period from 1868 to 1912, they noted the level of meat consumption, and so actively encouraged it. As pork was considerably cheaper than beef, it predominated.

One of the most popular ways to eat pork in Japan today is as tonkatsu, a thick pork chop that is breaded and fried to crisp and served sliced with a spiky sauce. A bone-in version was included in the menu Tim drew up in response to my request for a Japanese-influenced journey around planet pig. He served it on a metal platter, with a salt and sesame seed seasoning on the side, plus a rich, cider-based sweet–sour sauce. We debated who should get the curve of bone with its prime nibblage opportunities, until I enforced my rights as the instigator of the dinner and nagged at every last strand.

Before that, there were many things. We began with a small cup of twelve-hour tonkotsu broth, bobbing with pieces of smoked pork jowl, burnt garlic oil, nori seaweed oil, pickled ginger and spring onions. It was soothing and deep. It was a declaration of intent. Just as with this broth, many things and much effort had gone into this dinner. There was a disc of gyoza – dumplings – with a dense, fiercely meaty filling of aged pork collar, liver and heart, the individual packages linked by a crisp, lacy filigree of batter. Those stomachs had been sliced up and cooked down to a light funkiness, then mixed into a stir-fry with a heap of hispi cabbage, bean sprouts and a spicy miso sauce. A cylinder of *presa*, or shoulder, had been seared on all sides but left utterly pink at the eye. 'Don't eat it if you're pregnant,' Tim said, eyeing the group of mostly middle-aged men. It was served in tender slivers with fresh wasabi, garlic chips and an aged soy and vinegar dipping sauce.

A quick trip across Asia gave us the boned-out and sliced-up trotters, slow-cooked to gelatinous, then fried into a darkly caramelised Korean-style pancake with spring onions and garlic chives that had us picking at every last sticky, toasted piece. From Sichuan province came Tim's take on mapo tofu, because he's weirdly obsessed with the stuff: cubes of wobbly, ivory-coloured tofu, playing tag with cubes of wobbly, ivory-coloured brain, in a huge, unctuous, pungent sauce made with smoked pig's head and, as his typed-up menu put it, 'many kinds of pepper'. It was a slap around the chops and utterly absorbing, even though we were beginning to sway in our seats and wonder how much more we could take. There was a smoked octopus and pig's ear salad, which was all about the bounce and snap of tentacle and long-cooked cartilage, and from the island of Okinawa, deep in the south of the Japanese archipelago, a stir-fry of tofu, crescents of emerald-coloured bitter gourd, egg and spam (a taste for the latter had developed on the island during the American occupation after the Second World War). Tim advised us not to eat the gourd by itself but with the other ingredients because it was really bitter and astringent, despite washing and salting. He wasn't wrong.

At the end, as if determined to take us to the very edge, he brought up slabs of dark, bitter chocolate, dusted with fiery pepper, into which had been cooked shards of crackling. We nibbled them and, thanks to the multiple bottles of sake, swayed gently in our seats some more. There were highs and lows. I could live happily without ever meeting the spam and bitter gourd dish again; however, a day which started with the Korean pig's trotter pancake would always be a good one. At the end I studied Tim's printed menu of ludicrous, gargantuan, shameless excess. How many of these dishes should make their way to my last supper? Or was this the kind of thing you only did in the middle of a life lived well, rather than at its end?

I make a list of the pork preparations I have most enjoyed over the years. I am detailed and meticulous, for this is a serious business.

During my road trip in Northern Ireland to find the source of Andrew Rooney's apparently famed oysters, I had stopped off to see an old friend called Peter Hannan. Together with his brother Jim, he runs Hannan Meats from an unassuming industrial estate in Moira. Hannan became famous in London because of his beef, from short-horns raised on clover. Famously, it was dry-aged in a room lined with blocks of pink Himalayan salt. I couldn't quite work out what impact the salt had. Certainly, it would be hygroscopic, removing moisture from the air. Perhaps it had an antibiotic effect, killing off less wanted bacteria from the air which could give long-aged beef that slightly high, funky taste. Either way, a Hannan côte de boeuf really was a special thing. It had won many awards.

However, I found his way with pork even more entrancing. In a part of the world famed for its bacon, he had turned it into a performance piece. He had taken to dumping cured bacon rib cuts, huge meaty things the size of a Sunday-lunch joint, in a sugar pit for a couple of weeks. The afternoon I stopped by, he was in his demonstration kitchen, just across from the shop, roasting up bacon joints for a couple of restaurant chefs who were considering using his meat. He knew how to show it off to its best advantage. The key was to roast it long and slow, below the 140°C burn point, until the skin had gone a golden reddy-brown. The deep-cured, smoked meat fell apart. The crisped fat dissolved on the tongue. It was rich. It was so rich it made you curse the limits of appetite. As ever, Peter laughed while he sliced it up, nudging the plate towards me with an encouraging shrug and a 'Go on now'. I did as I was told. Repeatedly.

Then there are the cracklins I was served at the restaurant of Louisianan chef Isaac Toups in New Orleans. Toups, a huge bald-headed man, with a beard like a Siberian forest, likes to play with the city's culinary traditions, but he stays true to the essentials. His cracklins are one of those: thumb-thick pieces of pork belly, simmered long and slow in fat, and then finished fast until crisp and brown, before being tossed in a mix of salt and spices and served warm. He pushed a large bowl of them across the counter at me, then said I should not eat them all because he had a whole load more dishes coming up. It was a futile request, like trying to get a dog to stop mid-coitus. These demanded to be eaten. First, they shattered under the teeth, before seeming to dissolve into intense gusts of aromatic porkiness. I troughed them.

There's the dish of small ribs served to me at Baiwei, a pretty basic Sichuan caff on the edge of London's Chinatown. They are braised, then deep-fried and heavily seasoned with a mixture of salt, cumin, chilli and a little sugar, before being buried inside a heap of dried red chillies which you have to pick through. The first time I ate the dish, I regarded it solipsistically as a plateful specifically designed with me in mind. I thought that the second and third time too.

I added the thick-cut, maple-cured bacon at Peter Luger's, the famed Brooklyn steakhouse, to the list. I hadn't enjoyed the steak that much; it just wasn't that great a piece of meat. But oh, the sticky, sweet-salty bacon with its dissolving fat.

I put one other thought on the list, then sat back and stared it. If I was going to do the job properly, then there was something important I had missed out. I have to go to St John. To not go there would be a dereliction of duty.

Fergus Henderson's restaurant, which first opened in a converted Clerkenwell smokehouse in 1994, knows more than most about ways with pigs. As a chef, he is celebrated for promoting 'nose to tail' eating; for a belief that if you bang an animal on the head, you have a responsibility to eat as much of it as possible, not least because if you go only for the prime cuts, you're missing out on the best stuff. The vast majority of those noses and tails, and the various bits in between, served at St John belong to pigs. The entry on my list that had brought me up short was the memory of a dinner at St John nearly twenty years ago, when a group of friends who had met on an Internet food bulletin board – it was that long ago – ordered a whole piglet. It was a sizeable animal, roasted for eight hours in their bread oven. It fed twenty people, from nose to tail.

I ask St John whether they might now see their way to doing me another special menu, this time of just extremities. They swiftly agree. Once more I gather the *Kitchen Cabinet* crew, and we set about eating around the edges of a pig. There is a dish of tails, braised long and slow, before being breadcrumbed and deep-fried. They are a light orange in colour and curl around each other. The crunch of the breadcrumb carapace gives way to the soft, gelatinous skin and the meat behind it. The bones are soft and chewy. It is a hands-on business.

A jellied terrine of pig's ear, the curving lines of white cartilage looking like the ridges on a hillside given over to terrace farming as shot from the air, proves a textural challenge. There is softness and then startling crunch. We have a stew of gelatinous pig's trotter and lardons of smoked bacon with tomatoes into which quails' eggs have been broken. It is a huge slap of savouriness. Because it is on the menu that night, we get an extra dish of pig spleen wrapped in bacon. It is served cold in round slices and has a sweet, dense, liverish quality, cut through by the cornichons on the side.

The main course comes in two parts. There is a large platter of slow-cooked pig's tongue with broad beans and a bright herby sauce. Finally, the centrepiece: half a pig's head, first braised, then roasted so the skin crunches.

'This is so much better than the suckling pig at Pearl Liang,' Professor Barry Smith says, as he pulls off a piece of the deep-bronze skin, and we all agree.

I say, 'It belonged to an older animal, one that has led a proper life.'

I find myself wondering if we risk being accused of obscenity for this carnival of feet and ears and noses and spleens. I am still mulling the argument made by my friend Zoe Laughlin: that it is about working out how much immorality and hypocrisy you can cope with. But making a point of eating the bits that others would leave behind, of making sure that as little as possible is wasted, does at least add a dollop of responsibility and thoughtfulness to the affair. I realise immediately that there is one person who would have examined this subject brilliantly: a man

I last saw in this very room but whom I will never see again. There is a ghost hanging over this dinner and, indeed, my entire endeavour.

I was working at home, in June 2018, when I learnt via Twitter that Anthony Bourdain had killed himself. I closed down what I was working on and awaited the inevitable email from one of my editors, requesting an instant piece. It came about five minutes later. I wrote about the way *Kitchen Confidential*, his memoir of life as a stove jockey, part culinary pirate, part fierce and wired junky, had freed food writing from the prison of the twee and the prissy, given voice to something muscular and aggressive which was far closer to the furious business of restaurant kitchens during service. In his world nothing was cooked with love; it was all cooked with fuck-you attitude.

We weren't close friends, though we had met a few times and I admired Tony greatly. Later, he would become a vocal supporter of the #MeToo movement. Arguably, though, in giving a voice to the sweaty, bandana-wearing rabble of the kitchen, he also seemed to endorse tacitly a world of machismo and casual violence, which, fifteen years after the book was published, would become the focus of a pushback. The kitchens of *Kitchen Confidential* read like scary, misogynistic places, and no one should be scared of going to work. Eventually, some of those scared people would indeed find a voice to testify about what had happened to them.

The curious thing is that the Bourdain who emerged from the almost instant stardom his book bestowed in 2000 was nothing like the Bourdain on its pages. The drug habit had gone. He was clean in so many ways, charming, a model of good manners. In 2004 he gave a quote for my novel *The Apologist*, despite the fact that my review of his second book, a rambling travelogue called *A Cook's Tour*, had been less than ecstatic. (He admitted in the Introduction that it was written to fulfil a two-book contract and, compared to *Kitchen Confidential*, it felt like that.) His quote read: 'A very funny book about apologies by a man with a lot to apologise for.' I wore the slap-down as a badge of honour. Later that year, we were paired at a book event in south London on food writing. Hundreds of people came. All of them were there for Tony. He wore it extremely lightly.

The last time we met was in June 2016 at St John, on the Sunday evening after Britain had made the decision to leave the European Union. St John is closed for dinner service on Sundays, but it opened for Bourdain, who was shooting an episode of his food travelogue series *Parts Unknown* for CNN. This one was on London. Fergus Henderson and Bourdain were very close friends. In the show Bourdain would describe Henderson as the 'most influential chef of the last two decades. He changed everything.' The first time Bourdain ate there, he'd walked into the kitchen, dropped to his knees and pledged undying love. 'St John,' he said in the show, over drift shots of the stark white interior, 'I love you and I need you more than ever.'

Bourdain asked me to come and have dinner with him on camera and talk London, food and the utter shit-storm calamity of Brexit. Fergus would be cooking, a rare occurrence these days. His well-documented Parkinson's disease had removed him from service years ago. But tonight he would be there at the stoves.

We sat in the dining room. The tables, stacked with chairs, had been pushed back. The lights were off; we had our own television lighting, dropping a golden glow around us. As filming experiences go, it was a revelation. The process of documentary television is mostly a nightmare of hurry up and wait, of reshoots and close-ups and 'Just do that again and again, and once more, please.' I'd come to hate it so much that I'd quit *The One Show*, for which I was a food reporter. I couldn't stand the process any more.

'We don't do any of that,' Tony said. 'No retakes. We just shoot.' He had become fascinated by the process of film-making, he told me, though he rarely intervened with his crew. Before we started shooting, he was quiet, polite and self-contained, as if holding everything back for camera.

After a suicide it is tempting to use hindsight to imbue almost anything with significance. But it's impossible for me not to look back
on that dinner and review it from that perspective. Fergus served us
roasted bone marrow with parsley salad and sourdough toast, the dish
for which he is now most famous. There was skate wing poached in
court bouillon with shaved fennel and green herbs. There was a pig's
head and potato pie in a golden pastry crust, like something from a
comic book, and devilled kidneys on toast, which tasted of Madeira
and cayenne and just the hint of urea. There was pickled calf's tripe.

Across the table I enthused to Tony about 'these foods that have
about them the faint whiff of death'. I told him that they were the
ones which 'remind you that you are most alive'.

Tony nodded. 'It's the scent of your own mortality.'

That night at St John I had been revelling in the nowness of
everything. I had been tapped up by a brilliant and important man
to take part in a great show. There were any number of journalists
in London he could have asked, but he asked me, and I was full of it.
Later, after the news broke, I found myself wondering whether ending
it all had been a long-term preoccupation of his.

After our braised pig's head and the pig's tongue with green sauce,
we were stuffed. Dessert was not in any way a necessity, but I did
feel something was required to give the evening a full stop. The
ever-changing menu at St John often lists madeleines, fresh from the
oven, courtesy of a fifteen-minute wait. It takes that long to whip up
the batter and bake them. They arrived at the table still hot, and crisp
at the edges. We did not have Proust's tea to dip them in. We didn't
need it. We weren't trying to remember. We were profoundly happy
in the moment.

We paid up and trailed out into the cavernous, semi-industrial bar
area, with its metal top and its bakery sales point and its blackboards
scrawled with possibilities. I thought about the time I had spent in

there, especially when the *Observer* offices were just a short walk up the road. And suddenly I knew exactly what I had to serve at this meal of mine. I had eaten my way through the pig and round the pig and over the pig, and had found numerous accomplices. We'd all had a ball. But all those different dishes and preparations and platings, however fabulous they were, had made my head spin. How was I to choose?

And then it came to me. Where pig is concerned, I'd missed out the obvious.

I knew exactly what I had to do.

Crispy belly pork teriyaki with red chilli and spring onions

No, it's not this. You'll have to wait for that. Meanwhile, the recipe I'm giving you involves pork belly. It was always going to be a pork-belly dish. This hot, sweet and lightly sour stir-fry has the benefit of being completed very quickly once the preparation is done, so you can set it up in advance. And while it isn't my last supper dish, it's a serious whack of flavour and texture that just might become yours.

Serves four, along with other dishes, or two with just rice

INGREDIENTS

Three 200g skin-on pork-belly strips, each 3–4cm wide

One red chilli, chopped

Four spring onions, each of them topped and tailed and cut into three

A knob of salted butter

Salt and pepper

Tabasco

For the sauce:

30ml soy sauce

40ml orange juice

3tsp runny honey

1tsp sesame oil

A thumb-sized piece of ginger

One clove of garlic

Heat the oven to 200°C.

Slice the belly pork across the strips into 1cm pieces. Spread in an oven tray and season with salt and pepper. No need to add extra oil; they'll produce enough of their own fat. Roast until the skin is crisp, turning them around occasionally so they don't stick. It should take about forty-five minutes to an hour, depending on your oven and the pork. They can be used the moment they are roasted or left out of the fridge for up to a couple of hours.

Meanwhile, mix the ingredients for the sauce in a measuring jug. Grate in the ginger and the garlic. Stir.

Heat a tablespoon of vegetable oil in a cast-iron frying pan. When hot, throw in the chopped red chilli. Cook for a minute over a medium heat, then throw in the spring onions. Finally, add the pork. Stir-fry for a couple of minutes, until the pork is reheated.

Pour on the sauce and turn up the heat, but keep everything moving. It will thicken quickly, but because of the high sugar content from the honey, it could burn, and you don't want that. You'll only blame me.

When it begins to thicken, whip in the butter until the sauce is glossy.

Throw in a dash of Tabasco, according to taste. Four or five drops, if you like it properly fiery. Whisk again.

Serve with boiled, steamed or sticky rice. Your call.

▶ 5. 'All of Me', Gerald Marks and Seymour Simons (1931)

A Friday night in 2010, and I am sitting at the end of the bar of the Ivy Club, a fancy private joint above the famous Theatreland restaurant of the same name. Here, the whisky sours are both strong and stupidly expensive. I often come on a Friday night. I appear live on *The One Show* on BBC1, talking about that week's food news, and then get the cab from the studio to drop me off at the door. The supple, dextrous house pianist, Joe Thompson, is an old friend from university, where he cast me in a student production of *Cabaret*, as a transvestite. On Friday nights there's always a jazz trio: Joe, on piano, with a bassist and another instrument, often sax or guitar. The musicians are always glorious; indeed, they are some of the biggest names in British jazz and they like to come for what is a relaxed gig in a room largely populated by people from the world of theatre, who know what they're listening to and show their appreciation accordingly. It's not just a joy to be here, so close to the action; it's a privilege.

I have been at the end of the bar listening and nursing those whisky sours for about an hour, when Joe stands up, looks at me and says, 'You're on.' He knows I play piano. He's even given me a few lessons. By this point I have taken jazz-piano night classes. I've also played in front of audiences, though not with much finesse. Way back at university, when we first met, I discovered my wife Pat had an unexpected jazz voice, full of soft, airy highs and big, throaty blues tones. She had sung with a youth big band and knew one end of a jazz standard from the other. In the 1990s, while we were trying and failing to make children, we had performed a few times in bars as a piano/voice duo, as a way of taking our minds off infertility. But it was very basic, raw stuff. And, crucially, no other musicians were involved.

Now I am being asked to sit down and play with two other people: a roaring, percussive bassist called Robert Rickenberg, who has played with everyone from the Dankworths to Mark Murphy and Will Gaines; and a guitarist called Chris Cobbson, who is a regular part of Courtney Pine's line-up.

Robert says, 'What do you want to play?'

I say, nervously, '"All of Me"? In C?'

It is the only jazz tune I am confident I can get all the way through. The chord changes are straightforward and there aren't too many twists and turns. But I only know the chords (and even then, only very basic ones) because I play it to accompany Pat. I certainly can't play the melody over the top with my right hand. But that's okay because Chris can do that. And so we play. It is utterly thrilling. Just an hour or two before, I had been live on TV in front of millions of people, but my heart hadn't moved. Now it is fighting to get out of my chest. To be deep in the river of that music, to have the soft wondrous pull of the bass behind me and Chris's guitar floating over the top, is to live in the moment. All I have to do is hang on. I want the feeling again. I want to play again. The music really does have all of me. For the next week I practise playing both the chords and the melody. The following Friday I return to the club, promising to do the whole thing. But I don't just want to be the guy with that one tune.

And now – stifle the yawn – here's Rayner with his party piece.

I go home and learn 'Summertime', followed by 'Softly, as in a Morning Sunrise', followed by 'Black Coffee'. Each Friday night I come back and try out my new project. (Eight years later, I still often do that with a new tune: play it straight off with no rehearsal at the Ivy Club on a Friday night. It's a good test of whether I really know it.)

I learnt vast amounts of what I needed to be a jazz pianist in the bar of the Ivy Club, and I continue to do so: the basic structure of tunes, how to count, how to bring soloists in and out. I discovered that musicians care deeply about their food because they spend so much time on the road, wondering about lunch or dinner. As a result, many of them read my reviews and were curious and patient enough to let me sit in with them. In truth, it was ludicrous. A musician of my then mediocre abilities should never have got to play with guitarists like Jim Mullen and Nigel Price, the saxophonist Nigel Hitchcock or the trombonist Mark Nightingale. But in the Ivy Club on a Friday night Joe Thompson had created that rare thing: the jazz scene, a space in which musicians could gather and play together with very little pressure. As well as overseeing the music in the bar, Joe also booked musicians into the Ivy's private rooms; some Friday nights, when the various gigs around the building were on a break, you could have three bassists, a brace of tenor sax players and four pianists at the bar. And they were all happy to talk music, in between talking restaurants.

In 2011 I was invited to take part in an event called '5 × 15', in which five people are asked to talk for fifteen minutes about a personal passion in front of an audience of hundreds. They probably assumed I would opt to talk about an ingredient; braised otter perhaps, or roast swan. Instead, I asked if there was a piano available. They said there was. In which case, I said, I wanted to talk about playing one for thirty-five years and not being especially good at it, because we generally only talk about the things we're great at. And yet many of the things that give us huge pleasure are not those we'll ever excel at. I talked for eleven minutes about my love of the piano, the way just the mere presence of one in a room makes me think better of that space for what it means could happen there. At the end Robert Rickenberg joined me on stage to play 'All of Me'. I imagined it would be the only time I would play anything close to jazz in front of a major audience.

I was wrong.

Afterwards I was approached by a woman from Jewish Book Week, the literary festival held every year in London. She said she'd enjoyed what I'd done very much. 'Could you do it for an hour?'

I frowned. 'I can't do "I'm shit but thank you for listening" for an hour.'

She shrugged. 'Well, how about we give you a year to get ready?'

In a moment of either stupid courage or vanity, I said yes. I wasn't worried about the patter between the tunes; that I knew how to do. But I needed both a repertoire and, I concluded, a full band. The latter wasn't tough. I had access to those sparkling professional musicians from the Ivy Club, who were always up for an interesting gig. Robert Rickenberg agreed to play bass, and Dave Lewis – a lyrical player renowned for his ability to improvise top lines that felt like they had been composed long ago, and a regular with the late John Martyn and now with the Blockheads – joined on tenor sax. As for the singer, well, I slept with her every night. She couldn't say no. Together, Pat and I shaped a list of ten tunes that we felt we could do justice to, or at the very least get to the end of. All we needed was a name for our ensemble. I put the question to Robert. He said, 'You're the one getting the gig.' Fair enough. The Jay Rayner Quartet was born. If nothing else, it meant everyone knew who to blame.

On a Sunday evening in February 2012 we performed our first hour-long gig. It was in Hall 2 at King's Place, in London's King's Cross, which happens to be both the building that houses the offices of the *Observer* newspaper and home to two major concert halls, complete with a bunch of beautiful Steinway grands. A terrific piano can do wonders for a novice pianist's playing. I claimed it was the chance to play one of those instruments which had encouraged me to say yes to the booking. In truth, I just wanted to see whether I could actually do it. (You can decide for yourself, because it was videoed. That recording lurks even now in the dustier recesses of Vimeo.) Sure, the playing lacked subtlety. It was clunky in places. But we got through every tune. What's more, the audience seemed to enjoy it. My one regret is that the audience didn't include my mother Claire, who had died in 2010 and therefore didn't ever get to see me play. But my dad Des was there. It was the only gig he was able to make it to, but it was the one that mattered. Because as Pat and I agreed afterwards, after all that effort it could not be a one-off. It was too much fun. Somehow we would have to do that again.

And yes, we played 'All of Me'. We still do, sometimes. How could we not?

As for the recording, it has to be Oscar Peterson's, from his 1959 album *A Jazz Portrait of Frank Sinatra*. Oh, how it swings. One day, if I practise really, really hard, I might just be able to work out how he's doing what he's doing.

Salad

There was one particular detail in the death-row-meal academic papers I studied that stayed with me: the fact that three condemned prisoners, with just hours to live, chose Diet Coke as their drink of choice. The first explanation I can muster is that these people liked the taste of artificial sweetener, relished that dull tingle along the edge of their tongue. They craved it, even when there was no good reason for drinking it. This raises so many questions. Generally, in America you end up on death row for having killed someone, for having such a callous disregard for the life of another, or such a complete belief in the righteousness of your own needs or demands, that you are willing or able to kill. And yet to be a Diet Coke-drinking death-row inmate, that same person must at some point surely have made a decision based on the minute calibrations of personal health.

'Ooh, I'm fatter than I would like to be. I'd better cut out the sugar.'

It seems such a thoughtful, considered position, compared to what is required to make a killer. There are convincing explanations for this apparent contradiction, mostly rooted in mental health or a personality disorder: a sociopathic ability not to feel anything about anyone else, while still seeing to your own precise needs and desires. Which is all well and good, but it comes down to this: only someone who is in the grip of a mental illness or, more likely, that personality disorder would choose Diet Coke as part of their last-ever meal.

And so to salad.

My younger son asked me what foods I would be exploring during this last supper of mine. I told Dan there would be a chapter on salad.

'Why? It's not like you have to be healthy.'

'I like salad.'

'More than chips?'

'Can't there be a place for both?'

He is fourteen. As he has never knowingly eaten a salad, I could see this was a stupid question.

Once, I was like him. Eating salad was, for a very long time, a choice I could never imagine making. It happened occasionally, but so did double maths. Necessarily, I must retell the story of how, as a small child, I picketed the family home in response to the challenge of salad. It was a hot summer's day in 1973, and my mother had decided that cold smoked-mackerel fillets with salad leaves would be the thing. I scowled, slipped from the table and found the cardboard used to stiffen my father's shirts when they came back from the laundry. Armed with that, along with a ruler, some Sellotape and a black felt-tip pen, and I was ready to go. I scrawled 'I want proper dinner' across the board and marched up and down outside the house, like the strikers I had seen on the telly. I would have been six years old. I knew it was funny, but I also meant it. Cold smoked-mackerel fillets? With salad? How bloody dare they?

Now a parent myself, I look back on that incident and sense in my late mother a 'Sod it, this will do' moment. I adore my children, but sometimes, especially through the smaller years, making sure there was a proper meal on the table was a drudge and bore. I could make a huge effort and it wouldn't always be met with enthusiasm. So perhaps she thought, 'Smoked mackerel and salad. It's quick, it's easy, I like it and the little bastards better not complain.' But I did. She made me eat it anyway.

Salad didn't become a genuine choice until the advent of Joe Allen, the restaurant in London's West End, which my parents treated as a members' club from its opening in 1977. Their Caesar salad was like nothing I had come across before. Each portion was served in its own large rough-carved wooden salad bowl, with its own salad servers so you got to toss it yourself, which felt curiously subversive, as though you had become your own waiter. It was pretty true to the original 1924 recipe devised by restaurateur Caesar Cardini, who put it together from ingredients at the back of the fridge, after the Fourth of July celebrations had cleared out the kitchen at his hotel in Tijuana, Mexico. In time the Caesar salad served across London would become a monstrous, adulterated beast, pelted with pieces of griddle-marked chicken breast with the texture of moist cotton wool. There would be roast-vegetable Caesar salads and prawn Caesar salads and salmon Caesar salads. Worst of all, there would be those given the silver flash of *boquerones*, those vinegary anchovies which are a consolation prize for anybody hoping for salted anchovies. Terrible food crimes have been committed in the name of the Caesar.

It's not that the original is regarded by everyone as perfect, although I happen to think it is. It's that the adjustments made to it by chefs who think, say, that wheels are too round are not better. At Joe's the salad was made with whole leaves of romaine, like green canoes, which arrived under a snowfall of grated fresh Parmesan. Even that was a revelation. In the 1970s Parmesan was still a dry, finely ground something in a plastic pot which smelt of vomit (literally so; they both contain isovaleric acid, which gives vomit its distinctive smell, and which becomes more concentrated and, therefore, obvious in the dry-dust version of Parmesan). There were seriously garlicky croutons in Joe's Caesar, and a creamy dressing made with egg yolk and the big hit of Worcestershire sauce. It may or may not have included extra pounded salted anchovy; there is a view that the addition of anchovy is unnecessary because there's so much of it in the Worcestershire sauce.

These things were an irrelevance to me. I just knew it was unexpectedly delicious. Unlike too many floppy British salads, the leaves crunched and tasted of something. There was garlic and salt and creaminess and a whole bunch of good things. I ordered a Caesar to start every time I went to Joe's, and my parents would look at me adoringly, the more so as time passed, because as adolescence hit, much like a hurricane making landfall, it became clear that looking after my body was not a priority. My waist measurement passed the forty-inch mark at some point in my early teens and then stormed ahead. A genetic tendency to varicose veins, combined with that weight, meant that my calves bloomed with peaks both green and purple before I was fifteen. We had no culture of exercise in my family, and I liked to be a part of my family's culture. In the standard way, I was introduced to smoking cigarettes at teenage parties and took to it with enthusiasm. I mastered asking for 'ten-bee-and-aitch' very quickly, not because I especially liked Benson and Hedges, but because I could say it quickly and, therefore, with what sounded like nonchalance. Its repetition made me sound discerning, like I was a chap who had a brand. In the early months of smoking I adored the way my knuckles smelt after a fag had been between them. A few years later, during my first weeks at university, I would give thanks for cigarettes, for giving a lonely boy a long way from home a way of looking like he was engaged in something important. Smoking done properly could always be made to look important, and I was terrific at it.

And then there were the recreational narcotics. If my body was a temple, it was a deconsecrated one, or perhaps a place into which devil-worshippers had moved.

And yet, at Joe's I ordered salad and looked like I meant it. To my poor parents I imagine this was important. I suspect they saw it as a reason for optimism. If so, I had plenty of ways to undermine their hope. After all, this was my adolescence, and I was determined to do it properly.

In May 1983, when I was sixteen, I became a famous juvenile delinquent. It wasn't the plan. Until the bright spring day when a couple of boys in the year above me at school told me a scandal was about to break and I was to be at the very heart of it, my delinquency had been a private affair. I smoked dope with my friends, with vaulting enthusiasm. I was good at rolling joints and prided myself on always obtaining my own narcotics. I didn't expect others to dive into the criminal underworld to score for me. I went direct to source. Later, after I'd packed it all in, I concluded it was less the high that interested me than the subculture: it was those men in their dank squats, blankets hung over the windows both to keep the heat in and to stop the light escaping, so the place looked abandoned; the particular way you had to knock on the window to gain entry; the joint you knew you had to roll for the dealer before you could leave. I was an avowedly middle-class Jewish boy from the suburbs who could recite bits of T. S. Eliot and had a quiet love for MGM musicals, but by darkness I could be something entirely other. I could be edgy and dangerous. Or at least feel edgy and dangerous. Inevitably, it would be my fascination with that subculture, my insistence on scoring my own hash, that would be my downfall.

That summer, having auditioned year after year, I was finally cast in the school play, a co-production between the fee-paying Haberdashers' Aske's boys' and girls' schools, which stood side by side in rural Elstree, just outside London. That year it would be *The Taming of the Shrew*. I was cast as a cleric, not one of Shakespeare's most famous characters or, to be fair, one of his characters at all: he had no lines. Still, I put my back into it. The play had a Victorian setting, and I decided my Jew-fro of mad, curly black hair needed to be smoothed down into something shiny and brilliantined. Keeping it like that for a whole night was, however, tricky. It was my mother who came up with the solution: K-Y Jelly. The sexual lubricant sets hard if left for a little while on hair; it did the job perfectly and turned me into a talking point, which was exactly what I wanted.

By tradition, the last-night party would be held at the home of the leading man, which that year was in Golders Green, north-west London. The school would lay on a coach to get us there. It was going to be an all-night affair, which we knew presented challenges. There would be booze, lots of it, but we were a thoughtful, overeducated lot. We knew that if we laid into the bottle, we'd all get too pissed too quickly. It would be far better, we agreed, in what even now I regard as an extremely sensible secret planning meeting, to get a load of dope and just get stoned. About a dozen of us, the self-regarding core of the party, handed money to one of our number, who said he was willing to score on our behalf. That offended my highly developed moral code. It felt like the others were soliciting someone else to commit a crime. I said I would get my own.

The play was a triumph, and so was the party. One person in our crowd declined the joints and instead drank so much he poisoned himself and threw up everywhere. Patrick was never punished. Indeed, a few months later, he was made head boy. He went on to be a teacher of religious education and, weirdly, for a God-fearing Christian, headmaster of a Jewish school. The rest of us rolled our joints, got gently stoned and pushed on until dawn.

It took a while to find out who had grassed us up, and we never found out why they felt the need to do so. I often wonder if they look back and cringe at what they did. I seriously bloody hope so. It may have been over thirty years ago, but a part of me still hopes they're reading this right now and dying a little inside.

The storm broke about a week after the party, as senior teachers fanned out across the campus like the Stasi to feel appropriate collars. The school told us we were washed up, a perfect example of disappointing wasters. In reality, it turned out fine: we became teachers and barristers and psychotherapists, playwrights and journalists. But at the time it was a proper trauma. We also never quite worked out why the school felt a party at a private house was anything to do with them. But they did, and the parents went with it. By the time I found out what was happening, around a dozen kids in the lower sixth in both the boys' and girls' schools had already been put on notice that they were going to be suspended. The search for the source of the dope was under way. I was told by my friends that I had to own up to bringing a couple of joints to the party, which is what I did.

I was interrogated by the head teacher. He asked me if I had not in fact brought much more with me, a whole stash of my own. I denied it. They let me go and said they might have further questions. A few days later, I was dragged back in. They had a witness, they told me. The deputy headmaster, a brisk little man called Mr Carlton who talked through his nose in a high-pitched whine, read from a statement: 'You were seen heating a piece of hashish cannabis resin . . .' – even as the incident was unfolding I found myself bemused by this outbreak of ignorant tautology, hashish being the cover-all name for cannabis resin – '. . . on a safety pin over a flame, crumbling it into a joint and . . .'

I should have held the line. I doubt they could have proved anything. Instead, I folded. I admitted everything. They called my parents, who came and collected me.

A dozen kids were suspended for between one and two weeks. One person from the girls' school was expelled completely. On 20 May 1983 I was suspended indefinitely, with no promise that I would be allowed back in to complete my A-levels come the autumn term. (Spoiler alert: I was readmitted.)

My poor father was both livid and baffled. My mother was more understanding, although within a couple of weeks she would also end up feeling terribly guilty, courtesy of a call from the *Daily Mail*. Two of my friends had flogged the story to the paper for £30, which seemed indecently cheap. It was a page-three lead: 'Drugs Dilemma of an Agony Aunt'. In London's *Evening Standard* it was 'Private Agony of Claire Rayner', a legend they slapped all over the billboards they used to advertise that night's paper across the capital. In the *Harrow Observer*, our local paper, it was front-page news. So I should bloody think. (In the late 1980s, when I finally made it into the offices of national newspaper groups to help them produce student supplements, it occurred to me that they would have all these reports in their newspaper cuttings libraries, which journalists used to research the background to stories. I became unduly paranoid that someone would call up the file on me and decide to revisit my past. As if anybody would care. One by one I went around the cuttings libraries – from the *Mail* group to the *Telegraph*, from the *Guardian* to the *Express* to

The Times – ordering up the files on myself. Most of them had one. I destroyed all the cuttings and returned the files empty. As far as I know, I have the only complete set.)

My poor old dad found it excruciating. Des worried about what he called 'the family business'. Claire made her living as an agony aunt, and a very good living at that, offering advice on how to navigate life's chicanes. It had bought us a huge house in the suburbs, my expensive education, fabulous holidays and a nice lifestyle. Getting myself slapped all over the papers for being naughty and bad put that at risk. Claire saw it slightly differently. She told me that any teenager should be allowed to screw up, and to do so privately. But because of what she did for a living, my screw-up had become public.

Indeed it had. The parents of close friends of mine told their sons and daughters that they were no longer to associate with me because I was plainly an appalling influence. Usually, these friends told me this as they rolled me a consolatory joint. Being thrown out of school should have made me stop; in truth, there was only a dope-smoking hiatus of about a week. It would take the mushroom Cup-a-Soup incident eighteen months later to deal with that.

Despite my deep love for the Joe Allen Caesar, I was a long way off being salad-curious. It turned out I just hadn't met the right vinegar. The right vinegar is everything, because without it you can't make the right dressing. When I was a kid, salad dressing was something made by Kraft which came in a long-necked glass bottle that was kept in the fridge, a coagulated, jellied scab gathering around the screw top. They were a triumph of industrial emulsifiers, these dressings, water-based fluids and oils handcuffed together with a special kind of edible glue. There was the Thousand Island, the colour of pink fondant icing, with the sharp tang of malt vinegar and the blunt sugariness of, well, sugar. There was a blue-cheese dressing, which tasted to me like so many kinds of putrid wrongness in a bottle, and a vinaigrette that was always separated and needed vigorous shaking. At the bottom was the oil; at the top was something that glistened and shined, in which were suspended brutal, unfriendly pieces of raw garlic that meant us all harm. Those bottles of cheap, separated vinaigrette could have doubled as a poor man's lava lamp.

The only time my mother made her own dressings – a rather lovely standard vinaigrette with lots of Dijon mustard, and something dreadful involving breadcrumbs which I never quite understood – was when she served globe artichokes at dinner parties. These I liked because of the hands-on action: pull off the leaf, dredge through the dressing, drag leaf over teeth to get at the good bit, lob the now dead leaf into the bowl and start again, until you get to the artichoke autopsy: dragging off the fibrous choke in search of the yielding heart.

For the most part, though, salad dressings were a worry.

Then, one day at Leeds University, I had the extreme good fortune to meet the woman who would eventually agree to become my wife. Pat's mother Denise was from a mountaintop somewhere near Neuchâtel, in the French-speaking part of Switzerland. While she had lived in Britain for the best part of fifty years, she carried with her certain markers. One of those was a French accent that joyfully mangled the simplest of words and failed altogether at others. Another was a particular type of vinegar called Kressi. It was nothing special, in the sense that it was a mass-market brand to be found on supermarket shelves in Switzerland. On the other hand, it was everything. Pat's family had been obsessed with it all her life. Trips would be made from their home in the West Midlands to see the family in Switzerland every couple of years, and they would return with half a dozen bottles, like it was a rare vintage that needed to be cared for. Hers was the only family she knew of that regularly ate salad with their evening meal. She would bring friends home from school, and they would stare baffled at this bowl of leafy stuff. If they had ever met salad before, it certainly wasn't dressed; it was just a deathly thump of leaf matter. This was something different.

In time I would become a part of Pat's family, and I too would inherit the obsession. Occasionally, we would be given a bottle of Kressi by a family member returning from a trip to Switzerland. When the bottle got down to the last inch, I would begin to mourn. At various times I travelled across London in search of a replacement, buying a dozen different brands at a time. None would do the job, though there was for a while an own brand from Harrods which came close. It is only in the past few years that an enterprising wine merchant, Patrick Whenham-Bossy of Terra Wines, in Melton Mowbray, recognised that there might be a market for it. Especially if a particular, quite noisy food writer insisted on tweeting about it. He now imports the vinegar of the gods direct from Switzerland, and I do my best to help him sell it, simply to maintain my own supply.

Kressi has a light acidity and a deep, rounded flavour. Other white-wine vinegars make you shudder and bare your teeth. You have to work on them, pelt them with aromatics to get something out of them. Kressi isn't like that. As a child, Pat used to pour some into a saucer and mop it up with white bread while watching cartoons after school. I remember making a salad dressing with it for the first time, in the tiny galley kitchen of the first flat we shared together in south London: some finely sliced spring onions in the bottom of the bowl, a glug or two of olive oil, two caps of Kressi, a pinch of sea salt. Pile on the leaves – romaine, torn by hand, the thicker outer leaves as well as the hearts – and turn them in the mess at the bottom of the bowl. It was bright and crisp. It was invigorating. It was perfect. The salad years had begun.

In truth, it wasn't my vinegar epiphany that turned me into the kind of man who regarded a dinner table without a full salad bowl on it as incomplete. I am self-aware enough, or perhaps just old enough, to know that my taste for salad also developed alongside something rather significant: a growing sense of my own mortality. When I was a teenager, working hard to keep the stock price of Benson and Hedges high and the volume of vodka in the bottle low, the idea that I could be contributing to my own early death was entirely abstract and, therefore, not especially convincing. It was far beyond any visible horizon. I did worry about being too fat, but not because of the state of my heart. I worried about my weight because it meant girls wouldn't snog me. I was certain it was impossible to overdose on the kind of marijuana that I liked to smoke. The worst that would happen was I would fall asleep, and how could you not love an activity that ended like that? Even at university I was baffled by anyone who did sport willingly. Bunking off games to smoke in the woods was an item of faith among my crowd in the upper years at school. Sometimes, in the coldest months of the year, we took a small camping stove with us into those woods and heated up soup. We put a startling amount of effort into not doing games.

Once I had left behind the regimented demands of a school timetable, I certainly wasn't going to do voluntarily that which I had refused to do even when it was mandatory. I knew sport happened. I had walked past tennis courts full of people looking moist and anxious. I saw lads dancing about on five-a-side pitches in the floodlit cold. I just didn't see myself as a part of that. It was their culture. I couldn't get involved.

And then come my mid-twenties I began getting up early to go swimming at the local pool in Clapham, before work. I was doing this three times a week. Okay, I may have rewarded myself with chocolate cake from the brilliant Spanish cafe across the road, but at least the swimming came first. I moved from the pool to step machines, from step machines to weights to cross-trainers. It wasn't sport in the sense of pitting myself against anyone else's prowess. The thought of that horrified me, and still does; I knew it could never end well. But it was proper exercise and it became a quiet addiction.

I also started eating salad. I ate a lot of it. At home, before the onset of children, I developed the 'big salad'. It wasn't a very fancy name, but then nor was the salad: a vast heap of leaves with tinned tuna, freshly grated Parmesan and lots of cracked pepper. I shocked myself when I suggested to Pat one evening that this might be our dinner that night.

In this narrative, the crisp green salads made with Kressi vinegar with which we still end most meals eaten at home are not merely some marker of social class, although they are certainly that. (Look at us being so cosmopolitan with our salad servers and our continental vinegar and our romaine. You call it cos lettuce, do you? Well, I'm not here to judge, but how inelegant. We're so sophisticated and at ease with our fine tastes that we're practically French.) They are also a highly developed kind of self-care, which could be a handy euphemism used by teenage boys for a particular kind of 'me' time, but in this case isn't. It's a terrible phrase, and I hate myself for having used it, but the term is functional. It's not the overwrought quackery of 'wellness', used to flog chia seed flapjacks, smashed avocados on toast and brassica enemas on the false promise of miracle cures for diseases you don't actually have. It's just an awareness that maybe a bit of salad isn't such a terrible idea for a fifty-two-year-old overweight man who's prone now to reading the obituary pages and scoping out the ages at which people pegged out, just as a quiet warning to himself.

Which brings me back to those condemned prisoners ordering their cans of Diet Coke. Instead of being seen as a function of a personality disorder, perhaps it could also be seen as a form of self-care. Life has not gone as planned. Terrible crimes were committed and now, whether you approve of state-sanctioned execution or not, the end is coming. The moment for regret is long gone, and with it the time for pleading and self-pity. All that's left is a moment in which you look after yourself. In the circumstances, the ordering of Diet Coke comes across as a form of indulgence. But if this isn't a time for indulgence, then when is? It's now or literally never.

One summer's morning I get up at 4.30 a.m., just as dawn is breaking over London, and take a taxi to New Covent Garden fruit and vegetable market, at Nine Elms, Vauxhall, on the south bank of the Thames. The scuffed fifty-seven-acre site supplies 40 per cent of all the fruit and vegetables eaten outside the home in the London area, across restaurants, hotels, schools and prisons, as well as many independent greengrocers. Until 1974 the market was located in the original Covent Garden, which had been home to some kind of formal trading point since 1830. Traffic congestion at London's heart in the late 1960s eventually made that unsustainable, so it moved to this purpose-built site. It's a sprawl of blocky industrial warehouses interlinked by roadways and wide shadowed tunnels for the forklift trucks that ship produce about. It's a night-time economy, which functions while the city around it sleeps. Business kicks off around 10 p.m., and by 10 a.m. it's all over.

Anybody writing about food who uses words like 'nature's bounty' and 'field to fork' should come to a place like this once in a while, to these bleak, breeze-block shells, with their filthy thoroughfares and grubby walls from which the paint is peeling away. This is the reality of so much of our food. It's not a good or a bad thing. It's just how it is. There are stacks of knackered wooden pallets out the back of each unit, piles of cardboard boxes and huge refuse bins. Over the top of it all is that sickly-sweet smell of vegetal decay, the unavoidable stench that comes with being here at the hard end of the food-supply chain, where there is always some wastage. I visit the day after the 2018 World Cup Final, which at one point England seemed to be heading towards. The red and white of the cheap nylon flags of St George are still draped across many of the units, sagging markers for hopes unrealised. It's another hot day in that summer's seemingly endless heatwave, and there's a woozy, deadened air about the place, as if I've arrived just after the party finished.

The nearest I come to seeing anything rustic are the big wooden boxes filled with bunches of Italian flat-leaf parsley. Otherwise it's carton after carton of the bagged and the sealed and the date-stamped. Here is food from Poland and Italy, Portugal and France and the wealds of England. I'm directed to the Side Salads unit. The company sells exclusively for G's, one of the biggest growers of salad leaves in Britain, with a turnover of £400 million a year.

Side Salads is run by Nick Padley, hair neatly trimmed and combed, bright-eyed despite the hour. He's the fourth generation of his family to work in the fruit-and-veg trade. His great-granddad was over at the original Covent Garden. But now Nick is here at Nine Elms. Sixteen members of his extended family also work for various firms at the market. Fruit and veg is what the Padleys do, he says. It's what they've always done. He leads me into the cold room, where boxes of different salad leaves are stacked up. He picks up what I recognise as a round lettuce. 'We sometimes call that butterhead,' he says, lifting up a soft-leaved, deep-green specimen. 'An old-fashioned lettuce, that. Used for prawn cocktails, that sort of thing. Not very popular.'

We move along to the next cartons of shrink-wrapped product. 'Retail doesn't go for iceberg very much any more,' he says. 'But schools love it because you can get a lot of plate out of one of those.' He picks up an iceberg and bounces it in his hand, like he's weighing it. Generally, though, he says, people are moving away from 'whole-head lettuce. They want it bagged and ready to go.'

He shows me a big bag of pre-prepped leaves in blue see-through packaging, which makes it easier to spot if it falls into the food in restaurant kitchens. It includes leaves like escarole, can-can, red chard, lollo rosso and the frilly fancies of frisée. It's all springy and expansive. It's the bouncy castle of the salad world. 'Restaurants like this selection because it sits high on the plate. Whereas this . . .' – he picks up another bag, full of rocket, chard and baby spinach – '. . . this can collapse, but it tastes very good. Also very popular.' He shows me the bag. It's called 'babyleaf'. An awful lot of babyleaf is sold here at New Covent Garden. There used to be just two wholesalers doing it, but now everybody seems to have a babyleaf product.

The increasing popularity of bagged salads surprises me, because they haven't always had the best press. Everything Nick is showing me at Side Salads is unmistakeably of impeccable quality and completely safe, but elsewhere bagged salads have been shown to be prone to bacterial infection from the likes of salmonella. In 2016 the NHS even issued a warning, based on a study by the University of Leicester. It said that the bagging created a friendly environment for bacterial growth. Search online for academic studies into salad and the first hits will all be about the growth of pathogens. There are papers with names like 'Survival and Growth of Escherichia coli O157:H7 on Salad Vegetables' from *Applied and Environmental Microbiology* and 'Prevalence and Growth of Pathogens on Salad Vegetables, Fruits and Sprouts' from the *International Journal of Hygiene and Environmental Health*.

It's a blissful contradiction. The salad in this last supper of mine is meant to be the most benign element. Indeed, it's so benign that its very healthiness raises questions over whether it has any right to be a part of the meal. Why would your final meal on earth contain something which seems so specifically designed to keep you alive? And yet, as it happens, salad could be the quiet killer. In June 2016 British shoppers were warned to wash bagged lettuce as well as they could because of an E. coli outbreak which had killed two people and infected 150. Two years later, there were reports from the US that five people had died and 197 been taken ill as a result of an E. coli outbreak linked to contaminated romaine lettuce. My go-to lettuce, my leaves of choice, had been the medium for fatal contaminants.

Still, a meal without a salad feels wrong to me. It's like wearing shoes without socks. I know some men do it, but that doesn't make it right. There have to be leaves. The question is, which ones? I worry that at this last moment, I will turn out to be some appalling creature of habit, a role that I never thought suited me. Generously, Nick Padley gives me a bag of their babyleaf mix, in its shades of crimson and emerald, to try at home.

The working day is coming to an end at New Covent Garden, while in the rest of London it is just beginning. I take the bag back to my kitchen, and that evening give it the usual treatment: the spring onions, the olive oil, the Kressi, the sea salt. I ignore the romaine staring at me from the fridge – there is always romaine in my fridge – and throw on instead these soft leaves. It's a nice salad. No, it's better than that. Certain of the leaves are almost silky. A couple have a peppery edge. It's a denser salad than the bouncier version caused by the rigid structure of romaine's crisp, framed leaves.

But while I'm eating it, something niggles at me. Evidently, I eat different takes on salad. Part of my job requires me to do so. I have eaten salads containing pecans or blue cheese or mandarin segments, or all three. Outside the home I am salad-promiscuous and unashamed about being so. But inside the home salad means one thing, and one thing only. And it isn't what's in the bowl in front of me right now. I feel like I've been unfaithful.

It is the end of another day, and I am perched on the edge of the bed, strapping myself up. I might have liked Dr Kent's suggestion that my apnoea go untreated, but only because it made me feel less decrepit, tumbledown and knackered. Unfortunately, while it might have made me feel better emotionally, it didn't deal with the issue at home. I am still snoring. I am still being sent to sleep elsewhere or rolling over as Pat leaves me to my noise and rumble. My body is still playing dead.

I embark upon some research. The NightBalance device looks interesting. Apparently, it can be extremely successful in treating positional sleep apnoea like mine. The problem, as Dr Kent pointed out, is that while it is in use in certain European countries, it has not yet been approved for use by the NHS. But it occurs to me that perhaps the manufacturers need a few guinea pigs here in the UK. It turns out they do. I am to be one of the very first people in Britain to use it as a treatment. Accordingly, I go back to Guy's, where I am given training. It's a clever piece of kit. It's a small battery-powered pendant, rechargeable via a USB port, which not only monitors your position, but measures your responsiveness. Over the first few days that you wear it, strapped to your chest with a Velcro-fastened belt, it ramps up the level of vibration until it finds one that will actually rouse you enough so that you turn over. This also means that anybody else in the bed gets used to the feeling, which can transmit itself through the mattress.

I have started wearing it at night, and it really does seem to be having an impact. Pat reports that my body no longer seems to buck and jump. I am certainly responding to it. Wearing the pendant, strapped across my chest, feels a little like sharing the bed with another person. If I don't turn over immediately, the vibration ramps up and up. I have started to anthropomorphise it, to think of it as some nagging, scolding creature. Sure, it's non-verbal, but it still knows how to make me feel bad about myself. Previously, when I snored and ended up sleeping alone, the issue was confronted at most once a night, at the point when I made for the spare bed. But now the reminders are constant. Throughout the night the damn thing fizzes and buzzes against my chest. I begin to imagine it tutting and shaking its head, which is extremely peculiar given it is a lozenge of technology with no human features at all.

This weird emotional involvement aside, it is functioning well. It is stopping me from sleeping on my back. But whatever the graph might have said, I am still snoring. We are still sleeping separately. And there's something else: I am constantly tired, and becoming more so. Throughout the summer of 2018 the situation deteriorates. I turn fifty-two, and wonder whether middle age is meant to feel like this.

I feel the need for a mentor. I want a salad maven, someone to show me the way of the leaf. I know just the man. Yotam Ottolenghi came to Britain from Jerusalem, via Amsterdam, in 1997, on the run from academia. He trained at the Cordon Bleu cookery school, worked in some fancy restaurants and in 2002 opened his first delicatessen in

Notting Hill, with his name above the door. It became a raging success. It wasn't just that his food was delicious; it looked fabulous too. You couldn't walk past an Ottolenghi without being drawn in to the retail display: there might be huge platters of cauliflower and pistachio salad, heavy with the green of fresh herbs and the jewel-like glint of pomegranate seeds; he presented platters of watermelon and feta with olives and preserved lemon, of tomatoes with rhubarb and elderflower, or of Turkish-style vegetables with yoghurt and green chilli oil. He made vegetables the star, to be celebrated for their own sake. Through his recipes for the *Guardian* newspaper and the cookbooks which followed he gave us a fresh new lexicon: of za'atar and sumac, of dried limes and tahini and labneh and so much more.

Given all this, what would an Ottolenghi green salad look like?

He invited me to his house in north London, with its clean-lined, airy kitchen and its huge, gnarly wooden table, as if made from a slice straight down a tree. 'Not very practical,' he said, when I complimented him on it. 'But it was a good idea at the time.'

He made me mint tea, and sliced mini-cucumbers, his knuckles up high, with the blade against them, so as not to risk his fingertips, in the manner learnt by all trained chefs. I asked him if, as a child growing up in Israel, with an Italian-born father and a German-born mother, salad was a part of mealtimes.

'Always. My dad, because of the Italian background, always made a raw veg salad. Cucumber, cauliflower, tomatoes, onion. It's like crudités mixed together, all dressed with a really nice vinegar.' He starts preparing his own dressing. Over the years Ottolenghi has been accused of writing recipes which are endlessly complex, utilising ingredients many people have not heard of, let alone been able to find in the shops. He was forever suggesting alternatives, though he did little to disguise the fact that he found the accusation of complexity baffling. Why shouldn't good food take effort? Was it a peculiarly British thing to expect the good stuff to come easily? Still, the answer is the book he has just published when we meet. It's called *Ottolenghi Simple* and is, as the name suggests, a set of pared-down recipes which are still hugely appealing. 'The dressing is just four things,' he says. 'There's yoghurt, lemon juice, garlic and ginger.' He grates the latter into the yoghurt and then loosens it all with the juice and seasons it with flaked sea salt. In another bowl is a pile of springy lamb's lettuce, picked green herbs and the cucumber. You should only dress the salad when you're about to eat it, he says, because the salt in the dressing will draw moisture out of the cucumbers, which will make it watery. And yes, he says, you can use normal-sized cucumbers if you can't get hold of the small ones. Just make sure to remove the watery core before slicing. I make a note.

'We always have a green salad with meals,' he says as he works. 'It lifts and refreshes and creates a sense of balance.' He has become my salad Yoda. Salad was what happened when he was a kid in Jerusalem, and it's what happens now that he is a father of two boys in London.

He pours the dressing over the leaves, tosses them in it and portions the salad out. It's late morning, but no matter: we stand in a companionable silence, leaning back against work surfaces, forking up the salad. It is crisp and fresh and bright, and just a little alien. But that's the thing: it's Yotam's salad, not mine. A taste for snails in garlic butter or raw oysters or even a particular way with bacon sandwiches is shaped by family history and experience and appetite. But each of them is, in its own way, about the exceptional moment. The whole salad thing is different. It's about domestic culture, about the way things are done in particular households. It's not about the extraordinary or the indulgent. It is about the everyday. It's about what a table needs.

And so I return to my son's question, the one he posed so early on, when I told him that there would be a chapter on salad. My first answer – that I liked it – simply wasn't good enough. Finally, I felt I could do better.

Why, Dan had asked, was I even bothering? 'It's not like you have to be healthy.'

'No,' I now wanted to tell him. 'But I do have to be me.'

Yotam Ottolenghi's recipe for cucumber and lamb's lettuce salad

Serves four

INGREDIENTS

Five baby cucumbers (or one and a half regular ones, approx. 500g)

30g lamb's lettuce

10g picked mint leaves

10g picked coriander leaves

1tsp nigella seeds

For the dressing:

1tbsp lemon juice

1 small garlic clove, crushed

2cm piece of ginger, finely grated (approx. 10g)

20g plain yoghurt

Flaked sea salt

For the dressing, whisk all the ingredients together with ⅓tsp of flaked salt and set aside.

Take each cucumber and quarter lengthways. Then cut each long quarter diagonally into 0.5cm slices and place in a large bowl with the lamb's lettuce, mint and coriander. Gently mix the cucumber and leaves with the dressing and spread in a large shallow bowl. Sprinkle with the nigella seeds and serve.

▶ 6. 'The Ladies Who Lunch', Stephen Sondheim (1970)

Our first-ever show at King's Place was not an unspeakable disaster. It led to offers of other gigs. That was fabulous. I needed a reason to practise my playing, and avoiding looking clueless in front of an audience was exactly the right one. Even so, I knew that if we were going to keep doing this, we would need to justify it. Why the hell was the big-haired bloke off *MasterChef* on the telly, the one who waved his velvet cuffs over some poor sap's attempt at a duck pithivier, playing jazz piano with a quartet? The answer lay in the question: because of the intimate relationship between jazz and food. The music started out in what polite people call the bars and restaurants of New Orleans, and the more realistic ones refer to as brothels, where the punters could get drunk and fed, as well as laid. Lots of jazz tunes reference food and drink: there's 'Black Coffee' and 'One for my Baby', 'Cantaloupe Island' and 'Peel Me a Grape', 'Frim-Fram Sauce' and 'It Must Be Jelly ('Cause Jam Don't Shake Like That)'.

It felt like the right way to go, not least because the songs could be linked by stories from my life in the world of food journalism and broadcasting. But it wasn't enough. The song 'Black Coffee' gave me the other half of our repertoire. It's a big, roaring blues tune which quite clearly isn't about coffee at all. It's about a woman who's been done wrong, and who paces out her night waiting for the shit of a man who has done her wrong to come home, while she drinks cups of coffee. The lyrics could so easily have been a letter to my mother in agony-aunt mode. That was something I knew quite a bit about.

Plus, there were so many stories I had never told about Claire Rayner, even though growing up with an agony aunt was one long anecdote waiting to happen. There was the man who was so concerned about the shape of his erection, but so desperate to be

polite in his quest for advice, that he eschewed the technology of the
day – a Polaroid camera – and instead carved a version of it lovingly
from wood. He painted it all the right colours, varnished it and
sent it in a cardboard box to my mother. Claire opened it over the
breakfast table. I became slightly fixated on the nights of work this
must have taken; I imagined him, tip of tongue caught between lips
in concentration, as he in turn imagined my mother finally dealing
with his issue. (He had no issue. It just leant a little to the right.) A
couple of years later, at the height of the AIDS crisis, she was invited
onto breakfast television to demonstrate how to put on a condom.
Happily, she now had just the model to use.

One morning, in the days when phone numbers were more freely
available, a chap rang my mother and asked if she would mind
listening 'while I have a wank?' Claire was nothing if not polite. She
agreed to do so, put the receiver down on the desk and carried on
typing. She picked it back up again five minutes later and said, 'Have
you finished?' He said, 'Yes,' in a slightly tight, strangulated voice.
It wasn't just strangers who did things like this. A close friend from
New York rang her once in the middle of the night to announce that
one of his testicles was missing. She told him to go back to sleep and
it would be there in the morning. It was. Another happy ending.

We were told that the letters coming into the house represented
very real and serious heartache, but some of them couldn't help
being funny: there was the woman who knew her husband was
having an affair because she had found female footprints on the
inside of the car windscreen; another woman complained about not
being able to reach orgasm, and finished her letter with the plaintive
observation that 'I even bought a vibrator but the batteries ran out'.

So now we'd also do songs which drew on the joy and torture
of love and heartbreak: 'When Sunny Gets Blue' and 'Don't Go to
Strangers', 'But Beautiful' and 'That Old Black Magic'. With many
Johnny Mercer lyrics all you had to do was put the words 'Dear
Claire' at the top and they would be problem-page-ready.

We'd been playing irregularly for about eighteen months when I decided it was time to get ambitious. What I really wanted was to play the Crazy Coqs, a gorgeous art deco cabaret room which is part of the equally gorgeous Brasserie Zedel, located in a gilded basement space near London's Piccadilly Circus. It's an homage to the grand brasseries of Paris. The circular Crazy Coqs, which can seat only eighty, was run then by a formidable and extremely kind woman called Ruth Leon. She had been around the worlds of jazz and cabaret for decades and knew everything and everybody there was to know. At the insistence of a friend in the jazz world, who said we were ready, I emailed Ruth asking for a gig. I included a link to the video of our performance at King's Place. She replied within an hour offering us a late slot. Result.

The night of the gig, I was standing next to Ruth, watching the engineer prepare the stage for our soundcheck. Ruth nodded at the grand piano.

She said, 'You'd better be able to play that thing.'

I said, 'But, Ruth, I sent you the video.'

'Oh, I didn't watch it.'

'Why the hell not?'

She turned to me. 'Because if a man with your public profile claimed to be able to do this and couldn't, you would have to be a monumental idiot. Now go do your soundcheck.'

The Coqs, which has since become our home base, was important to us in another way. When Ruth booked us, she explained quite reasonably that our show needed a name, otherwise she would have nothing to put in the programme. The repertoire made that simple. We would give the audience *A Night of Food and Agony*.

But just choosing songs wasn't enough. A group of reasonable jazz musicians, or two great instrumentalists and one finding his way, could come up with passable renditions of most standards with no rehearsal. But that wasn't much different from jamming. We needed our own arrangements. It transpired that having my kind of sparse musical knowledge helped. It meant I had to prioritise ideas, rather than smart harmonies. If I first worked out why we were bothering to play a song, I could shape it. For example, I was looking for something to back up my mother's strongly held view that the great set-piece events in life were not always the best. The two weeks following Christmas were always the busiest for Claire and her secretaries. Families all over the country had spent an unnatural amount of time with each other over the festivities, and now wanted to get divorced or put their kids up for adoption. To express this, I suggested turning 'Get Me to the Church on Time', from Lerner and Loewe's musical *My Fair Lady*, into a slow blues. Robert, our bassist, suggested a minor blues instead, and we were away. Now it was a pre-wedding song, sung by someone who was not convinced getting married was a good idea at all.

Later, I decided we needed a signature tune which said both food and jazz. I alighted upon 'Food, Glorious Food', from Lionel Bart's musical *Oliver!* But I slowed it right down, threw in some soft Bill Evans-style chords and shamelessly played up the similarity between the song's tune and the great standard 'On Green Dolphin Street'. It worked beautifully, and for a while we opened with it, until I decided it was a bit of a downer.

And then there was 'The Ladies Who Lunch' from Stephen Sondheim's musical *Company*. It was the song that Pat did not want to sing. Partly, this was because she was suspicious of Sondheim in general: his music is tight and a lot of it is exceptionally prescriptive. You sing it his way or not at all. But there was also the problem of this song in particular. It was made famous by Elaine Stritch, playing the drunk, caustic Manhattan socialite who is far too bright for the world of long lunches and Martinis and charitable events with which she fills her days. She has observed these women, has been one, and now wants to raise a glass to their ludicrous lives. Everybody rise! (There is no better song to celebrate in a chapter on salad than 'Ladies Who Lunch'.)

Stritch didn't so much sing it as rage at the audience in the dark. Hers was a voice enthusiastically tempered by cigarettes and liquor. If there was a tune in there, she didn't bother to make it immediately apparent. The raw power of the performance made Stritch's name. It also put Pat off the song. There was no way she was doing it. Too show tune. Too grandiose. Showing her YouTube videos of Broadway legend Patti LuPone doing it more melodically didn't really help. Sure, you could hear the song, but 'Ladies Who Lunch' was still taken as an excuse to go so far over the top it was almost asphyxiating up there. Pat said no again.

I was not deterred. I love the musicals of Stephen Sondheim: there's a caustic wit, a love of wordplay and a profound understanding of human relationships in his lyrics. Slowly, I worked on the Latin rhythms underpinning it and the chord voicings; anything to turn it from a rant to something more subtle and underplayed. It took months before I had a version to take into rehearsal with the rest of the band, but even then it wasn't right. Pat wasn't sold on it. As she has always said, if she doesn't believe in what she is being asked to sing, she can't do it justice.

What emerged from that session was an arrangement which made me feel that the hours at the piano hadn't been wasted, though it took Dave and Rob's acute musical knowledge to get it there. Dave was, like Pat, suspicious of something so show tune. He insisted we took the whole structure apart, before putting it back together again into something that worked for us. Rob showed me new chord voicings. It was, as all our best arrangements are, a collaborative act. We played up the sense of dismay and disappointment. It's an actor's piece, and Pat sings it like she's lived it. At the end of that rehearsal she admitted she had been won over. Which is why, in March 2017, when we recorded two live shows back to back at the Crazy Coqs for our live album, we included it.

Which also means that for my playlist I get to choose a track off *A Night of Food and Agony: The Jay Rayner Quartet Live at Zedel*. It's my last supper, and I want to hear my extremely talented wife sing.

Is that okay with you?

Good.

Chips

Here they are in reverse order: my all-time top five fried-potato experiences.

5. The fries at McDonald's, Marble Arch, London, c.1980

I am thirteen years old and sitting in front of a tray of McDonald's finest product. I have tried the burgers before. At some point in the mid-1970s my mother returned from an official event at the American embassy carrying a big box of McDonald's burgers. They were a little chilly by then, and the bright-orange cheese had solidified. Nevertheless, they were enticing. I ate one or three.

This time it's about the fries, fresh out of the bubbling oil. Marble Arch is the location of the West London Synagogue, home to Britain's Reform Jews. They have a youth club for over-thirteens called Contact, which is held here late on Sundays. Each week I take the Tube from Harrow, spend a couple of hours being mouthy with my mates, experience a little light religious indoctrination, perhaps watch a cheery film about the Holocaust, and then pop around the corner to the nearby branch of McDonald's, which opened not long ago, close by the famed (now demolished) Marble Arch Odeon. These chips – fries, if we're using the correct language, but to me they're just chips, and always will be – are a high point of my week. This tells you what kind of adolescent boy I am: a fat one with cellulite, nascent breasts and an overly developed interest in dinner.

British chips are too often soggy and pale and under-fried. These aren't anything like British chips. They are hot. They rustle in their greaseproof bag. These are mostly crunch and, being so, completely addictive. They cost 24p, which means I can afford to buy them with my pocket money. I love them. I come here to show my love most Sundays. I am nothing if not devout.

4. Triple-cooked chips, Hind's Head pub, Bray, November 2004

I had heard an awful lot about these chips in the years before I finally got to try them. I had heard about chef Heston Blumenthal's rigorous experimentation, designed to create what he believed was the perfect specimen. It was a major part of the modus operandi that had won him three Michelin stars at the Fat Duck, but which he liked to apply to every new food project. In his book *In Search of Perfection*, published in 2009 to tie in with the BBC TV series of the same name, he detailed that process. He had concluded that the ubiquitous double-frying method – once in low-temperature fat to cook the potato, followed by a shorter dip into high-temperature fat to make it crisp – wasn't good enough. It didn't produce a chip with the right balance of crunch outside and pillowy within.

He investigated in detail the qualities of the right potato for the job. It needed to have a significant quantity of 'dry matter', which is to say, a high ratio of potato to water. Just north of 22 per cent was about right. The potatoes needed to be well stored, at between 7 and 9°C, so the starch doesn't turn to sugar, resulting in overly dark chips when they're fried. While he would later decide that a potato variety called Arran Victory is best for the job, the better-known Maris Piper also turned out to be a good bet.

Blumenthal concluded it was all about removing moisture. At one point he tried pricking each raw chip individually multiple times, so as to create a hole for the release of steam, but even he realised that was ludicrous. Eventually, he settled upon a method that involved boiling them until they were almost falling apart, then chilling them in the fridge so the moisture evaporated. Next, they had to be fried once and again allowed to chill in the fridge, before being fried a second time: boil–fry–fry. Hence 'triple-cooked'.

A great chef is not defined by their ability to come up with the complex and the intense. Their greatness lies in their ability to reinvent the simple. The late French chef Joël Robuchon proved his talent by changing the way high-end kitchens make mashed potato. He did this by putting in less potato and more butter; a lot more butter, until it became less starchy side dish, more condiment you could slather on a friend. Likewise, Blumenthal did it by changing the way chips were made. The triple-cooked chip is his major contribution to the world of food. They now turn up on menus all over Britain and beyond. Whether they are actually made according to the method Blumenthal outlined is uncertain, because frankly most of them are unexceptional, despite how they are listed on the menu. They are rarely crisp enough or satisfying enough or even just cooked enough.

But the ones that I finally try at the Hind's Head, the pub next door to the Fat Duck which Blumenthal has recently bought, are a delightful thing. They come as part of a meal that features none of the familiar Blumenthal whizz-bangery. Instead, it is all about pub classics: pea and ham soup, a steak-and-kidney suet pudding and a steak with a deep, glossy bordelaise sauce, dotted with pearls of bone marrow. The chips accompany the latter. They are indeed craggy on the outside, giving them lots of crisp surface area. They are fluffy inside. They are quite a thing. I get it.

So why have I listed them only at number four? It's partly because they inspired so many truly crap chips, the product of lazy chefs who like to put certain words on their menu – 'I didn't cook these chips twice; oh no, I cooked them thrice' – but can't be bothered to learn how to do these chips properly. But mostly it's because to make the method work, they have to be thick-cut. However much I like these ones, I really can't ever love a thick-cut chip.

3. *Pommes Allumettes at Chez L'Ami Louis, Paris, September 2006*

Five years after I ate at L'Ami Louis, the late, thrillingly brilliant A. A. Gill, restaurant critic at the *Sunday Times*, wrote a piece for *Vanity Fair* magazine in which he dubbed this ancient Parisian bistro the 'worst restaurant in the world'. He did it with real enthusiasm. He pricked the bloated self-regard of the American plutocrats who gum up its tiny tables, the ones he said were draped in 'labial pink' cloths. He slagged off the narrow, dark-brown, wood-panelled room, which reminded him of a 'second-class railway carriage in the Balkans'. He spewed vitriol at the famed slabs of foie gras pâté, with their 'coating of pustular yellow fat'.

He had a point about the foie gras. Everybody I knew who had already been there warned me not to order it, including the chef Simon Hopkinson, who, as a long-term regular, had been able to book me the table. They all said I would have no space left for anything else if that was my starter. I suppose I should have acknowledged Gill's other criticisms too. I should have been cowed by his fully vented spleen, but I am made of stronger stuff. He was right about its almost cartoonish Parisian clichés. But here's the thing: I love a grand, cartoonish cliché, and the French know how to take theirs very seriously indeed.

I chose L'Ami Louis as the restaurant by which to mark my fortieth birthday, and I'm not now going to dance on the grave of a great night out just because Gill got a terrific 1,000 words out of it. I went to L'Ami Louis for one thing, and one thing only: the chicken and chips, or to be more exact, the *Poulet de Bresse avec pommes allumettes*, which is to say, a whole roast chicken with matchstick-thin chips. This will now cost you the best part of 100€. For that money you get a flavourful, crisp-skinned bird, the legs complete with their scaly blue-grey claws, and a pile of chips about a foot high. I grabbed handfuls of them for my plate, and yet the pile never seemed to subside. They were golden and sharp-edged. Because they were so thin, there was precious little by way of soft, fluffy innards, but that's missing the point. You eat them in bunches, in mouthfuls, in heaps. They are riveting in a 'lunch falling into your lap' sort of way.

I loved the chicken, I really did. But I bloody adored the pommes allumettes.

2. The chips at Parson's, London, 2017

It's a fish restaurant, so they do chips. Those chips could have been an afterthought. That's how too many other restaurants treat them: as something so far down the list of priorities they get forgotten about. It's London's badly kept, dirty secret that many of the big, glamorous restaurants, the sort of places that crow about making their own bread, buy in their chips pre-cut and frozen from behemoth corporations like McCain's. In the hunt for financial advantage, for crumbs of profit margin, they think it makes sense not to pay an in-house member of staff to peel and cut the potatoes when they could outsource that to someone else. Who's going to notice? Parson's has a brilliant menu full of peppery brown shrimp croquettes and clam chowder, baked brown crabmeat pissaladière and sea trout tartare. Against all that, who really cares if any thought has gone into the chips?

I do.

I really do.

Happily, so do they.

There is a story that Van Halen's backstage rider in the 1970s included a clause demanding bowls of M&Ms, but with all the brown ones removed. If any were found, they could cancel the gig at no cost to themselves. It was always assumed to be an ultimate rock-diva request. Many years later lead singer David Lee Roth explained that the clause was there to make sure the venue had really read the contract and, in particular, all their notes on stage wiring. If any brown M&Ms were found, it meant they may not have paid complete attention. How could you be sure they'd taken due care and attention to wiring up the sound and lighting desks properly if they could miss a clause like that? (There's another version of this story in which a band demands a copy of that day's newspaper, with all the 'O's on the front page coloured in.)

I feel the same way about chips in a restaurant. If the kitchen takes care over something so simple, so quotidian, they must surely have put their backs into the rest. The chips at Parson's are delightful. They are crisp outside and soft inside. They are not too thick. They rustle against each other, like leaves in a dry autumn. Throughout my lunch there I eat them compulsively, and feel a deep sadness when I clock that the bowl is now empty.

1. *The chips at Ken's Fish Bar, Half Moon Lane, south London, 2014*
   to present

You know Ken's on Half Moon Lane. It's in the middle of that small shopping parade, the one just before the road swerves off towards leafy Dulwich. You should do. It's the fish-and-chip place that you want near you. Happily, it's near me. Not that everybody is aware of how good it is; for a long while I wasn't. Being in a generally prosperous, gentrifying inner London suburb, we also have a fancy fish-and-chip place near us. It's been there for many years. The waitresses wear uniforms. There's a full gluten-free menu and lots of laudable sustainability certification. Their fish and chips are lovely. They really are. When you wait for your takeaway, they give you a small cone with four or five chips in it to help you deal with your hunger, which is ramped up by seeing order after order being prepared. For a very long time I was committed to them because the place was bright and shiny, the food was good and the staff smiled easily.

Then Pat said, 'You know, the chips at Ken's are better.'

'Ken's? That bog-standard place down Half Moon Lane?'

'So much better.'

My teenage elder son joined in. Ken's was only a three-minute walk from his school. 'Love a bit of Ken's,' Eddie said.

One takeaway night, Pat brought back pie and chips from there for our youngest. I tried one of the chips, which is a tricky manoeuvre when you have a child fiercely patrolling the perimeter of his dinner.

I snatched a couple. He growled.

Pat looked at me, with an eyebrow raised.

'I told you . . .'

'But . . .'

Ken's is just our local chippie, a place that has been serving the community for decades. You really would drive past it and not give it a second look. But oh, the chips: better than the ones I love at Parson's, better than Heston Blumenthal's triple-cooked version, better than McDonald's (that was plainly about nostalgia) and the L'Ami Louis matchsticks (which was about the moment). They crunch in the right places and are soft in the right places. They are hand-cut and golden and glorious. They are what potatoes are planted for, and I'll punch anyone who says otherwise.

It is a bright autumn day, and I am standing on a street in Amsterdam, staring up at a garish shop frontage as the trams whirr and rattle past behind me. I have not been in the city for over twenty-five years; not since I was sent here by *Esquire* magazine as a very young man to live my life by the dice. The trip is an act of pilgrimage, for I have come solely to eat chips. My online research revealed that elsewhere in Europe, there is a museum dedicated entirely to deep-fried shards of potato. For a while I planned to go there. But it's in Brussels, and eventually the thought of schlepping all the way to Belgium to traipse around a bunch of exhibits dedicated to chips made my shoulders slump. I don't want to look at chips. I want to eat them.

This is the place to do so: a branch of the seventy-strong Dutch fast-food chain FEBO. It's named after the first two letters of the words in the Amsterdam street address of the original shop on Ferdinand

Bolstraat. FEBO is an automat. The walls are lined with small, coin-operated cupboards with transparent doors, behind which can be seen a selection of hamburgers, hot dogs and croquettes, the latter fresh out of the deep-fat fryer. You choose what you want to eat, drop in a couple of euros, which unlocks the door, and grab your order. Who would have thought that a food concept based on easy access to fast food without human interaction should prosper in a city famed for its coffee shops selling cannabis? More seriously, it baffled me that nobody has opened an automat in the heart of London's Soho. One of these on Wardour Street would go down a bomb.

I first came to Amsterdam in 1982, at the end of a youth-group coach tour around Europe. We quickly found our way to the Leidseplein, the well-known square at the heart of the city, home to the famed Bulldog Palace cafe. From there it was only a few metres' stumble to this FEBO on Leidsestraat. After that initial visit, all of my Interrail trips around Europe ended right here on this stretch of pavement. However heavy the pack on my back, there was always the promise, at the end of the journey, of a joint smoked without the paranoia of arrest, followed by a crisp-shelled, deeply savoury minced-beef croquette puffing gusts of hot, nutmeg-spiced air at me as I satisfied the munchies. But the thing which drew me here more than anything else was the chips. In truth, the chips themselves weren't special. What made them so was the satay sauce that went with them, a hangover from the Netherlands' imperial adventures in Indonesia. Most Dutch people I have spoken to over the years are profoundly embarrassed about the country's colonial past, which they regard as being at odds with their generally liberal worldview. The only saving grace is the impact of Indonesia on their food: the numerous restaurants serving the Indonesian *rijsttafel*, or rice table, an elaborate multi-course menu.

And this satay sauce.

For the chips, I have to go to the counter at the back, which is not something I recall having to do. I was sure you got them out of the cupboards too, but memory is not always reliable. I definitely remember that the sauce canisters were on the side and you added it yourself. The server confirms this was so. He tells me that, these days, he does it to stop the bottomless sauce option being abused. The chips are fried to order. They are very good: hot, crisp, salty in all the right places. But it is that sauce which really rocks me back on my heels. It is exactly as I remember it, a kind of loose, soft, highly spiced, sweet–savoury peanut butter, with a piquant kick. I stand out in front of the shop on the street, as I always used to do. This was never the kind of food you moved off to eat; you stayed where you were to scoff it immediately. At night a crowd of stoned, hungry kids would huddle under the glow of its signage. They probably still do. I stand here now on the pavement, as the late-autumn light begins to drain from the sky, and dredge the chips through the muddy-brown sauce. I begin to worry that there is not enough sauce for the chips.

And all of a sudden, the years seem to fall away. I am that sixteen-year-old kid again, hungry and hopeful in equal measure. And all because of a carton of chips and sauce.

I am staying at the Hotel Pulitzer on Prinsengracht, the same grand hotel that the dice sent me to for my first night when I was here for *Esquire* all those years ago. I decide that I will start the night by going to the bar and rolling myself some drinks for old times' sake. That afternoon I had wandered the streets trying to find a shop that would sell me a pair of dice. After three or four failures, I suddenly realised I had the answer in my pocket. I downloaded a dice app. Now I sit here at the bar, shaking my phone. In my notebook I have written down a set of numbered drinks. It reads:

1 – Champagne
2 – Vodka and lime
3 – Neat whisky
4 – Negroni

5 – White wine

6 – Gin and tonic

I hope for a 1, 2 or 5. I will be okay with a 6. I roll a 4. The barman mixes me an impeccable Negroni, which is to say, it's awful: that terrible mixture of sickly sweet and bitter, as if it's some twisted narrative on the cruelties of life in a glass. I grimace as I drink it.

A British woman is sitting next to me at the bar. She says, 'You don't look like you're enjoying that very much.' I tell her I'm not, and wave the phone at her. 'The dice made me do it.' She is amused, but insists on trying her luck at the dice game. Her list looks similar to mine, with the addition of a margarita, which she says she likes, and a whisky sour, which she says she hates. I tell her that if she gets the whisky sour, we can swap. It's one of the curiosities of life that while I dislike neat whisky, I don't mind a whisky sour.

She says, 'But that means I'd end up with a Negroni, and I don't like those either.'

She shakes the phone and rolls a 6. I laugh. She has a Negroni of her own.

We sit there sipping our terrible drinks. 'This game is awful,' she says eventually, before draining her glass and saying her farewells.

I turn over the phone so it's face down on the bar and can't see me cheating. I order a glass of wine and sit there getting gently drunk. To one side is the hotel's back door, which opens up onto Keizersgracht. Back in 1991 that was where the car that took me to the brothel drew up. I think back on that night, on the young man I had been in the vice-slicked city. The story about me going to a brothel, declining sex and sitting in a bath with a hooker is funny, and probably reflects reasonably well on me, but deep down didn't I regret it? My sexual experience at the time was limited. However seedy, it had still been an opportunity. I flew home from Amsterdam to Pat, with whom I had been living for a few months by then, and blurted out what I had done, or to be more precise, what I hadn't done. She laughed and said she wouldn't really have cared. I've never believed her. I suspect she felt able to say that because I hadn't done anything. But what about me? What did I feel, even now? No, I was very happy being the man who went to Amsterdam and declined to have sex with a prostitute. I was fine with that.

But there are other things I genuinely do regret. In 1989, as the Berlin Wall fell, I didn't just jump on a plane and go to witness it for myself. That, I do regret. The cold war had been a constant through-out my life. I was fascinated by politics and history. I had a degree in political studies, during which we had looked in detail at the stand-off between East and West. Now it was coming to an end, and I could be a bystander at a moment of history, and all for the cost of a cheap plane ticket. I decided I had too many other important things to be doing in London. I had deadlines. I was twenty-three. Sitting at the bar of the Pulitzer I fall to brooding. I think about the other things I did not do.

It is the summer of 1986, and I am backpacking my way alone around the eastern Mediterranean, from Greece to Turkey and back again. I am skilled at using the efficient Turkish bus system and always book the same seat: the one in the aisle of the front row, next to the passenger door. It has extra leg room, which I need. Compared to most Turkish men I am tall, and these buses are not built for me. I have decided to travel from the coastal tourist town of Bodrum to go and see the famous carbonate mineral pools that form terraces down the hillsides at Pamukkale, a good four hours and two buses away. The glossy pictures I have seen in guidebooks make it look quite the thing. I board the bus and find, sitting in the seat next to mine, a woman who, from the perspective of adulthood, I imagine was in her late thirties or early forties. All I know then is that she is much older than me. I also know she is attractive. She is wearing very short shorts, a boob tube and an awful lot of dangling gold jewellery. She has a small rat-like dog by her feet, who is also wearing gold charms on its collar. She smiles and babbles at me in what I assume is Turkish as I sit down. We set off.

It seems she wants to be friends. She talks to me, but I do not understand a word. She touches me incidentally, rather than accidentally: on the knee, on the shoulder, on the chest. She laughs at what I imagine to be her own hilarious jokes. The bus stops for a break, and unbidden she brings me back a drink from the stand outside. I thank her. Within a few minutes of pulling off again, she seems to doze off. Her head drops onto my shoulder. I rather enjoy it, this head-on-shoulder business. It's flattering. It's sweet. Her left hand rests itself on my knee. And that's fine too. Really. I'm not complaining. An attractive woman feels very comfortable in my company, and so ... hang on, what the f—!

I am wearing only three things that day, and two of them are my espadrilles. The other one is a pair of turquoise dungarees; yes, turquoise dungarees, and if you are judging me on that, you are missing the whole point of this story. I have nothing on underneath the dungarees because it is high summer and I'm bored of washing stuff and pants seem superfluous and I am eighteen years old and that's how it works.

As she seems to sleep, her hand has come off my knee and journeyed its way inside the bib of my dungarees. Her fingertips have found my right nipple and started to squeeze. I lean forward in my seat slightly. What do I do? How do I tell her to stop? Come to think of it, do I actually want her to stop? I really don't know. This is both brilliant and terrifying. I think about forcibly removing her hand, but I am twice her size and, in my paranoid state, I wonder whether she might accuse me of getting handy with her, rather than the other way around. She is the one here who speaks the local language. While I am thinking all these things, I realise her fingers have relaxed their grip on my nipple. Her hand is now slipping downwards inside my dungarees over the soft slope of my belly. I sit completely still, staring out through the windscreen at the long, straight Turkish road ahead of us as it shimmers in the early-afternoon heat. Finally, her fingers find their prey and grip.

And there we sit: her hand, my penis and me.

Suddenly, she lets go, whips out her arm and howls with laughter, like it was all some hilarious cock-gripping prank. Then she says, in curiously perfect English, 'Come to İzmir with me tonight.'

I say, 'No, I have friends I must meet,' inventing them. When the bus reaches the interchange, I kiss her on the cheek and get off. She looks huffy.

Later, this story became my first-ever piece for *Cosmopolitan* magazine. I tried to make it more than just a salacious anecdote. I used it to ask whether a woman could ever sexually harass a man, concluding at the time that she could not, because the physical power remained with the man. All of this was my way of saying I had enjoyed the experience, though it had also terrified me. I was lousy with virginity back then, a state which felt like it was clinging to me like moss. (During the same trip two lovely young women invited me to share their hotel room overnight. The next morning they took all their scant nightwear off, lay on their beds naked and invited me to give them a massage. And that's exactly what I did. I gave them a massage, then went off and had breakfast. I later told this story to a friend, who stared at me, slowly shook his head and said, 'If you fell into a barrel of tits, you would still have come out sucking your thumb.') This moment in Turkey surely would have been the perfect way by which to remedy the whole virginity situation? Perhaps, but I bottled it.

I order another expensive glass of mediocre white wine and try to reach a conclusion. Described like this, yes, these are things I regret. How could I not regret failing to follow through on the sexy bus lady when, from the perspective of middle age, it's not a frightening encounter, just amusing? And yet no life experience happens in isolation. Had I dived straight in, had I gone to İzmir, perhaps I wouldn't have returned to Britain as the bundle of enthusiasms and insecurities and overcompensating wisecracks who met Pat a few months later. I would literally have been cocksure, and I imagine that would have been extremely unattractive. Maybe my relationship with Pat wouldn't have worked out the way that it did. Maybe we wouldn't have got married. Perhaps we wouldn't have become parents to our two boys. That is unimaginable.

It's not the greatest of insights, is it, this idea that we are the sum of all our interactions, that life is just one long chain reaction, but it does help. It makes sense of what went before. I especially like the fact that if I hadn't come to Amsterdam in search of the chips with satay of my youth, I wouldn't have ended up here at this bar, rolling the electronic dice, getting drunk on appalling cocktails and mentally putting the world to rights. Chips are brilliant.

In 1970 a young chef from south-west France called Pierre Koffmann came to London and went to work at Le Gavroche, a standard-bearer for French gastronomy in the British capital. It would be the first restaurant in Britain to win one, then two, and finally three Michelin stars. Later, the restaurant's proprietors and head chefs, the brothers Albert and Michel Roux Sr, installed Koffmann as the head chef of their second restaurant, the Waterside Inn at Bray. In 1977 Koffmann opened his own restaurant, La Tante Claire, in London's Chelsea, serving a menu full of gutsy Gascon classics. He was famed for his glossy braised pig's trotter, stuffed full of chicken mousseline, sweetbreads and morels, which took days to make. People travelled to his restaurant just to try his reliably tumescent pistachio soufflé, the colour of jade jewellery. In the early 1980s he won his third Michelin star, which he kept for years. Many of the big names of British cooking passed through his kitchen in the 1980s and '90s, including Gordon Ramsay and Marco Pierre White; the latter even put Koffmann's pig's trotter dish on his own menus, in homage to his mentor. Koffmann in his pomp was said to be a fearsome head chef who led from the stove and didn't suffer the slightest imperfection. If you worked for Koffmann, you worked very long hours.

Koffmann closed the restaurant in 2003, after the death of his wife Annie. Around that time, he met his new partner, Claire Harrison. The daughter of a potato merchant, Claire has gone on to work across the potato industry. 'I met Pierre over a potato harvester,' she told me, when I called her to discuss chips. Koffmann had come to investigate the complexities of potato growing, and there was no better guide than Claire. 'Potatoes have been my life,' she said. 'When I was a kid, we used to sit around the dinner table discussing potato varieties.'

Koffmann returned to run a couple of other much-loved restaurant ventures; by popular demand, the pig's trotter and the pistachio soufflé had one last outing. By all accounts he had mellowed by then and was a less terrifying figure at the pass. Finally, on New Year's Eve 2016, he worked one last service, then closed his restaurant. At which point Claire put him to work testing potato varieties. The idea was simple: to come up with a range of potatoes specifically aimed at chefs which were perfect for the intended job and endorsed by the great Pierre Koffmann. 'People say Maris Pipers are what you need for chips,' Claire said, 'but it depends what time of year it is.' The quantity of all-important dry matter differs from season to season and variety to variety, as does the sugar content. Apparently, the starch in potatoes acts as a kind of natural antifreeze, protecting them against frost. As the weather gets colder, the starch gets converted to sugar, which has an even lower freezing point. It protects the potato, but it makes it distinctly sweet and results in very dark chips, because sugar burns easily. Nobody likes a sweet or burnt chip. Or if they do, they're weird and will never be a friend of mine.

Claire sent me a briefing note. It said: 'The potatoes you see bright and shining in supermarkets are kept at 3°C as this temperature maintains the skin finish. Unfortunately, the everyday shopper tends to buy with their eyes, so retailers demand a bright skin.' But that bright skin can only be achieved at the expense of flavour. 'Our motto', Claire said, 'is the right variety for the right time of year for the right job.' In the autumn of 2017 they launched Pierre Koffmann chipping potatoes, complete with a picture of his face on the bag and, underneath it, his signature. The variety inside the bag would change depending on the time of year, but you would always know that what was in there would be ideal. Koffmann had literally signed off on them.

'Pierre was a bit resistant to having his face on them,' Claire said, 'but we got there in the end.'

It was intriguing. Chips are meant to be straightforward. They aren't like a pig's trotter stuffed with chicken mousseline, sweetbreads and morels, which is extremely complicated to make. They aren't like a pistachio soufflé, a dish which is so tricky most kitchens make two for each single order in case one collapses in the oven. Chips can come with anything and everything. Chips are made by everybody. And yet, it seems, we are always at risk of getting them completely wrong.

My younger son, Dan, does not like sweet things. Confectionery goes unmolested by him. Chocolate, given to him at Easter, will go off before he eats it. If he ever eats it. Occasionally, when working from home, I have stolen from my own child's chocolate stash while he was at school, when the need for a sugar hit overcame me during the day. I'm not proud of this, but it had to be done. It's not like he wanted it, and I do so hate waste.

For his fifteenth birthday we asked Dan what kind of cake he would like for when his mates came over to kill each other via the medium of computer games. He said, 'I don't want a cake. I want a steak.' He wanted a slab of beef with a burning candle stuck in it.

I was therefore required to cook seven long-aged sirloins, each the thickness of a paperback novel, for a bunch of eager teenage boys. More importantly, there would have to be chips to go alongside them. This was not a task to be taken lightly. Steak, I know how to cook: allow it to come to room temperature, heat pan to smoking, oil and season the steak, a minute or so on each side, depending on thickness. And then rest. Chips are another matter. I very rarely cook them. There's just too much admin. It's all about the vat of bubbling oil, which also needs to be dealt with when cooled. Deep-frying at home is a pain. Still, a birthday promise must be kept. I asked my local greengrocer what variety of potato I should use for chipping. The hot summer of 2018 had, he told me, done massive damage to the British crop. He directed me to reds, with their ruby, slightly mottled skins and waxy flesh. He never identified the exact variety, but they were definitely red. I took them home and peeled them and cut them up so they looked like chips. I gave them a first fry in vegetable oil at 130°C, until they were just coloured, as I'd always been told I should and as I'd done success-fully a couple of times before. I drained them on kitchen paper and left them to cool. I turned up the heat on the oil.

There was one problem: I was using a saucepan filled with oil, rather than a deep-fat fryer with a built-in temperature regulator. I was dependent on a probe thermometer and manual management of the flame to get this right. I thought I'd got it to 160°C. Within a minute of getting the first batch of chips back in the oil for the second fry I knew I had gone far beyond that. The chips had gone very dark indeed. I concluded that not only was the oil too hot, but these pota-toes had a higher than usual sugar content. They had gone so dark that there was only one word for them: burnt.

I had burnt my son's birthday chips. I was a terrible father.

I scooped them out as quickly as I could, turned down the heat and stepped back from the stove. I was supposed to be someone who knew about food. I was supposed to be a form of expert. Even if I argued that you did not need to be a trained chef to review restaurants – and I do believe this – you should have some basic skills. I liked to think I had these skills. This pile of dark-brown chips, gently fizzing on their plate in front of me, suggested otherwise. There was no doubt about it: I was very much in need of professional help.

Crispy new potatoes

There are a few self-appointed language snobs who tell me that the 'y' at the end of 'crispy' is redundant; that the word 'crisp' will do it. They are wrong. 'Crispy' has its uses. You can prove this by identifying sentences in which it is redundant. Cotton shirts can be crisp. Trouser creases can be crisp. Linen can be crisp. None of these things are ever crispy. But something coated in batter and deep-fried until it forms tiny undulations, air pockets and a lacy filigree of golden nodules which shatter beneath the teeth most certainly can be called crispy.

Because of their exploded surface area these new potatoes are most certainly crispy.

Serves four to six as a side dish, but do not underestimate just how many of these people will eat

INGREDIENTS

1kg waxy new potatoes like Charlottes, skin on

Vegetable oil

Salt and pepper

Boil the new potatoes in lightly salted water until done – approximately fifteen minutes, or until a fork goes right into them. Don't worry if one falls apart while testing. It's what you want.

Drain the potatoes, then lay them out on paper to cool for a couple of hours. This will reduce the moisture content.

Heat the oven to 200°C.

Pour half a centimetre of vegetable oil into a large roasting pan. Put it in the oven for ten to fifteen minutes until it's good and hot.

Put the potatoes on a plate and crush them with the back of a fork. You don't want to mash them. You just want each one to look like it's burst out of its skin, presenting lots of craggy surface area.

Take the roasting tin out of the oven, drop the potatoes into the oil, turn them until they are properly coated, then pop them back in.

Roast until golden brown and, yes, crispy, checking every now and then and moving them around a little with a spatula. It will probably take between forty-five minutes and an hour, depending on your oven. Check a few by eating them. This is your prerogative.

Drain on kitchen paper, sprinkle with generous amounts of salt and cracked black pepper and serve.

▶ 7. 'Come Fly with Me', Frank Sinatra (1966)

You have seconds.

A minute at most.

If you are going to get the audience on your side, especially an audience that don't quite know what they have signed up for, you have to do everything you can to assure them they are in safe hands, and you have to do it damn quickly. The bookings that the jazz quartet got at the Crazy Coqs led to opportunities at Pizza Express Dean Street, one of London's great jazz clubs, and later to an annual Sunday-lunch booking at the great Ronnie Scott's. Each new gig seemed to be a calling card for another: to the festivals at Bath or Buxton, at Snape Maltings or Cheltenham, and, eventually, to Cadogan Hall, one of the big dates at the London Jazz Festival.

However grand or prestigious the gigs might be, however much faith the bookers might have put in us, I can't quite shake the feeling that the audience might well be there partly out of curiosity. Could this man, the one who reviews food on *MasterChef* and restaurants for the *Observer*, really do this? Let's see if the dog can walk on its hind legs, and if so, for how long? Hence, I fixate on openings. Because if you don't get the beginning of a gig right, everything else is going to be so very much harder.

And when I think about openings, what I'm thinking about are the first couple of minutes of what I regard as one of the greatest live recordings in the jazz cannon: Frank Sinatra at the Sands Hotel in Las Vegas, in 1966. No, Frank is not at his very best. The glory years of his Capitol Studio recordings are behind him. But it doesn't matter, because what he has instead is complete and utter control of the space. (Almost literally so: he had bought shares in the place, alongside mob bosses like Meyer Lansky and Frank Costello.) He has been playing the Sands since 1953, and he knows it well. He also knows his audience.

There is a drum break, followed by the driving ra-ta-ta-ta of the hi-hat and, beneath it, a sprinkle of piano chords. The announcer's voice breaks through: 'The Sands is proud to present a wonderful new show. A man and his music . . . the music of Count Basie and his great band . . .' Now the horn section, under the direction of a frighteningly young Quincy Jones, kicks in. This is a big band at the height of its powers. It's a roaring, supercharged musical beast. It pushes into a four-chord turnaround, a grooving holding pattern for the vital piece of information: '. . . and the man is Frank Sinatra.' The audience explodes. This is the moment they've been waiting for all night. Perhaps they've been waiting weeks or months, forever checking and rechecking their tickets. And now he's here.

The mood alters. The energy levels rise. You may not be able to see it, but you can hear it. He's walked on stage. There's a key change, and the whole orchestra drops down into a vamp. Frank waits until they've settled into their rhythm. Now, casually, he says, 'How did all these people get in my room?' Because be in no doubt: while you might have bought a ticket, the room remains his. Frank Sinatra can now do anything he damn well wants. What he wants is to sing 'Come Fly with Me'.

I don't have Count Basie's horn section, not to mention that rhythm section. I'm no Frank. But I do have cracking musicians and an audience of people who have taken the chance and bought a ticket. They deserve reassurance that everything's going to be okay.

Which is why I focus on the first minutes like my life depends on it, because it feels like it does. Who the hell am I to lead a jazz-piano quartet? I taught myself to play piano and talk at the same time, specifically so I could hit the keys and immediately address the audience. They need to know I'm comfortable here in this seat, however nervous I might be. We hunted down the biggest, most joyous songs we could find: a jump-and-jive Cab Calloway number like 'Everybody Eats' or the roaring blues of 'It Must Be Jelly'. Then we go in as hard as we can.

And each time we do that, in my head I hear the ra-ta-ta-ta of the hi-hat raising the musical curtain on one night at the Sands Hotel, Las Vegas, in 1966.

Sparkling Water

6.35 a.m. The radio bursts into life. The intense urgency of right this very minute is barked at me by BBC Radio 4. I roll over in bed, dragged from my dysfunctional sleep, and try to focus on what I know is lying on the floor beside me. A couple of discarded books. A pair of shoes, scattered where they fell.

And between them: the empties.

Immediately, I feel guilt. I know Pat will be appalled when she sees this. She will take it as proof that my habit is out of control. I start working up my explanation: that one of the bottles was almost finished when I brought it up, which is why I brought up the other one. And anyway, don't you remember the takeaway we had last night, the Sichuan? All that double-cooked pork with chilli, and the lamb with cumin, and the tongue-numbing peppercorns with the beef? And the salt? Taken in context, finishing a whole bottle and a bit isn't really that much.

I get dressed on my side of the bed, then attempt to sweep up the bottles while Pat is out of the room waking the boys for school. Perhaps I can get the bottles into the recycling without her noticing. But she's faster than that. She stands now in the doorway, looking from me to the empties and back again.

'That's a hell of a haul.'

I say, 'It's not like I've got a coke habit or something, is it?'

'That doesn't stop it being . . . problematic.'

I know what she means. I'm not a plank of wood; I understand the issues, but I'm really not ready to confront them. I push past her, out the front door and down the path, hoping I'm too early for the neighbours. Maybe they wouldn't think anything of it. Then again, it happens so often, this dash to the recycling, that they're bound to have formed an opinion by now, or at least raised a quizzical eyebrow or talked about it to their significant others: 'Did you see him this morning? Again, with the bottles?'

'How many?'

'Two.'

'He's escalating.'

I have made it to the big dirty-green recycling bin without incident. I'm safe. I'm hidden from view by the huge privet hedges. I fling open the lid and look in at the other empties, the ones that arrived here in the previous few days. The way I'm going I'll end up filling the damn bin all by myself, which would be shameful, if I had some real sense of shame over this, rather than just a fear of being confronted about it. I throw in the two bottles and watch them bounce down to join the others. I close the lid and head inside for breakfast, wondering if I have enough of a supply in the fridge.

My name is Jay Rayner and I am *not* addicted to sparkling water. I just bloody love the stuff. I love the burst and fizz on the tongue. I adore the cleanness of it, the way it keeps on fizzing and bursting as it streams down my throat. Nothing is as refreshing. Still water is just an opportunity to drink sparkling water that's been missed. It's dullness in a glass.

There was a time when I was getting through eight of those two-litre green plastic bottles of Highland Spring a week, or perhaps if they didn't stock that, a generic own brand from the supermarket. I really would put one on the floor next to my bed, especially if it had been a salty takeaway night and it was a hot summer. And if there was only a little bit in the bottom of the bottle, yes, I would take up two and thrill to the chilly condensation that would form on the outside as I carried them up. And no, before you raise the flag, I'm not diabetic. I've had myself checked over. There's nothing especially abnormal about drinking sixteen litres of water in a week. It was just that I tried to make sure all of it was fizzy. Why wouldn't I? Fizzy is good. Fizzy is great. Fizzy can make you feel like you are drinking something grown-up, even when you're not drinking anything at all.

In my line of work, that can be helpful.

It is a January night early in 2009, and I am in a pizza place on the edge of downtown New York, feeling anxious. I am here to meet and interview the New York superstar chef Mario Batali, the big beast of the city's food world. At this point he has ten restaurants here, plus three in Vegas and two in Los Angeles. *Molto Mario*, his show on the Food Network throughout the 1990s, garnered him a huge following. He is very recognisably him: huge round head, sculpted beard to help you work out where chin ends and neck begins, sandy hair pulled back in a ponytail, a barrel of a chest.

We won't be sitting still for long, he and I. We are due to go out on the town, crossing from one of his restaurants to the next, with the aim of helping me get to the soul of the man. The interview is to mark the release of both a TV series and a book about a gastronomic road trip he has taken across Spain in the company of, among others, the actor Gwyneth Paltrow. This is such an innocent time. Eventually, Paltrow will rise to be seen as the enemy of appetite, a profoundly dippy, goggle-eyed ambassador from planet woo and bunkum, a proponent of a raw vegan diet who will be fined $145,000 for making unsubstantiated claims on her website *Goop* about $66 jade eggs that are to be inserted into the vagina, where, apparently, they 'clear chi pathways in the body, and invigorate life force'. She will be laughed at for saying underwire bras cause cancer and that a colon cleanse is just the very best thing. Right now, though, she's Batali's best pal and exactly the right woman with whom to tour a country famed for its dry-aged, hand-sliced ham.

I should be excited. I should be thrilled by the prospect of a night on the town with the superstar chef, the one we're all on first-name terms with. On seeing my media visa, the US immigration official at JFK airport had asked me the nature of my work in America. I told him who I was interviewing, and he spread his arms wide and bellowed, 'Mario!'

Yes, him.

But I am not excited. I am very anxious. I am dressing up my concern as a professional consideration. Fitting this interview into each other's diaries has been tough, and this is the last possible evening it could take place. At 6 a.m. tomorrow I must be at the airport for the daytime flight back to London. By the time the plane lands, I need to have written 3,500 words on Batali, which I must file the moment I get Wi-Fi. The concern is: booze. Mario drinks. He drinks like he has a stunt liver in his back pocket. He is renowned for his appetites, for the way he treats rich, artery-clogging, liver-misting, mind-blowing ingredients like they were narcotics. Again, these are innocent times. Eventually, those appetites – all of them – will be his downfall. Because in the depths of the #MeToo movement, he will be marked out as a serial groper and assaulter of women who plainly thought he was entitled to go nose down in the trough of everything. And frankly, no one will be surprised.

Right now, though, we are still in the period when men like Batali are lionised for wanting everything to be more and now and bigger and heavier and triple-sized and front and centre of the table. My fear is that if I play along out of some desperate need to be thought one of those guys, I will be crippled by the morning and incapable of writing anything worth reading. I will end up with a dismal hangover, and we know how much I hate those. I will miss my deadline. I have never missed a newspaper deadline. Accordingly, I have a strategy: I will join Batali only on every third alcoholic drink; for the other two I will drink sparkling water. Because somehow sparkling water manages to look like a real drink.

Almost certainly it will be San Pellegrino. It's a blunt object, but it will do the job. The fact is that unlike Europe, America doesn't have

much of a sparkling-mineral-water habit. If you want water with bubbles, you are most likely to get soda out of a gun, straight off the
mains, so that it comes with the authentic tang of chlorine. Even if it
comes out of a mixer bottle, it will be violently carbonated. But Batali
likes to play up his Italian roots, loves to talk about his three years living there getting to understand offal and *agrodolce* sauces and hand-
shaped pastas. I know he'll stock San Pellegrino, and that will be my
get-out-of-jail-free card.

The night is as full-on and brutal as I had expected. Batali's PR man,
who is with us, attempts to match his client drink for drink – 'Have a
whisky sour'; 'Try this fabulous Barolo'; 'Where's the grappa?' – and
ends up face down on a table. Batali himself becomes garrulous, then
noisy, then excessive, then glassy-eyed and unpleasant.

Early on I ask if he likes being famous. 'I do, and I have no problem
telling people that – because it's one way I can give people love and
joy as a restaurateur.'

On food: 'In the end the only reason I am motivated to do what I do
is for the hedonistic pleasures of the table.'

To the female sommelier who asks him whether he likes the choices
of wine: 'This wine is treating me like a hooker in Florida, baby.'

He orders razor clams and foie gras and salty quail, and lumps of
ham hock roasted in treacle until black. He makes dribbly, lascivious
comments about various female British chefs. He slips outside to
chain-smoke, tells me he loves his wife and wants to live to eighty-
five. He bitches at me about Gordon Ramsay, because Ramsay had
called him 'Fanta Pants' on account of his bright-orange cargo shorts.

I ask him if there's anything I've forgotten to ask him.

'You didn't ask me if I fucked Gwyneth.'

I thank him for interviewing himself and mentally clock the bra-
vado of a man who looks like Batali and thinks that anybody, including Paltrow herself, would even consider that a possibility. I ask the
question.

He drags deeply on a cigarette. 'No, I didn't fuck Gwyneth.'

We end up at the Spotted Pig, the Greenwich Village take on a British gastropub which he opened a few years before with the British chef April Bloomfield, and which is famed for its Roquefort sauce-covered burger and its celebrity clientele, who come here to hang out after hours. It is a venture to which I gave the first serious review, during a previous trip to New York. It's one of the reasons Batali is giving me so much of his time. He leads me to the very top floor, where there is a door secured by a numeric keypad. He's so slammed he can't recall the number. Eventually, we get into a room. It's rammed. He orders a bottle of Fernet-Branca, the black, bitter liquor that signals the end of all hope and sense. My sparkling-water habit has served me well. I know that if I leave now, I'll be okay. I tell Batali I'm going, that I'm done. He looks at me, baffled. He is only just getting started.

I make my flight, hangover free. Thank you, sparkling water. I panic when I discover that there is nowhere at my seat to plug my laptop into, which I thought there would be. I will have to write the piece racing against the feeble battery life as we tip down over the North Pole and head back to London. I thrash out 3,500 words in just under three hours. I click 'save' repeatedly as I go, and the computer dies as I type the last words. In truth, it has not been hard. As I left the Spotted Pig I had decided I would hang Batali with his own words. I was certain everybody would see exactly what sort of ludicrous, unself-aware shmuck he was.

Eight years later, in December of 2017, in the heat of the #MeToo movement, which began with the revelations in October of that year about film producer Harvey Weinstein's appalling treatment of women, Batali is named as a sexual harasser. According to a report on the food blog *Eater*, he had a history of crude language, unwanted touching and sexualised power play directed at women in general, and his own staff in particular. That third-floor space with the numeric keypad that he couldn't get into was known within the business as 'the rape room'. Batali didn't deny it. 'I apologise to the people I have mistreated and hurt,' he told *Eater*. 'Although the identities of most of the individuals mentioned in these stories have not been revealed to me, much of the behaviour described does, in fact, match up with ways I have acted. That behaviour was wrong and there are no excuses. I take full responsibility and am deeply sorry for any pain, humiliation or discomfort I have caused to my peers, employees, customers, friends and family.'

A few days later, the journalist Helen Rosner wrote a brilliantly savage piece for the *New Yorker*, in which she shone a spotlight on the way the things for which he was now having to atone were the darker flip side of the very things so many of us had celebrated him for: namely, his appetites. As she said, 'Batali has always in a sense been selling sex. It's there in his worshipful gazes at ingredients held aloft, his exhortations to his friends, viewers and dining companions to taste whatever rests on the tongue.' These were the appetites we allowed men. We did not allow them to women. She referenced my piece: 'Every woman who appeared – in person or in reference – was defined relative to Batali's sexual proclivities.' I might have thought I was hanging him with his own words; in truth, all I was doing was helping to build the myth.

The only comfort I could take in any of this was that my sparkling water-fuelled ability to take dictation during that night with Batali had seriously pissed him off. I heard through a mutual friend that he was furious with me for reporting word for word the exchange about whether or not he and Gwyneth Paltrow had had sex.

A couple of years later, I gave a mixed, though mostly positive, review to one of chef Dave Chang's restaurants in New York. Chang was furious and tweeted abuse at me about the poor journalistic standards of British reporters. Batali saw his chance to wade in. 'Hey chang Jay Rayner is more into Jay than anything else.' (Given the nature of the book you're holding in your hands, I'm not even going to attempt a defence.)

I replied, 'I have been called self-absorbed by @mariobatali. As that's come from a master of the vice I shall have to take it as a compliment.'

We have not communicated since.

I am standing in a spartan office in south-west London, all cream-painted bare brick and industrial windows, trying to take my interviewee seriously. Michael Tanousis, a south Londoner from a family of Cypriot Maronites, is stocky and dark. A thin gold necklace nestles in chest hair beneath a white linen shirt. He is focused and intense. Mostly, he is intense about mineral water. As a student at Stirling University, he tells me, he studied philosophy, and the mark of that study is still on him twenty years later.

'There's an absence of language or terminology to express the experience of water on the palate,' he says. 'If you don't have a word to describe what you're experiencing which someone else can recognise, then you can't communicate it. Wine has a language. Water doesn't.'

Between us we are apparently going to try to find a shared language. Michael runs a company called Aqua Amore, which, as its name suggests, supplies a wide variety of bottled waters both to the hospitality business and retail customers. In 2017 he took a course at the Doemens Academy, near Munich, which started out in the early nineteenth century promoting expertise in brewing and has since moved on to cover mineral water as well. The qualification Michael received allows him to describe himself as a water sommelier. Accordingly, he has laid out a tasting of sparkling waters for me, ranging from 'effervescent' – those that just make the tongue tingle – through 'light' to 'bold' and finishing with 'classic' – fizzy waters which assault your palate with bubbles. This is the bit I am trying to take seriously. This sort of overcooked connoisseurship, this nerdy attention to minutiae, makes my palms itchy. We know I can barely pay attention when someone is giving me tasting notes on a wine, and that at least has alcohol in it. How I am supposed to pay attention to water in the same way? Just by coming here I fear I have become precisely the sort of person I hate.

Except this water tasting was my idea. I was the one who sought out Michael, and with what felt like good reason. If I love it so much, surely I should seek out the best example there is? And might it not help if I knew a little about it?

But I'm still trying to focus. He starts by getting me to try two well-known brands of still water, Evian and Volvic. Both are produced by the same multinational company, Danone. Evian has 491mg of minerals per litre. Volvic has only 131mg per litre. Yeah, whatever.

Except . . .

Michael asks me if I know the work of the psychologist Professor Charles Spence of Oxford University. It so happens that I do. Alongside his work on the role music can play in our experience of food, Professor Spence has also studied the impact of shape. He has shown how rounded pieces of chocolate taste softer and creamier, whereas sharp, geometric shapes of the same chocolate are experienced as more acidic. It sounds nuts, but I've done the experiment, trying the two shapes blind, without knowing they are the same recipe, and it's true. The effect was first recorded in 1929 by a German-American psychologist called Wolfgang Kohler. In 2001 neuroscientist Vilayanur S. Ramachandran and his colleague Edward Hubbard staged similar experiments and adopted the words 'bouba', for soft and rounded, and 'kiki', for sharp.

Michael asked me if I was able to use those words to describe the waters I was tasting. I sipped both. Blimey. I was. Evian was thicker in the mouth and rounded. It was definitely 'bouba'. Volvic was crisper and more metallic. It was 'kiki'. Or was I reacting to the names of the waters themselves? 'Evian' is a more rounded word than 'Volvic', which is dominated by a sharp final consonant. I'm suddenly unsure of myself. I do know, however, that these two waters are not the same.

We move on to the tasting. For the first category, 'effervescent', we try a Finnish glacial water called Veen, which is about as mineral free as mineral water gets, with just 22mg of trace elements per litre. It's being put up against Badoit, famed for its high levels of bicarbonate and sodium. Badoit is familiar to me. It is the taste of the overtly foreign, stumbled across on childhood trips to France. I remember drinking it for the first time and wondering who had done this to my water. It bounced and vibrated in my mouth. It was distinctly flavoured. Now it is just the taste of a very hot summer's day on holiday. Against it, the Veen really is sharp and metallic. Michael tells me that being devoid of flavour itself, the water is dragging in anything it can from the tongue and reflecting it back at me. I'm not across the science in enough detail to make any sense of this. All I know is that there is an almost sour edge to it.

We work our way through the various categories. We roll our eyes knowingly at that blunt old stager Perrier, categorised as one of the boisterous 'classic' waters. What it lacks in subtlety it makes up for in familiarity. I nod appreciatively at San Pellegrino. The marketing of the brand is so strong that it seems to be the water of choice at every public event I go to. Sometimes I am employed to present trophies for particular trade bodies: it might be the Highland and Islands Food and Drink awards, or the Homewares awards, or the East Midlands Innovation Network awards. I am nothing if not eclectic. The script is studied. The jokes are honed. The velvet jacket goes on. I stay away from the booze until I'm off the podium and the job is done. Nobody likes a drunk awards host. I sustain myself through these evenings by drinking sparkling water, and these days it's almost always San Pellegrino. It is the taste of pleasure, deferred.

But it is the 'light' category which really draws our attention. On one side there is the low-mineral choice: Speyside Glenlivet, which, as its name suggests, is from Scotland. On the other there's a very high-mineral choice: Châteldon, from France. I have met Châteldon before, in a Moscow restaurant which was so up itself it had a water menu. Based on its provenance, they were charging £12 a bottle for it, when in France you can get a box of twelve for 12€. It is certainly illustrious. Châteldon comes out of a hole in the ground in the Auvergne at a refreshing 5°C, becoming naturally carbonated en route. It's been doing that since 1650. Louis XIV's physician told the Sun King that it was good for his health, and so it became the official water at court. I know Louis XIV had his faults, but you've got to admire a man who had his own mineral water.

We sip our waters. Speyside is brusque and hard-edged. It leaves your tongue feeling like it's been stripped. But the Châteldon is just lovely: it is the Goldilocks of sparkling mineral waters. The bubbles aren't too big or too small. The water isn't too rounded or too sharp. I would usually hesitate before describing a glass of water as delicious, but that's the only word that describes what I'm experiencing. Michael agrees. From the fridge in the corner of the room he takes out a bottle of white Burgundy, a Chardonnay by Louis Latour. We sip the wine and try it against the two waters. The Speyside merely emphasises the bitter edge to the wine, hiding all its mellow butteriness. The Châteldon makes the wine sing again on the tongue. It's like hearing the echo of a song you dearly love.

And now I have become precisely that person I claim to hate. I am a mineral-water perv.

Pat had no objection to the amount of sparkling water I was drinking. It was the plastic bottles the water was contained in that bothered her, and reasonably so. According to a report by the House of Commons Environmental Audit Committee published at the end of 2017, the UK uses 13 billion plastic bottles every year, of which 7.5 billion are recycled through local authority schemes in Britain. Around half of that recycling involves plastic made from polyethylene terephthalate, or PET, a form of polyester used specifically for drinks bottles. The fact these particular bottles can be recycled is demonstrably a good thing, but that doesn't disguise the volume of resources required to maintain my sparkling-water habit.

It got me thinking. Part of my job is to eat out in restaurants more regularly than most people. At base this is once a week for the review I have to write, but being both curious and greedy, I might end up in another two or three during the week. Eating out is supposed to be an addition to normal life, rather than the focus of it. In the UK it is regarded generally as a luxury. I began to wonder: was I a one-man greenhouse-gas machine? Had my chosen career, weighing up the virtues of one rib-eye steak against another, one intriguing way with flame-grilled cauliflower against another with clams, gifted me a vast carbon footprint? As I mused sardonically upon my own death, should I really be worrying about the death and destruction I was helping to foist upon the planet, albeit incrementally?

This is not virgin territory for me. My 2013 book *Greedy Man in a Hungry World* looked in detail at middle-class perceptions of sustainability around food: localism, small-scale production, farmers' markets and so on. I wanted to see whether they stack up. In the main, while they do have a certain narrative value – it's nice to buy stuff from neighbours, and who doesn't love wandering a farmers' market, fondling a luxury chicken, yours for £27? – they are not the route to a genuinely sustainable food supply chain. What I learnt was that if you are to calculate true environmental impact, you have to do it in the round, by considering far more than, say, just the fuel used to transport food from where it is grown to where it is consumed. You need to do what's called a 'whole lifecycle analysis' on the food's production, which means looking at the carbon embedded not just in fuel, but in farm buildings and machinery, fences and fertilisers, and even examining the lifestyle of the farmer. It turns out that a farmer's trusty Labrador creates a bigger carbon footprint than the Land Rover it is transported in.

What matters is how the food is grown, not where. I found my way to a report which showed that lamb raised in New Zealand and transported by sea to Britain while frozen has a smaller carbon footprint than lamb raised in Britain. Why? Because New Zealand agriculture is generally powered by renewable sources of energy – mostly hydro-electric – and the landscape is better suited to the task. Even though this has been confirmed by further studies, the finding drove people absolutely nuts.

What conclusions would I reach if I tried to carbon-footprint myself?

For a start, what could I say in my defence? In the positive column, I specifically get my electricity from a company which sells only renewable energy. (Any units my household uses are then returned to the grid from renewable sources.) Go me. I also no longer have a car. I was leasing a Toyota Prius because I thought that made me nice and green, but living in the city, with reasonable public transport links, I was using it less and less. Neither Pat nor I have any living parents to drive out to see, which was what we had once used the car for, and the kids are old enough to get on the bloody bus. I was paying a significant sum of money to park a big lump of metal and plastic outside the house. If we dumped the lease on the car, we could get car-pool membership for when a car was needed and use public transport for everything else. It worked perfectly.

I felt smug just saying the words 'Oh, we don't have a car.' Go us.

But that still leaves my lifestyle habits. I spoke to Dr John Kazer, an expert on environmental impacts with the Carbon Trust, which helps organisations to reduce their carbon footprint through efficiency and low-carbon technologies. He's done a lot of work on carbon-footprinting foods, in particular. So does the fact that I go to a lot of restaurants make me a bad person?

'From a philosophical point of view, leisure is the point of life,' Dr Kazer said, winningly. 'The reason we work is so we have leisure time.' Or, to put it another way, having a good time is not necessarily a bad thing. I knew full well that there were many people who would argue with this rather vociferously. Working out the point of life is the foundation of many things, including the motivational books business, university philosophy departments and the entirety of organised religion. I was short on time. I let it slide.

I had a simpler question: is eating in restaurants an okay thing to do? This is where it gets interesting. 'Cooking a meal at home for just two or three people is generally less efficient than cooking a meal in a restaurant for twenty or thirty people.' Resources are pooled. Relatively speaking, a smaller number of people are doing the work. 'For example, older people tend to have a much bigger carbon footprint than younger ones because they tend to live alone or with just one other person and cook only for themselves. They also stay at home and keep the central heating on.' This leads to a basic truth: if you really want to do something about your carbon footprint, be dead. 'There is a lot to be said for dying,' Dr Kazer added. I thanked him for the thought.

As to restaurants themselves, the Carbon Trust has been working alongside a number of them to improve their waste management. Restaurants are generally much better than domestic kitchens at managing waste. Every piece of food wasted in a commercial environment is money off the bottom line, in a manner that we don't tend to consider at home. 'The majority of waste in restaurants', Dr Kazer said, 'is on the plate. It's people not finishing what they've ordered.' I told him this was really not a problem with me. I was a champion plate-clearer.

But this led to another thought. It is hardly a secret that I am overweight. I can, and do, ascribe this partly to genetics. I know people who eat as much or more than me but who are not my size. I can be cross about this. But it also follows that I must be consuming too many calories for my metabolism and, therefore, more than my fair share of resources. Was this not proof of an oversized carbon footprint?

Firstly, Dr Kazer commiserated on the whole metabolism thing. 'I'm a small person,' he said, 'so I'm a more efficient unit. I'm certainly more efficient than someone who is six foot three.' I explained that I controlled my weight and its impact on my health through a lot of vigorous exercise. I wondered whether there was something a bit weird about expending all that energy to manage overconsumption.

'Not necessarily. The exercise is good for your general health, and that keeps you out of the grip of the doctors and the hospitals, which means you're not using up resources.' I sensed he was being kind.

Finally, I asked him about my bottled-water habit. For a start, the bubbles are CO_2, or carbon dioxide. Was I contributing to global warming every time I burped and farted the gas back out? On this he could reassure me. Generally, the carbon dioxide used to make drinks fizzy is a by-product of the fertiliser industry. During the summer, when mass agriculture needs less in the way of fertiliser, some factories close down for essential maintenance. In the summer of 2018 many more fertiliser factories than usual closed down at once, leading to an acute Europe-wide shortage of CO_2. There was not enough to keep drinks fizzy or to operate the machinery used to slaughter chickens. The brewers Heineken had to write to pubs asking them not to order too much of their beer. And there was certainly not enough for the sparkling-water business.

'The CO_2 in your sparkling water is regarded as the fertiliser industry's waste product,' Dr Kazer said. 'It's already been accounted for. It's nothing to do with the drinks industry.' Phew.

'But', he said, 'the packaging is a very big issue.'

I suspected he and Pat would have a lot to talk about.

In the spring of 2017 a team of burly Ukrainians came to our house in south London and ripped out the orange MDF kitchen that we'd had installed almost twenty years before. It was the start of a six-month build which would see walls knocked down, steel girders installed and the floor dropped by eight inches. During that time we turned our living room into a temporary kitchen. The surviving cabinets from the old kitchen were installed along the back wall and a supply of water plumbed in courtesy of a pipe banged through from the building site behind. It was all paid for by the legacy left after my father's death. Lose your parents; gain a kitchen.

Even a man like Des Rayner, with little interest in cooking, would, I think, appreciate the space that has emerged: the clean lines and the ergonomic distribution of cooker, fridge, work surfaces and sink. Mostly, being an exceptionally tidy man, I think he would have appreciated the way there was storage space for everything. The old kitchen had been a chaotic jumble of things piled on things piled on other things. It was that winning combination: both charming and irritating at the same time.

But now here we are with a place for everything.

One of those places is at the far end of the main work surface, where the back and side walls meet. A corner always needs something in it, and ours is no exception. After my morning with Michael Tanousis, I went and stood in front of the object that fills that corner. I was ashamed of myself because, faced with Michael's intensity, I simply couldn't bring myself to tell him of its existence. I couldn't bring myself to tell him that to deal with Pat's unarguable environmental concerns over plastic water bottles, I had bought a SodaStream.

I had asked Michael what he thought of them, and he'd thrown a massively dismissive shrug back at me. 'If it's tap water, it's just cleaned-up piss.'

Cleaned-up piss.

I ran my hand over the soft, curving, lift-up back of the SodaStream, where the CO_2 canister went. Over the two years since I'd bought it I'd come to adore it. I liked the semi-industrial way the heavy CO_2 canister screwed in at the back. I loved the way the plastic bottle full of water, awaiting carbonation, fitted in at the front. I loved the satisfying farty noise the machine made as it indicated the correct carbonation pressure had been achieved. Most of all, I loved the guilt-free access to fizzy water whenever I liked.

Then again, Châteldon. I had a decision to make.

Sparkling water

Serves one

Fill a glass with the sparkling water of your choice.

Add two ice cubes.

Squeeze in the juice of half a lime.

Drink it while looking like you know exactly what sophistication is. What more do you want from me? It's fizzy water.

▶ 8. 'Cantaloupe Island', Herbie Hancock (1964)

I finally realised I had to get serious about jazz piano when I found myself watching an old episode of *Star Trek: The Next Generation* and envying Data, the android who is constantly questing to understand what it is to be more human. One particular scene was set on the holo-deck, a brilliant device which allowed the writers to place the crew wherever they wished them to be whenever they got bored of outer space. In this case the crew were in a 1960s Hollywood nightclub. Data finds himself at the piano, leading a big band. And suddenly, courtesy of his programming, he can play 'All of Me'. Oh, to be running Data's software. I was jealous of a robot, which is, frankly, pathetic.

Which is why I went to the piano and learnt the chords that I was eventually called upon to play at the Ivy Club.

Over the years I would listen to the jazz canon. I would hear a recording and think, 'If I want to call myself a jazz pianist, I ought to be able to play this.' It was a longing to be a better version of myself. Herbie Hancock's seminal 1964 tune 'Cantaloupe Island' was one of them. It has a killer groove. You will know it, even if you don't know it, even if you believe you hate jazz, as it is forever being used as a bed on adverts and TV shows. (That's one of the curiosities of jazz. It is regularly described as a marginal genre, a redoubt for the self-absorbed and the pretentious and the tiresome. And yet, in adverts and TV dramas, in restaurants and airports, lifts and toilets, it is the soundtrack of our lives. We all of us have urinated to some of the greatest jazz solos ever played.)

As our live shows became more regular, I suggested to the quartet that we come up with tunes specifically designed to spotlight our musicians' talents. Together, Pat and our bassist Robert Rickenberg came up with a bass and voice version of Irving Berlin's 'Blue Skies', later followed by Joan Armatrading's 'Love and Affection'. For the sax, Dave Lewis suggested 'Cantaloupe Island'. I had no choice: I had to learn it.

It turned out to be one of the most joyously satisfying tunes I have ever got my hands across. It's not simply a pleasing chord progression (in truth, the main groove is only three chords), it's also an intensely physical experience, with a driving rhythmic form that drags you in and won't let you go. Plus, whisper it, I found the piano part was pretty straightforward. Or maybe something else had happened: maybe I was just better at playing the piano. Gigging 'Cantaloupe Island' felt like a turning point for me. Not to mention it's named after a type of melon. It deserved its place in a show called *A Night of Food and Agony*.

It also gave me the chance to duet with a bona fide Hollywood film star. In the autumn of 2018 Jeff Goldblum released his first album as a jazz pianist. He too had been playing with an ensemble, the Mildred Snitzer Orchestra (named after an old friend of his mother's from Pittsburgh), alongside his main career. He is an extremely accomplished, knowledgeable and dedicated pianist who can seriously swing. Finally, Decca Records, having seen him on a British TV chat show accompanying the singer Gregory Porter, signed him up. The *Observer* agreed that I should interview him over a piano: about the tunes that shaped him, the appeal of having a sideline as a musician, and how it compared to his acting career. The interview took place over a terrible digital keyboard in the small bar of a fancy central London hotel. He was charming, exactly the Jeff Goldblum you want him to be. He was unquestionably aware of his own reputation and charisma, and yet somehow managed not to come across as smug or irritating. The first track on his live album is 'Cantaloupe Island', possibly the one tune that we both know, and at the end of the interview I suggested we slipped out to see if we could duet on the Steinway in the foyer. Out there the afternoon crowd was taking tea, while a young woman serenaded them with a bit of French classical piano.

We advanced upon her from two sides. She came to the end of a piece and looked up. I said, 'This is Jeff Goldblum.'

She blinked, slightly startled. Indeed, it was Jeff Goldblum. She said, 'Would you like to play . . .?'

And we did. It was a small piano bench for two big Jews, but we found a way. I took the groove to 'Cantaloupe Island' at the bottom and Jeff took the tune at the top, though occasionally we swapped over, wrapping our ludicrous frames – he tall and lean, me broad-shouldered and soft – over and across each other. To save the moment we broadcast it live across Twitter to an audience in the tens of thousands.

I know how this reads. It reads as if I'm showing off. Well, obviously I bloody am. I got to play 'Cantaloupe Island' with Jeff Goldblum. You bet I'm showing off.

The Sweet Spot

When I was a kid, there were two sorts of homes: those that did cake and those that did not do cake. The homes that did cake always had one on the go, a golden-domed, open-crumbed, buttercreamed plate of loveliness and possibility, sitting innocently to one side in a suburban kitchen. You didn't even have to see it to know it was there. The house smelt of baking, in an age and middle-class environment that saw certain mothers staying at home and doing these sorts of things, possibly out of boredom. I found the unmolested presence of this cake mystifying, for I knew that if such an object were to enter my family's house, it would not survive long enough to be looked at. It would not be eaten so much as inhaled, by a houseful who would regard it much as a prisoner might look at contraband smuggled into prison: it should be dispatched immediately lest the guards get wind of it and take it off us.

Clearly, ours was a house that did not do cake. My mother believed we liked it far too much, for where sugar was concerned we, apparently, lacked an off switch. We were a household of people who battled their weight, in the way gardeners battle bindweed, certain that the small victories are only that; even if it appears to have been dealt with for now, it will be back one day. We all of us went on diets of one sort or another from time to time. My first was when I was eight. It involved eating an awful lot of eggs. My breath stank. There was another at the age of twelve and a third at sixteen and so on. Perhaps we should simply have accepted that we were Shtetl Jews, with metabolisms built for a winter on the Russian steppes when the Cossacks are coming. Then we could have given ourselves to cake, as some sort of birthright.

But we didn't. Led by Claire, we came to understand that in our house certain foods had to be regulated, or at the very least not actively entertained and encouraged. There was, for example, no standing supply of chocolate in the house, and with good reason. It would have been eaten. By me. My friend Richard Lindsay, who was sporty and fit and thin, the good-looking friend no adolescent fat boy should ever have, lived in a house with what they called a 'chocolate drawer', and it was just that. It was a drawer in the kitchen that was always full of chocolate: the purple-wrapped promise of Cadbury's Dairy Milk; the garish primary-coloured cellophane wrappers of individual Quality Street emptied out from their tin; dimpled discs of minted chocolate covered tightly in gold or silver foil, a rare sugar-boosted currency. I would watch Rich open the drawer, take just the one square or a single Quality Street, then close it again. Later, I would come to wonder whether my inability to take just one piece came as a result of the stigma attached to it by my family's culture, or whether that family culture was a direct response to the lack of an off switch. I suspect it's the latter. One afternoon, when I must have been six or seven years old, my siblings sent me round to the local newsagent's repeatedly to buy family-sized bag after family-sized bag of Revels, those soft- and toffee-centred chocolates for busy people on the go. Or greedy bastards who need a hit. (Oh, for the orange creams. But what were the coffee creams doing in there?) My older sister just kept telling me to get more. On the fourth occasion the person behind the counter said, 'You'll get fat.' Well, duh!

It's the same to this day. If there is chocolate in the house, I will eat it because, you know, chocolate. Then three days later my wife will reach for some. Pat will find it's all gone and gaze at me with a mixture of outrage, dismay and pity.

To which I will say, 'You don't like chocolate enough, or you would have got in there.' This answer does not go down well.

When cake happened to my family during childhood, it was in unexpected outbreaks, like the sun breaking through on a cloudy day. For example, Des had just happened to be near Louis, the Hungarian patisserie in Hampstead, and look what he'd brought back with him.

And yes, the chocolate éclair was his and leave the mille-feuilles for your mother, but you can have the doughnut. Or perhaps it was a plate of sticky glazed Danish pastries from the bakery around the corner, which in retrospect I realise made awful Danish pastries. They were always soggy and covered in those sliced almonds that bend rather than crack. None of us ever wanted the one with the soggy lump of apricot in the middle, because that was eating fruit when you should have been eating cake.

My mother may have baked from time to time, but it's not something I recall in any detail. Claire was always better at getting other people to do the things she had little or no interest in. Our birthday cakes would arrive pre-iced from a local baker, bearing the legend, in blue against white, 'Now Jay is seven', or whatever digit we had attained. The cake would sit in its white cardboard box for a couple of days, on the dining-room table in clear sight. None of my birthday cakes were a surprise; it was enough that there was cake in the house – that was the surprise. If she wanted something more exotic for a party, she would look to Anya, the aged mother of her Hungarian hairdresser, Maritza. Anya and Maritza had fled Hungary in 1956, during the failed uprising against the Soviet-backed government, with just a couple of suitcases and a head full of cake recipes. While Maritza made her living tending to the hopeful looks of the women of north-west London, Anya baked. Her speciality was Dobosh, an extraordinary multilayered affair of extremely thin slices of sponge glued together with chocolate buttercream, topped with a shiny caramel surface that would crack under the whack of a spoon. As family lore has it, I first met Anya, who never learnt to speak English, when I was around one and still speaking toddler scribble. We bonded over this lack of language. When I turned eighteen, she made me a Dobosh all of my own. It was so rich and complex that I was able to store it in the freezer and eat slices straight from there. The sponge was too thin to get ice-hard, the buttercream too luscious to freeze. What I recall most was the sense that this cake was mine, that no one else had rights to it. In a house that did not do cake, this was something very special.

Dessert, like high-thread-count bedsheets and colonic irrigation, is an indulgence. It's never necessary. Sure, for certain meals a cake can be an important signifier, but even then it's not about the eating of it. At a wedding it's about the cutting. At a birthday party it's about the blowing out of the candles on top. Mostly, it's just about the fact that someone bothered to get one. The eating happens because you needed something to cut or blow candles out on. I've always liked the quote from the great American food writer Julia Child that 'A party without cake is just a meeting,' while knowing that it wasn't worth drilling down too much on the role of that cake. The fact is that if you rush into a restaurant, desperately hungry, you don't call for the dessert list, or at least you don't if you have any shame. You look at the starters and mains. That's where the acceptable fuel is. Dessert is the thing you do after the thing you came to do.

A friend suggested to me that if I really was building my last meal, one eaten without any sense of guilt or recrimination, then every single course should be of cake. I've tried a meal like that: a dessert tasting menu by the New York-based pastry chef Dominique Ansel, who is famed for creating the half-croissant, half-doughnut Cronut. The Cronut is a delightfully outrageous thing, full of flaky, buttery pastry, light cream filling and raucousness. It's the full Elvis Presley indulgence, in classy Louboutins. I queued for twenty-five minutes to try one, in the depths of a frigid New York winter, because I thought it was the sort of thing a man like me should be able to say they've tried. Weirdly, having eaten it, I didn't begrudge a moment of the line, and I hate queueing for anything.

The dessert tasting menu was nothing like this. It was a push for greatness by a cook who had missed his own point. It was themed on the American Dream and was, therefore, a bit of a nightmare. There were fruit purées served on a paper cut-out of a house with a white picket fence, to celebrate the cult of individual home ownership;

capitalism was marked by a 'cigar' made with a soggy tuille and chocolate ganache; the tech age was represented by a fake Apple Mac,
circa 1989 – you stuck in a floppy disc and, in return for your self-
consciousness, it spat out a mediocre waffle. This and four other overwrought courses cost $135. It's a big no to the cake-only last supper.

I want to tell you it was a man who argued for a last meal of guilt-
free cake-eating, but it wasn't. Too many of these guilty relationships with food are profoundly gendered. It's the magazines aimed at
women that reference 'guilt-free' alternatives to things you should
not feel guilty about in the first place. Perhaps my own feelings about
dessert represent my unlikely guilty-female side, or perhaps I'm just
indulging in the same sort of gender stereotyping. I have every right
to be just as weird about sweet things as anyone else.

Then again, the association of sugar with guilt and the forbidden,
so familiar to me from childhood – perhaps for good reason: by the
age of thirteen I really did have an arse the size of Wyoming – feels
increasingly mainstream. We talk of sugar taxes. Our bookshops are
filled with titles like *I Quit Sugar* or the *Sugar Detox Plan* or *50 Low
Sugar Meals for the Oven*. Most of them are written by the scientif-
ically illiterate. They generally fail to recognise that just pushing the
refined granulated stuff to the side does not remove sugar from your
diet. It doesn't matter whether it comes from agave syrup or molasses
or the cement in Willy Wonka's chocolate factory. As far as your body
is concerned, it's all still sugar, ready to be converted into glucose,
which results in the release of insulin and, hence, weight gain. At the
same time as we fret about this, we watch *The Great British Bake Off*
and quite rightly salivate over the wonders that sugar can perform.

We are, in short, more fucked up over the sweet spot of the meal
than any other part of it, and I am more fucked up about it than most.
But that's okay because now, as I pretend my death is imminent, is
precisely the moment for me to shed my inhibitions and examine my
true self. What exactly do I want? Untrammelled by anybody's expec-
tations or prohibitions, what do I crave? There is no dessert menu

for me to choose from for this meal, or to be more precise, there is, but it is seemingly endless. I am allowed the run of history's dear sweet trolley: tiramisu to the left of me, Paris Brest to the right, Eton mess and clafoutis right ahead. I consider Dobosh, but I realise that underlying those gilded memories of soft sponge and chocolate cream and crisp caramel is another one: of nausea. A little goes a very long way with Dobosh. You need only a tiny slice, and where's the fun in that? It has to be something you can seriously eat. In any case, Anya is long gone and I have never found a Dobosh to match hers. I think too about a classic rum baba: a beautiful, bronzed, cylindrical loaf of booze-boosted, syrup-soaked savarin with, on the side, a dollop of cooling whipped crème Chantilly. But the very thought of it bores me, as if I am trying to pose as some Burgundian count revelling in the bourgeois good life. I like to be more subtle about my revelling.

And then it strikes me. I know exactly what I want. It's not an intellectualised choice. I cannot attach to it any personal stories of great significance. But every time I think about serving one of these, I smile and quietly sigh. If I see it on a restaurant menu, I have to order it. The only issue is that if this is going to be my last supper's dessert, it has to be the best example, the swoon-worthy version that leaves you gasping, and I'm just not sure where to find one of those.

Naturally enough, I start looking in Paris, because what I want is a classic and the French capital is meant to be good at those. In this I have made a strategic error, which is to underestimate the ability of Parisian food businesses to treat their own iconic dishes, and the customers they are selling them to, with complete and utter disdain. My depressing experience with L'Escargot Montorgueil and their dried-out snails, like so many withered, elderly scrota, should have educated me. Still, I do like to travel hopefully. It is both rather sweet of me and a failing. It is a failing which has led me to a primped and carpeted belle époque tea salon on the fancy rue de Rivoli, overseen by sturdy waitresses in white pinafores, where the kitchen has dedicated itself to buggering up my favourite dessert of all time: the Mont Blanc.

The first mention of it is said to be in a fifteenth-century Italian cookbook. Accordingly, it was supposed to be a favourite of the Borgias, who ate it between bouts of political infighting and incest. It's so called because the combination of cream and chestnut purée is meant to resemble the snowy peak of the great mountain on the Italian–French border. The classic version – various countries have their own take – has meringue, either as a base or mixed heavily into the whipped cream. It is then topped with sweetened chestnut purée, extruded in almost spaghetti-like strands to create a kind of chestnut coiffure. The presence of chestnut is the one constant in all versions of the Mont Blanc. In a conversation with the chef Michel Roux Jr, for a 2013 BBC series, the American cookbook writer Dorie Greenspan, who spends much of her time in Paris, came up with a brilliant explanation for how the chestnut purée and the meringue work together, or at least an explanation which spoke directly to a man like me, brought up on Hollywood musicals. She said it was like Fred Astaire and Ginger Rogers. 'Fred Astaire gave Ginger Rogers class, and Ginger Rogers gave Fred Astaire sex appeal,' she said. 'With chestnut purée there's the need for Ginger Rogers.' That's what the meringue does: it gives the chestnut purée sex appeal. A great Mont Blanc has smooth cream and crunch from the meringue and earthiness from the chestnut. It is all the good things, corralled in one place.

Or at least it is when done well.

Roux and Greenspan were filmed discussing the joys of the Mont Blanc at Angelina, the Paris tea room founded in 1903 by confectioner Antoine Rumpelmayer and named after his daughter-in-law. Apparently, the likes of Proust and Coco Chanel used to hang out there, though not necessarily together. I watched the video on YouTube a few times; studied the close-up shots of Roux's spoon slipping through the chestnut to the cream beneath; imagined that moment of silky anticipation for myself, like a wet-lipped teenager mentally pacing out the narrative beats of a first kiss. Which is what happens when a kid with a sweet tooth grows up to be a fifty-something man with a sweet tooth.

I arrange to visit Angelina and ask to meet someone there who can talk me through this wonder of cream, meringue and chestnut purée and its history. I am greeted by a young public relations executive called Natalie, who tells me exactly the Angelina story I had just read online. I ask her how long she has worked with the company. She smiles uneasily. 'One month.'

She's doing her best. Happily, I am introduced to Pascal Léger, the suited and booted maître d', who has been here for twenty-one years and is across the details. He has trouser creases you could slice your finger open on. The chestnuts come from the Ardèche, in south-eastern France, he tells me. 'There are so many good patisserie houses in Paris,' he says, 'so we have to be the best. The texture of the chestnut is what we're looking for. It needs to be done as a noodle.' Thirty per cent of all the patisserie they sell every day are Mont Blancs, which is good going given they charge a whacking 9.30€, although that does include their special editions. Sometimes they flavour the cream with passion fruit or pineapple or coconut, which sounds to me like an awful idea, but then I'm not flogging Mont Blancs. They sell 230 on a weekday and 330 at a weekend, plus 400 to go. In all, 4,000 are made for their various outlets in France, in central kitchens at Colombes, on the outskirts of Paris. A large proportion of them are blast-frozen for their journey. I imagine all those whorled and spiralled Mont Blancs, tray after tray of them stacked up in all their creamy, light loveliness. Pascal fills me in on a detail that I hadn't clocked: the Angelina group, with its five cafes in Paris, two in Versailles and myriad others across the globe, was bought up ten years before by the Bertrand Group, a French catering giant with 250 restaurants across the country and a raft of brands. The Angelina Mont Blanc has become a commodity. Given the price tag, it must be a valuable one.

We are getting on so well that I ask him how often he eats one. I imagine myself in his job, rationing myself to just the one a day, or perhaps two, the eating of which I would say was 'for quality control purposes'. I might confect a knowing wink. He leans in. 'The thing is,' he says conspiratorially, 'I don't really like chestnut.'

'Oh?'

'No, not at all. I have perhaps eaten ten of them in the past twenty-one years. But I do have a hot chocolate every day.' I can't pretend: I am disappointed in Pascal.

And then mine arrives, and I am left alone to eat. They serve it in a branded paper cup of the sort used for scoops of ice cream, which I suppose makes sense, even though it's hardly sexy. Now that I can see it up close, it's clear the chestnut purée noodle topping really is a piece of work: an extraordinary example of soft-matter engineering. It almost seems a shame to sink my spoon through it. But only almost.

In I go.

The first sign that something is up comes when my spoon meets resistance. This dessert is meant to be light and ethereal. It should be a cloud in a cup. This feels like something I will need to shovel. I break open the chestnut carapace and discover why. The whipped cream has been over-beaten, so that instead of being aerated loveliness the butterfat has started clumping together, making it thick, heavy and greasy. You don't even need to taste it to know this has happened; you can see the granular texture. I try a couple of spoonfuls. It's miserly on the meringue, more of which might have mitigated things, but only a little. It's heavy and cloying and, frankly, just grim. I lay down my spoon, my Mont Blanc half eaten, my dreams and culinary hopes in tatters. I am the seven-year-old kid who keeps getting the coffee cream in the bag of Revels. A waitress comes and collects the plate, but does so wordlessly. She does not ask if there's a problem.

I head upstairs, past the ornate cornicing, the flower displays and the garish murals of pastoral scenes, the flounce and polish that 9.30€ pays for, to the toilets. I need a consoling wee. This tea room can seat a couple of hundred people at a time, and yet there are just two toilets for the men, one cubicle and one urinal. The urinal is taped over to indicate it is out of order. The seat in the cubicle is broken. Angelina is the worst kind of culinary institution: it's the sort that has stopped attending to the details.

I explain the issue to another friend in Paris, who directs me to the shop of renowned pastry chef Gilles Marchal, on a narrow hillside lane in the 18th arrondissement. Marchal, who grew up in Alsace-Lorraine, made his name as the head pastry chef at the Hotel Bristol and the Plaza Athénée, before spending five years as head of chocolate at Maison du Chocolat. The shop is his first solo venture and, while they make a range of cakes, it is dedicated to the madeleine, the light, fluffy, shell-shaped sponge cake which, when dipped in tea, took Proust's protagonist on a journey into memory. He flavours them with orange and raspberry, with salted butter caramel and black truffle and so much more besides. Some are filled; some are not. The door handle is in the shape of a madeleine. His logo is a madeleine. Do I need to tell you that his madeleines are lovely? No, I do not.

He comes out to meet me in the small shop that fronts the bigger bakery kitchen behind, which is staffed mostly by studious, intense-looking young pastry chefs from Japan. He is a tidy, elegant, middle-aged man in spotless whites. He is a reflection of his shop, which is a clean, modern space with square glass cabinets, as though it were selling not cakes but watches. Marchal tells me he is very respectful of tradition. 'I would not exist without the great patisserie houses because they educated and trained me,' he says. I ask him what he thinks of Angelina and its Mont Blanc. 'It must be good or it wouldn't sell that many every day,' he says. It strikes me as a classically Parisian response: an unwillingness to challenge that which has achieved a certain status.

In April 2017 I published a less than positive review of Le Cinq, the renowned Michelin three-star restaurant of the Georges V hotel and of chef Christian Le Squer. When I say less than positive, what I mean is it was an utter blood-drenched, furious shitbagging. I hated the 300€-a-head place and everything it stood for. I have detailed the response to that review elsewhere – in the Introduction to *Wasted Calories and Ruined Nights*, my second collection of negative restaurant reviews – so I won't go through it again. But what was most striking was the outrage on the part of both some French journalists and many French readers, who emailed or tweeted me directly. The restaurant had already received three Michelin stars, they told me. Who the hell was I to question whether it was any good or not? The ribald, insolent, scabrously British tradition of calling out the grandiose and the high status, which can be found in the work of seventeenth-century playwrights like George Farquhar and George Etherege, cartoonists like Hogarth or, more recently, Ralph Steadman and *Private Eye* magazine, is not exactly part of French culture. My review of Le Cinq was so shocking in France because that sort of writing simply isn't the done thing. Equally, Angelina has been around so long and is so successful that it simply must be allowed to be called good.

I didn't push him. In any case, Marchal told me he is interested in moving things on, in making 'lighter and more refined' versions of classics. That, he said, was what he had done with his Mont Blanc. My heart fell. I didn't want something refined. I just wanted a recognisably classic Mont Blanc.

Marchal's was a lovely piece of work, but it was set in a pastry-tart shell which, despite its thinness and crispness, immediately made it a heavy item. The shell was there, he told me, to make it portable, rather than a dessert to be served in a restaurant. It was light on the meringue, and the strands of chestnut purée were laid in neat parallel lines across the top of the flat surface, in an obsessive-compulsive way which, in turn, made me slightly anxious. The light cream underneath was not split. It was topped with a caramelised pecan. It was undoubtedly a Mont Blanc, in that all the required ingredients were there. It just wasn't my Mont Blanc.

* * *

I decided drastic action was called for, so I flew to Tokyo.

I'd love to leave that sentence just sitting there: I was so outraged by substandard cake that I immediately flew over 5,900 miles to rectify the situation. It is the sort of gesture a man searching for the perfect dessert should make. But it's not quite true. I did go to Japan, but there were a few months between my disappointment in Paris and my flight. And when I flew, Pat was in the seat next to me and our two boys were in the row in front. It was a family holiday, posited on the fact that first Eddie and then Dan had spent years in their bedrooms engaging with Japanese culture through anime, manga, games and ramen. Eddie was about to turn nineteen, which meant this would probably be the last grand summer holiday he would ever be prepared to join us on. I suggested we go and engage with the real Japan. It was to be an adventure: we would visit temples and eat ramen and yakitori and ramen, and shabu and tempura and ramen, and so on. This is my family we're talking about here; food had to be a big part of it.

It occurred to me early on, however, that in this grand Japanese expedition there was a self-serving opportunity. Because foodwise the country isn't just good at its own stuff, it's good at everything. That culturally embedded nerdy attention to detail, combined with a willingness to bring in ideas from other traditions, means that as well as eating, say, great tonkatsu in Tokyo, you can also eat great pizza. We did just that one lunchtime at our hotel. The Mandarin Oriental, high up a tower block in Nihonbashi, boasts a simple marble bar on the thirty-eighth floor knocking out the best pizza I have ever eaten, made in front of you by a chap from Rome who has done this and only this for most of his working life.

Similarly, the Japanese love French patisserie. That cadre of intense Japanese pastry chefs in Gilles Marchal's kitchen in Paris was not an aberration; I have come across Japanese pastry chefs working in high-end restaurant kitchens all over the world. If it is precise and delicate and, best of all, stupidly expensive, the Japanese love it. This is a country that fetishises the growing of fruit to be given as a gift. In the fancy florist's in the lobby of my hotel, I found a £200 mango. It was a nice-looking mango and came in a pretty box, but for that sort of money I would hope it would peel and slice itself and then jump into my mouth. If they were prepared to splash that sort of wedge on a mango, they would certainly be happy to go big on cake.

I went from the lobby down a few escalators and into the network of subway stations, food courts and shopping malls that cross beneath the streets of Tokyo. There I found the entrance to the flagship branch of the Mitsukoshi department store. Like Peter Jones in Chelsea, it is the sort of place you should head for in the event of nuclear war, because nothing bad can ever happen there. Most importantly, I located the basement food hall, a glittering, shiny maze of edible, spendy loveliness: varnished oak and polished glass stands filled with the best in pickles, candied fruits, sugar-crusted jellies like costume jewellery or ludicrously identical boxes of fruit salad; there were a couple for smoked fish, and one for teriyaki and another for tonkatsu and a little sushi. There was everything, all at its most hyper-organised, glossy and contained.

Naturally, there was cake. There was so much cake. There were huge, vertiginous sponge cakes and tiny iced fancies. There were éclairs and mille-feuilles, and individual lemon tarts, gel-glazed and topped with berries placed just so. On the stand for the patisserie company Mademoiselle C I found precisely what I was looking for: the Japanese take on the Mont Blanc. I had been told in advance that they adored them. As early proof, in one shop I found a small box of dark choc-olates with a picture of a Mont Blanc on the front. In another I found a Kit Kat festooned with images of chestnuts. Japan loves Kit Kats and sells them in mind-boggling flavours, often as limited editions: you can buy them flavoured with wasabi or baked potato, pumpkin or melon, milky tea, soy sauce, and so much more besides. It was natu-ral there'd be one dedicated to chestnuts. Both of these confectionery items had a creamy flavour profile that gave a whisper of the Mont Blanc. Neither of them nailed it.

Happily, standing at the Mademoiselle C concession inside the Mitsukoshi food hall I was finally in front of the real thing. The chestnut was in the obligatory noodle form, but instead of a dome the cake was almost a cylinder, rising high above its foil-cup base. I watched the assistant carefully tuck it into its box – with gel packs for the long, arduous journey up the forty floors above me – then seal it with an ornate label and finish it with a ribbon. It cost 500 yen, or roughly £3.50, which compared to the Angelina offering felt like a bargain. I did a little more shopping before heading back up to the lobby at ground level and a shop called Sembikiya, which also did a Mont Blanc for 860 yen, or £6.15. It was a lot for a single cake but, hell, this was a serious business. Another box. Another gel pack. Regularly, these lifts up to the hotel above were filled with glitzy people clutching bags bearing legends like 'Dior' and 'Chanel', the booty from a raid on the glitzy malls of Ginza.

Me, I had cake.

Back in my room I set to work. The Mont Blanc from Mademoiselle C was a classic example of how different an item with the same name could be. There was no meringue. Instead, there was a thick sponge base flavoured with matcha, the ubiquitous green tea powder. It wasn't unpleasant. I could see the skill that had gone into it, but in no way was it the sweet thing I had been looking for. Next, I cracked open the Sembikiya version. Again, it was a twist on a theme: pastry case below, filled with almond cream. Next, a big pillow of whipped cream, and above that the chestnut purée, shaped into petals. Right in the middle, just in case you hadn't had quite enough chestnut, was a whole marron glacé, a syrupy crystallised chestnut. Naturally, I ate it. Not eating it would have been rude, and I like to think I have impeccable manners. But the whole experience didn't make me happy.

Two down, one more to go, because just as I was about to leave Mitsukoshi I had noticed one more stand, selling nothing but Mont

Blancs. It was the Tokyo outpost of Angelina. With a weary shrug I handed over my 500 yen and watched the sales assistant go through the endless boxing procedure: fold, place, wedge; here's the gel pack; here's the label; here's the ribbon. I didn't know whether I was meant to eat it or marry it.

Now it was in front of me on the desk in my hotel room. It looked exactly like the one I had been served in Paris. Still, I had to give it a go, if only for the sake of being a completist.

I lifted my spoon, slipped it through the chestnut purée and . . . it kept going. There was no resistance at all. Greedily, I scooped up a spoonful. It was light and fluffy, with the perfect balance of meringue to a cream that had been whipped, but not overly so. I ate it piece by piece, and as I scraped at the last of the cream in the pot I knew immediately I could do another one. And perhaps another one after that. It was happiness and deep sighs and hopefulness in a paper cup. It was everything I wanted the Mont Blanc to be. And it was here, in Tokyo, thousands of miles from where it was born. Which was utterly useless to me.

My family home did eventually become a house that did cake, but not until long after we had all grown up and left. In their seventies my parents hired a housekeeper to look after them, a warm, patient and hugely caring young woman from the Philippines called Flora.

My mother struggled with the appointment that she had made. Claire felt it turned her into the grand lady of the house, a role that was at odds with her working-class beginnings in the slums of Hackney. I pointed out that she was paying Flora well and had provided her with a self-contained flat at the top of the house; and that, most importantly, Flora wanted the job. All of this was true, but there was something else: I was, like so many adult children, utterly delighted. I wanted to know Claire and Des were being looked after.

And they were, often through the medium of cake. Every time I turned up to visit, there would be a new one in the kitchen, sitting under glass.

The first time I saw it I bawled, 'Cake!' like one of the talking dogs in the Pixar movie *Up* spotting a squirrel.

'I know,' Claire said. 'Isn't it fabulous? Flora bakes them every week. Once one is finished another one comes along.' As someone who had never baked much she saw this is as something of a miracle. There were moist almond cakes, the surface mosaiced with slices of nut. There were lemon drizzle cakes and ginger cakes.

My parents were slipping gracefully into older age, which meant the household had also slipped on its dietary axis. In 2003, courtesy of a botched anaesthetic during an operation, Claire had toyed heavily with the possibility of dying. What had started out as breathing problems on the operating table soon turned out to be pneumonia. Within twenty-four hours it had cascaded into sepsis and multi-organ failure. She was put into a coma, and we were told that she was unlikely to survive. For weeks she lay unconscious in the intensive care unit of a hospital in north-west London. For much of it she was on a gently rolling bed engineered to avoid bedsores, surrounded by monitors beating out a feeble rhythm, the call and response of the human body at the very edge of life. She made it, courtesy of the right antibiotics administered early enough. She was seventy-one when she entered the ICU and, by her own admission, a very large lady indeed. Across those first few weeks, and the months of recovery that would follow, the weight fell off her. The Rayner instinct to eat had simply gone. A large, round woman went into that hospital; a small, thin one came out. Meanwhile, my father, anxiously separated from his life partner, seemingly decided to keep her company by not eating much at all either. She eventually returned home for seven more good years of life, but during those years, as it does in older age, her appetite subsided. Theirs stopped being a house that had to regulate its intake of sugar. Cake, liberally administered by Flora, became a fine and good thing.

Claire died in 2010, leaving Des more in need of baked goods than ever, whether he knew it or not. The cake was still there under its glass lid, but it took longer and longer to be eaten. In 2014 he developed the neurological disorder which would prove to be the last great event of his life. Des's appetite, not just for the best of Flora's baking, but for life itself, really had gone. In those last few months it was obvious to all of us that he'd simply had enough.

Over the years I had reported on issues regarding hospital food in Britain. The consensus was always worryingly simple: the food was terrible, which was why patients didn't want to eat it. There were dreadful statistics about elderly people coming out of hospital more malnourished than when they went in. It was true that the outsourcing of hospital food services in Britain had done great damage to the quality of the cooking, as managers pursued ever tinier crumbs of profit margin. But the more I dug into the subject, the more complex I realised it was. It wasn't just about whether the apple crumble tasted nice. With the elderly it was also about their ability to access the food on the tray in front of them. Did they have the wherewithal to feed themselves? Did they need help? Was the food of a consistency they could manage?

There was one other thing. Over the years campaigners would claim the magic bullet was good cooking. Celebrity chefs, with no knowledge of mass catering or geriatrics but still touchingly keen to help, would be hired to write smashing new menus, oblivious to one brutal fact. Sometimes it didn't matter how good the food was. Sometimes it didn't matter how much care and attention had been lavished on it. Sometimes elderly, ill patients just didn't want to eat, and my father was proof of that.

When Des died in April 2014, there was still one of Flora's cakes on the counter in the kitchen, waiting to be eaten.

A spring night in 2008, and I am at Leeds station about to get a train home. I have been filming in the city all day and haven't eaten, and now have a problem: it's so late there is no guarantee of catering on the train, and the only thing that's open in the station is a branch of Burger King. I can't pretend I've never eaten their product before. In a few years' time I will conclude that I shouldn't be ashamed of these things. Almost everybody eats fast food from time to time, and regardless of my job I am part of almost everybody. I will willingly say that I prefer a Whopper to a Big Mac. But I am just embarking on a TV career and have become increasingly self-conscious. What if anyone sees me, the critic from *MasterChef*, ordering from a fast-food joint like this? What will they think? Oh, the shame. My self-importance meter is set to 11.

I hesitate. Maybe I can make it all the way to London without eating. No, I really can't.

I decide to take my chances. I queue up and, big surprise, nobody recognises me, not the other customers and not the staff. Who the hell do I really think I am? George Clooney? I head for the train, seek out the emptiest of the carriages and unload my hyper-tasty, salt-boosted, slutty bounty of carbs and fat and protein. Just as the train pulls off another passenger comes up the carriage from behind me, looks down and barks, 'You're Jay Rayner. What are you doing eating a Burger King?'

I smile apologetically. 'I'm hungry.'

No one who earns money by working on television should complain about this sort of stuff. I'm not being forced to do it. Being on TV is a choice, which brings with it many advantages, especially if you have an ego the size of Texas. But it does mean you have to be aware of screwing up in public. One of the reasons I joined a members' club in London is because it has a no-photography rule in the main bar. That means I can get blind drunk and fall off a bar stool and no one will ever have pictorial evidence of my disgrace.

So far I have navigated this successfully. However, the impact of my dysfunctional sleep is now causing me to worry greatly. My drowsiness feels pathological. At certain times of the day I don't just feel a little sleepy, a dizziness overcomes me. I start to lose focus, both visually and mentally. I try to deal with it by 'resting' my eyes. And suddenly I am unconscious. This happens repeatedly at my desk in my office at home. I lean back in my chair for a moment and I'm gone for ninety minutes. Happily, nobody can see this. I don't even have to admit to Pat that it's happened. It's my own private shame. I'm like a toddler who can't get through the day without a mid-afternoon nap.

The problem is, I travel a lot for work. The vast majority of that travelling is by train. It is now rare that I get through one of those journeys without falling asleep. My eyes close. My head lolls back. My mouth drops open. At which point I have no control over whether I snore or not. Sometimes I shock myself awake and know full well that a giant, roaring bout of snoring is what did it. I then look across the carriage and smile at a fellow passenger. When our boys were small they would, as all small kids do, fall asleep on car journeys. Back would go the head. The mouth would drop open, slack. We used to refer to it as 'catching flies'.

It is surely only a matter of time before a truly awful picture of me catching flies turns up on social media. There could even be audio. How appalling would that be? We are meant not to be too precious, to accept that things like this come with having a public profile, but I do like to have a modicum of dignity. Right now I am at risk of losing all of mine.

Back home I send Dr Kent another email. I tell him the time has come.

When Henry Harris was a small child, his family went on holiday each year to a hotel called the Villa dei Pini – the villa of the pines – in Fregene, a town perched on the coast, just to the west of Rome. It had been built in 1937 by a local prince, before being turned into a hotel which played host to the likes of Orson Welles, Federico Fellini and the entirety of the king of Yemen's harem. In those days Henry's father,

Lewis Harris, ran a restaurant in Brighton called Le Grandgousier, which fought the good fight on behalf of eating well at a time when such impulses were still viewed suspiciously in England. Harris family holidays often revolved around eating well, and those at the Villa dei Pini were no exception. Meals were served at tables set outside amid the pines.

Henry, being an August baby, would always celebrate his birthday while on holiday with a cake from the kitchens: meringue and whorls of cream topped with chestnut purée, dusted in turn with icing sugar for the snowy peaks. They called it a Monte Bianco, which made sense, given the origins of the dish in the kitchens of the Borgias.

For many years it remained a childhood memory, until Henry went on a trip to Paris with his then girlfriend, now wife, Denise in 1986. By this point he was a restaurant cook, working for a much-admired chef wunderkind called Simon Hopkinson at the latter's first restaurant, Hilaire. They were shortly to open Bibendum for designer Terence Conran. It would be a temple to classic bourgeois French cooking: escargot bourguignonne, soupe de poisson, steak au poivre and crème brûlée. These were all the dishes that both Hopkinson and Harris had come to love. Hopkinson told Harris to visit Angelina on the rue de Rivoli for hot chocolate, poured from a silver pot, and a Mont Blanc. Angelina was still in family ownership and presumably a very different place to the one that exists today.

'It was a reminder of the dish of my childhood birthdays,' Henry Harris says now of that Mont Blanc. 'We had to go for a lie-down in the Tuileries Garden afterwards.'

Henry and I are talking over lunch in the downstairs bar of a pub recently renamed the Hero of Maida because of its location in London's Maida Vale. Formerly, it was called the Truscott Arms and had been famous for its Sunday lunches, but a rent dispute had resulted in the previous landlord's departure. Harris is the chef director here, working across this and three other sites on behalf of an operator. We have been friends for many years, Henry and I, but we haven't seen each other for far too long. Happily, I'm re-meeting him as much for his food as for his company. After Bibendum and a couple of head chef jobs for others, he set up his own restaurant. It was called Racine, and it celebrated the kind of French country cooking he so loved. We met for the first time at an industry party, just before he opened Racine, and I asked him what the plan was. He said, 'To never cook with lemongrass or sear a piece of tuna ever again.'

He kept his word. I ate at Racine regularly from its opening in 2002 because it was so unapologetic about its overt Francophilia. I loved his steak tartare and his saffron and mussel mousse and his Wiener Holstein – breaded veal schnitzel with a fried egg, salted anchovies and veal jus. When I was researching a novel about a siege in a restaurant kitchen, he let me work a shift alongside him at the stoves. He made me pin-bone red-mullet fillets and laughed at how arduous a job he had given me.

Racine was where Henry finally put a Mont Blanc on the menu, and that was where I first ate one. That was where I stumbled across its insanely clever culinary juggling act: of light against rich, of crisp against soft.

In 2015 Henry closed Racine. It was intended to be a neighbourhood restaurant, but over the years too much of the property around where it was located on the Brompton Road, in London's Knightsbridge, had been bought up by people looking for an investment rather than somewhere to live. The neighbourhood restaurant mislaid its neighbourhood. I missed Racine hugely.

So now I am sitting over a lunch of Henry's great dishes and relishing every moment. To start I have calf's brains, sautéed in brown butter with capers. It is the sort of dish that makes certain people want to run away in search of a hug from somebody reassuring. Brains look just like brains. That shouldn't put anyone off. They are delicious: rich, creamy, with a slightly crisp carapace. There's the nuttiness of the browned butter and the sharpness of the capers. I follow that with a leg of grilled rabbit. It's the French farmed stuff, wild rabbit being tough as the proverbial and only good for braising. The burnished leg sits on a lake of thick mustard sauce. It's draped with bacon.

Henry has a halved soft-boiled duck egg with smoked trout and a watercress mayonnaise to start, followed by grilled onglet with garlic butter. We start talking about my gastronomic hike through the dishes for my last supper. This is the sort of chatter that makes Henry very happy indeed. Some chefs just cook, but the good ones also eat. Henry eats. I tell him about the Avery wine dinner and the blind tasting of the 1971 Penfolds Grange against the Petrus. After he ran his restaurant in Brighton, Henry's late dad set up Harris Vintners, which traded in fine digestifs, but especially Armagnacs. Serious wine is something he, and by association Henry, knew a lot about. I describe the moment of the reveal, and Henry nods slowly, as if he is imagining himself at the table.

We talk about snails and the disappointment I'd had in Paris. At Bibendum Henry would have knocked out dimpled tray after dimpled tray of the things for years. He too had been to L'Ami Louis in Paris, though a fair few years before me. 'I remember looking down the narrow restaurant,' he says, 'to where the hatch from the kitchen into the dining room was open. There was a cook with a fag in one hand while he stuffed snail shells with garlic butter. I remember thinking how happy he looked in his work. Mind you, I was still a smoker myself then.'

I say, 'We all were.'

He asks me about my plan for the pork element of the meal, because he assumes there must be one. He laughs when I tell him what I'm thinking. He suggests a couple of ways to make it better. It is the kind of ingredient-obsessed conversation I need to have.

He looks at my empty plate and says, 'Shall we go downstairs?'

We stomp down to the basement kitchen, where Henry gathers his ingredients. One of his cooks has already made him discs of meringue, according to the recipe passed down to him by his mother Gaye. 'The secret is to make sure the oven is completely clean, so nothing can compromise the meringue. They mustn't be too biscuit-like. They need a squidgy centre.' I break one of the hockey puck-sized meringues open. It is perfect. For the cream he mixes equal parts whipping and double, and then beats it lightly with a little icing sugar. 'It has to be Chantilly, or what the great chef Michel Guérard called "an insubstantial cloud of white cream".' He hands me a spoon to taste. It is light and cool, the culinary equivalent of a newly laundered white cotton shirt. Next, he takes a pouch each of unsweetened and sweetened chestnut purée, which he mixes in a ratio of three to two. 'The sweetened stuff is very cloying. It needs to be brought down.' Now he reaches for the killer ingredient: a bottle of De la Mazière Armagnac, of the sort his father Lewis first imported to Britain (and which the company, now run by Henry's wife, continues to sell).

'It adds a savouriness to the chestnut. You don't need much.'

Finally, he assembles the dish, seeking out a cold plate for the job. First, a small dollop of cream is dropped into the middle of the porcelain, there to keep the meringue from sliding all over the place. A much bigger serving of cream goes on top of the meringue.

Henry shows me a solid steel potato ricer that he picked up in a kitchen supply shop in the Bowery, in Lower Manhattan. It looks like a giant garlic press. 'Best I've ever found,' he says. He fills it with the chestnut mix, then squeezes out the tangle of brown threads, which heap across the cream. He dusts the finished dessert with icing sugar from a shaker, wipes a couple of smudges off the rim of the plate and shoves it across the work surface towards me.

My spoon cracks through the meringue and I scoop up a substantial amount of the three parts. It is all the things I want it to be: sweet but also restrained; there is crisp and soft; and then there's the woozy, boozy hit of the Armagnac, which just lifts the chestnut away from the cloying. I eye the big box of meringues that his cook has made for him today; restaurant cooks are incapable of doing anything in small batches.

I say, 'Is this going on the menu tonight?'

Henry grins. 'I think it should.' He calls over his small brigade and goes through the method once more, while I carry on clearing the plate, happily. I think about this evening's diners at the Hero of Maida, and how grateful they should be to me.

Afterwards, Henry takes me on a tour of the building. As we pass by the bottom of the stairs, he says, 'A few days ago this area was stacked with sacks of Pierre Koffmann potatoes. They have his grinning face on them, and his signature.' We both know Pierre. We're amused at the way this man, once known as the most fearsome and demanding of chefs in the kitchen, has become in his later years everyone's cheery uncle.

I say, 'Are they what you use for chips?' He says they are. He tells me they are great for the job.

We head up the stairs, past the first-floor dining room. Shortly, he says, they will open four bedrooms so people can stay in his pub overnight. They also have two private dining rooms coming on stream. Right now, they are a mess of plaster and dangling lights, but if they end up anything like the rest of this pub, I'm sure they will be beautiful. I ask him how long he thinks it will take to get them finished. He thinks. 'A month or so?'

'Henry,' I say, 'I've got an idea . . .'

▶ **9. 'Piano Man', Billy Joel (1973)**

As an amateur musician who has somehow managed to get paid
for it, I have led a charmed life. When I play the piano in public, it
is almost always to an audience of people who, for good or ill, have
paid specifically to hear me do so. I have never been the background
music. I'm not complaining. It's lovely. It's hardly a spoiler to declare
I like being the centre of attention. But I am cringing a little, because
I know full well that most musicians haven't had the luxury of
always being listened to. There are gigs to be played because there
are bills to be paid. And to do it with skill, precision, lyricism and wit,
despite knowing that the people in the room may not be there for
you, takes huge reserves of talent, technique and forbearance.

Billy Joel's 1973 ballad captures what it is to be that musician in
the bar, the one providing a soundtrack to the lives of the regulars.
It has a clever rolling structure which is extremely satisfying to
play on the piano, and necessarily so, given the song's name. But
what really drives the whole thing home is the story-telling. He
sits and he watches and he listens. There's Paul, who's in real estate
and never got married; there's Davy, who has chosen a life in the
navy (we just about forgive him the blunt rhyme); and the waitress,
who is too smart for the menial job she has at the moment, so she's
'practising politics' on one of the guests down the bar.

This song just has to be on my playlist, because the jobbing pianist
in the bar–restaurant deserves to be celebrated. The bar gigs are not
always the ones they wanted. They learnt to play for an audience
who's listening. But they play equally well for those who aren't.
The greatest of them in London was a glorious man called Jimmy
Hardwick. He was employed to play piano at Joe Allen restaurant
when it opened in 1977 because, to secure a late licence, they needed
live music. Jimmy Hardwick was the live music. He played at the
restaurant until just a few weeks before his death in 2014, aged

eighty-eight. Jimmy could seemingly play anything, and during a long night at the piano would do so. His bible was the Great American Songbook, supplemented by those bits of the charts he deemed acceptable and every new musical as it opened. He would study those in detail so that the moment the lead actors came into the restaurant to eat – and they would eventually come into Joe's; every leading actor and actress did at one time or another – he could segue effortlessly into their tune. If you ate there often enough, you could work out who had walked through the door by which tune he played: if it was 'Big Spender', Shirley Bassey was in; if it was the theme from *Phantom of the Opera*, it was Michael Crawford. It was high camp, major jazz hands, and I adored it.

But what struck me most was Jimmy's playing: the way his hands lay across the keys, the effortless way in which he slipped from tune to tune, weaving melodies across one harmony to another. I quickly came to regard a real restaurant as one in which there was a piano player like Jimmy. It is part of the soundscape: the chatter of voices, the rattle of the cocktail shaker, the lyrical song of the piano. I still think that. I think better of a space with a piano in it because of the possibilities it presents. Things can happen in a room that is home to a piano.

I wish every restaurant had a piano man.

Supper

I decided to think big. After all, it's not often you stage your own last supper. Ideally, you should do it only once. That being so, it has to be good.

I went to my desk, opened a notebook, wrote the words 'Last Supper Guest List' at the top of a page, then sat back, my fingertips steepled as I thought. This, I decided, could be more than my last supper; it could also be the fantasy dinner party made real. It could be a dinner table stacked with the great and the good and the witty. The first name I wrote down was Barack Obama, because who wouldn't want him at their table? In brackets I wrote, '(And Michelle)'.

Next, Stanley Tucci. I like Stanley. We've met a couple of times because he now lives in London and his wife is a literary agent at the agency that represents me. He always seemed to like his food, and he'd made a great restaurant movie called *Big Night*. He's even co-authored a cookbook. He was definitely on the list.

Then Jeff Goldblum. Or my friend Jeff Goldblum, as I like to refer to him, casually. Look, we'd exchanged emails after I interviewed him and it was all friendly and good. He was brilliant at being Jeff Goldblum. I wanted him to do that at my fantasy dinner party.

How about Diana Krall, for when we had a moment around my piano? I could duet with her. Also, she'd probably bring her husband, Elvis Costello, and who wouldn't want that?

I put down Dita Von Teese because I'd always liked her whole retro, burlesque, sex-positive thing. But then I put a line through her name because I worried that it just made me look like a sad middle-aged perv. If you were going to be a sad middle-aged perv, one's last supper would be the right moment. The problem was, mine would be a faux last supper. I would still be alive the next day and I wasn't sure I could quite cope with Pat's eye-rolling over breakfast.

I scribbled a few more names: Stephen Fry, J. K. Rowling, Harry Connick Jr. This was going to be a killer dinner party. It would be the dinner party to end all dinner parties.

I'm not stupid. I recognised that this list presented logistical issues. How exactly was I going to get all these world-famous people to come to my house in south London for dinner? Quickly, I came up with a plan: I would get Netflix to pay for it. I would approach them with a proposal. I had not long before been a judge on the British-themed episode of *The Final Table*, the biggest TV cooking competition ever made, which Netflix dropped over Thanksgiving 2018. It was shot on the vast Sound Stage 27 of the Sony lot and involved twenty-four of the world's top chefs, a hydraulic judging platform that went ninety feet into the air, and me, alongside the British TV host Cat Deeley and the footballer-turned-pundit Gary Lineker. After the shoot, I'd been told by the producers that the executives at Netflix had loved my witty take-downs of these culinary superstars' attempts at reinventing the British cooked breakfast. I had described one cook's effort as the 'sausage of doom'. I could work a soundbite.

Apparently, what Netflix needed to really be convinced by a pitch was an idea of the image for the show screen, the picture you get as you scroll through the app. Mine would be a cracker: me sat at the head of my kitchen table, with Barack and Michelle Obama, Jeff Goldblum and Stanley Tucci laughing uproariously at one of my jokes. If Netflix got involved, maybe I could sell them on the idea of Dita Von Teese as well, just for a bit of glamour. I was thinking solely in terms of the visual. All these people would have to be flown into Britain on private jets, paid for by Netflix. They would have to be put up in hotel suites at Claridge's and the Savoy, paid for by Netflix. There would be shiny Mercedes S-Class limos idling at the kerb, paid for by Netflix.

I imagined the night of the dinner itself: those shiny black limos would draw up outside my house in London's inner suburbs; Obama's security detail would be stationed by my front wall, talking into their cuffs, while the neighbours looked on, trying to work out what the hell was going on over at Jay and Pat's place. It would be brilliant.

So anyway, Netflix passed on the idea. They told me they loved me 'as a talent', but that it was 'not the right creative fit for us at this time'. I took it on the chin.

In any case, the more I thought about it, the lousier an idea it seemed. I'd be on edge all evening. I'd be desperately worried that Barack and Michelle weren't having a good time. Plus, when I looked at the list of dishes I had compiled, a stone-cold fear overcame me. I could inflict this on my friends, but not on complete strangers, and especially not on world-famous ones.

I drew up a second list, this time of people I actually knew and cared about. Then I sent them all an email. The subject line read: 'I'm eating my last supper on earth and I need your help.'

Here's the email:

Hello.

For the last year I have been working on a book about my last meal on earth. It's called *Jay Rayner's Last Supper: One Meal, A Lifetime in the Making.* It's built around the idea that last suppers are wasted on those who are eligible for them: the terminally ill, the suicidal, the condemned. So I'm going to have mine now while I still appear to be alive. I go out in pursuit of the ingredients, using memoir to explain why they are significant, musing on mortality as we do in our middle years, and telling a few other stories besides.

It always had to finish with the last supper. Or *a* last supper. I thought about trying to come up with 12 disciples but even my god complex couldn't quite cope with that. I thought of trying to wrangle a bunch of seriously famous people, so it became a real-life version of a fantasy dinner party, but I realised a) it would be a nightmare to organise and b) the ones I really wanted wouldn't come anyway.

Thus, I've decided to invite you lot instead.

The guest list was forty names long because I expected many people would not be available. Almost all of them said yes.

On the corner of Royal Park Road and Brudenell Grove, in the Hyde Park area of Leeds, just north of the university, there was once a bottle shop called Glenton's. Google Maps still records its location, the shop now a digital ghost, even though Street View told me it had long since been converted back into the terraced house it originally was. It was run by Mr Glenton and his wife – I never knew their first names – and was a vital public service for the thousands of students who lived in the cheap, damp, slug-slicked, red-bricked accommodation crammed in around it. Glenton's was open all hours. They were willing to cash cheques and had a fine selection of the very cheapest, roughest wines, beers and spirits. I was a regular. For the most part I bought bottles of Thunderbird Blue Label, the self-described 'American Classic' produced in Modesto, California, by the vast drinks manufacturer Ernest Gallo. The website bumwine.com, which is dedicated to cheap booze brands favoured by those who are down on their luck and care more about cost than finesse, isn't hugely polite about it. 'If your taste buds are shot, and you need to get trashed with a quickness, then "T-bird" is the drink for you,' it says. This was a reasonable description of my needs as a student. I recall it cost less than £1.50 a bottle back in 1986.

If the drink choices at this event of mine needed to tell my story, Thunderbird was a good place to start. As a student on a budget I drank a lot of it. Hence, as my friends trooped into the upstairs dining room of the Hero of Maida pub on a dark late-November evening, they were handed a tumbler of the stuff over ice. A number of them sipped it, then looked at me and said, 'What in God's name is this?' I told them and explained the night's drink options were likely to get worse before they got better. One friend from Italy said it reminded her of sweet vermouth. I could see where she was coming from, though the impact of Thunderbird is cumulative. You sip sweet vermouth and move on. You slug Thunderbird all night, until your teeth are aching from the sweetness, and your head feels like it has separated from your body. We were being so much more civilised.

Dave Lewis, the saxophonist in my quartet, wandered up to me, his brow furrowed.

'Why do I know the name Thunderbird?' he said. 'It sounds like a lyric.'

I said, 'It is a lyric. Remember "Sweet Gene Vincent"?'

Dave's eyes widened. Released back in 1977, 'Sweet Gene Vincent' was the second single released by Ian Dury and the Blockheads, taken from their album *New Boots and Panties*, and with a first verse that memorably rhymes 'decline' with 'Thunderbird wine'. Dury died in 2000, but the Blockheads continue to perform his songs, and when he isn't playing with us – or any of the other outfits he is part of or leads – Dave is their saxophonist. 'I'll be playing it in a couple of days' time,' he said. Then he looked in his glass. 'I'm driving, so I can only have one drink. Should I wait for something better to come along?' I said he probably should.

I looked around the room. A fair slice of the *Kitchen Cabinet* crew, who had seen me through the multiple pig fests, had come. It was right they got to find out what final pig choice I had made. Over in the corner was Danielle Peck, now a highly regarded television producer and photographer, and my oldest friend. We had met at Contact, the Sunday-night Jewish youth club, when we were both thirteen years old, and used to make raids on McDonald's together for chips. Susan Jeffreys, one of the very first magazine editors in London to have commissioned me, was here with her artist husband, Phil Hood. There were friends from university and a bunch of musicians, among them Ian Shaw. He and I liked to tell people that we had first met in a sauna, which was true, though it was the one at Brixton's local recreation centre rather than anything more thrilling. Only later did I clock he was Britain's foremost male jazz singer, and when I started gigging, he became a very supportive close friend. I was certain I could make good use of his voice tonight. I had hired a keyboard. They couldn't get a proper piano up the steep stairs, so we'd made do with a digital grand. Robert Rickenberg had brought his bass. I had printed out the playlist, along with lyric sheets for 'Ghost Town' and 'Love Cats'. Those two, I had decided, would be a group singalong, with help from Ian and others.

Both of my sons were here with Pat, who was wearing the green and gold brocade jacket she had made to get married in back in 1992. I sipped my Thunderbird and scanned the room. Almost all the people I had wanted to be here had come to my last supper. Except for one.

I start with the simplest of questions.

'How are you?'

Jerry Burden purses his lips, looks down at his mug of tea and says, 'I'm not too good at the moment.'

It is both an honest answer and an act of quiet understatement, but that's the Jerry I have known these past thirty years. I met his wife Sarah first. It was the late 1980s, and she was training to be a teacher with a mutual friend. We were at an irritating house party in the West Sussex hills. Sarah, a striking blonde six-footer, came striding majestically across the lawns. There were a lot of people at the party pretending they were recreating the movie *The Big Chill*. Sarah had a precise way of communicating that she thought they were mostly knobs, just with a frown. She later brought Jerry – short for Jeremy but never that to me, unless I was looking for a child-like admonishment – with her to a friend's Burns Night celebration in 1989. He had finished a politics degree at Essex University and was training to be a nurse, at a time when male nurses were few and far between.

He had a thick Northern Irish accent, laughed quickly, was intense about Labour Party politics, which interested me, and football, which did not. He could wield your first name in conversation like a newly sharpened pencil.

Sarah, Jerry, Pat and I became friends, in the way of couples with too much in common. In the 1990s we survived the ravages of infertility together, theirs thankfully over much quicker than ours. Their twins Molly and Todd were born in 1996, followed a few years later by Edith. We went on summer holidays together, to America and Spain, our five combined kids growing up side by side. Some of them even went to the same schools. We bonded early over a love of good food, especially things that could be done with pig. We swapped novels we liked and ranted about ones that irritated us. We watched each other's careers move and change. Sarah became head of English at her school. Jerry swapped from nursing to NHS management and rose to the most senior ranks. We spent so many Christmases together we lost count.

On Christmas Day 2017 Jerry told us that he was booked in for a colonoscopy the day after Boxing Day. Few men get into their fifties without having a doctor shove a well-lubricated camera up their bottom to inspect their bowel. I'd had two, because I'm greedy like that. But I'd been stone-cold certain each time that I was fine. My late mother once said there were only two sorts of people: those who had piles and those who were about to get them. I'd been both, and nobody has ever died of piles. Still, it was worth a look.

There was something about the way Jerry alluded to the symptoms responsible for his referral over Christmas lunch which suggested the outcome was not so certain. They told him on the day of the procedure that they had found a primary cancer in his bowel. Shortly afterwards, he had various scans, which revealed it had spread to his liver. He started a complicated round of chemotherapy, at the end of which he was told that his condition was terminal. The cancer was inoperable. A transplant wasn't an option. He had between eight and twelve months to live.

So how was Jerry?

Jerry was dying.

I had already started investigating the jaunty idea of last suppers and what I might have for mine before Jerry's initial diagnosis. For a good few months afterwards, I had assumed that he would go through treatment, however brutal, but that he would survive. So did he. I could get on with writing my narrative, full of gallows humour, full of reflections on death and appetite and the unashamed joys of the overfilled table. But it became harder and harder to do this. Shortly after they learnt he was terminal, Sarah and Jerry had asked us over to their house to tell us in person what was happening. We shared suppers together after that, because we always had. We listened to the narrative and offered support to both of them as best we could.

I like to think of myself, at base, as a reporter, and yet I was failing to report something that was not just significant to me, but hugely relevant. I told Jerry that to write this book without his story in it wouldn't just make it incomplete, it would be a big fat lie. He agreed, albeit uncertainly. With customary modesty, he thanked me for thinking it was important. We made a date.

By the time we talked, he was on morphine to manage the pain from his diseased liver and anti-emetics to manage the symptoms, a cocktail of drugs with various side effects, including drowsiness. Mornings were best, I was told by Sarah, who now managed the diary. We sat across the table in my kitchen, and he told me about his most recent meeting with his consultant. He'd recently taken an eight-week holiday from chemotherapy and, although further treatment was an option, he wasn't minded to go back on it.

'People talk about extending life,' Jerry said, 'but, Jay, what I'm not seeking to do is extend dying.'

That made it sound like he was comfortable with the idea of death. He agreed that was so. He had been reading a lot recently, he said, and had come across ideas which chimed with his own. 'Death is associated with fear and horror. But rather than bringing pain and suffering, death actually brings comfort, clarity, truth and compassion. I wrote a poem – a very bad poem – in which I talk about death holding my hand.' I thanked him for not making me read the poem.

What strikes me about all this is the lack of bitterness. I have heard Jerry be angry. He has raged about bureaucratic mismanagement of the health service that has been his life's work, at the stupidity of politicians on all sides and injustices which needed to be righted. He had always put me to shame by taking action. He was treasurer of his local Labour Party, had paced out the streets of his neighbourhood delivering leaflets and knocking on doors. If I wasn't sure what I thought about a political moment, I asked Jerry what he thought. He was brilliant at clarity, forged in anger. Now anger seemed to be absent.

He agreed. 'I also wrote about that. Why wasn't I cross and angry? Why wasn't I angry about not being diagnosed earlier? Why didn't they get the chemo right first time?' He answered his own question. 'Being cross and angry takes up a lot of energy, and I don't have much energy, so it's futile. Also, I want to focus my energy on projecting love.' That wasn't him trying to make everyone else feel better, he said. It wasn't the sloganising of the greetings card. 'I'm just happier and more content that way.'

I asked if there had been any sign of the divine in these last few months. Had God revealed himself? Sarah may have been a vicar's daughter, but a suspicion of organised religion had been something else that had united the four of us. Jerry grew up in a Unionist family in Northern Ireland. He once told me that he arrived at university wearing a parka with a Union flag on the back. He knew all there was to know about the impact of religion and tribalism on people. Experience working on a kibbutz in Israel and witnessing the political battles on campus in the 1980s had shifted his politics dramatically.

'I've always listened to church choir music because I find it comforting. But no, no sign of God.' And no, he did not have any time for the endless military metaphors around cancers: the narrative of personal battles, which suggest that those who die of it were somehow just not equal to the challenge. 'I'm not fighting cancer. I'm living with it.'

Although he had become a manager in the NHS, it was his work as a nurse that informed what he did. He said it had been a privilege to hold not only babies moments after their birth, but also the hands of people as they died.

'I believe in a good death,' he said.

'What does that mean?'

'No one jumping on my chest. Dying in the appropriate place, which may not be home. It may be the hospice. With liver cancer, the death will be slow and insidious.' Sarah and his kids will need a break, he said. He had made a detailed death plan. Jerry had been meticulous.

'Even though I know I will die, probably in the next year, I don't have a terrible foreboding. I just wonder how it will be.' He looked over my shoulder into the garden. 'I keep wanting to say the phrase "I am a dying man". I wouldn't go around saying it at home because that wouldn't be fair. But it's quite nice to say it here. It's got a ring to it.'

He is indeed a dying man, but he is not yet dead. Sarah had given up her job a few months before so the two of them could spend time together. They had travelled up to Scotland to see Edith at university and then down England's east coast. As they travelled, they sent me photographs from the road of all the restaurants they were eating at. They were based on my reviews: the glorious East Pier Smokehouse, on the fractured coast at St Monans, in Fife, where they serve hot smoked mackerel with rugged salads or grilled lobster with butter, in boxes of pure cardboard; a bistro in Cromer called No. 1, which made mushy-pea fritters with mint jelly and a killer ramen; the Farm Cafe in Suffolk, which did one of the best cooked English breakfasts for miles around.

'Why wouldn't we use your reviews? You've been doing it so long you've got quite the body of work now.' I suggested he was eating his own last supper in part-work. He said that might be so.

It always came back to the food with us. Regularly, our two families would settle down for an early-evening supper together. These weren't dinner parties. They were just dinner. Or, as Jerry put it, 'In by six, out by eight. Marvellous.' We knew what each of us liked: deep, long-cooked tomato and chorizo stews; a porchetta of rolled pork belly and loin, stuffed with fennel seeds and garlic and lemon zest; beef stews boasting the contents of a whole bottle of good red wine; chocolate cakes with squidgy middles, with lightly sour dollops of crème fraîche on the side. 'Once we worked out that you were a tactile eater and messy shirts come with the territory, we were sorted,' Jerry said.

A few months before, Peter Hannan had sent me a huge box of his product from Northern Ireland: packs of his sausages, a few thick-cut sirloin steaks and two huge bacon rib joints. There was far too much for us, so I passed one of the joints over to Sarah and Jerry. The day they cooked it photographs arrived on my phone of the meat carved in thick pink slices. To say thank you for taking the time to talk to me, I'd located another one at Fortnum & Mason, the only shop in London to sell it retail. Jerry enthused, as I knew he would.

I asked him what his last supper would be. 'I'd revert to type,' he said. 'One of those bacon joints, potatoes, cabbage. Keep it simple.'

While there is no God in my universe, there are certain Jewish rituals that appeal to me. One of those is the uniquely Anglo-Jewish tradition of wishing the recently bereaved 'a long life'. Finding the right words in the face of death can be tricky. These phrases help, even though it may not be what the mourner wants to hear. You are telling them that while the person they loved has gone, they are required to live on. It is Sarah who, after thirty-five years, will be required to live on without Jerry. She's the one I will wish long life to, along with Molly, Todd and Edith. But looking across the table it is Jerry I want to bestow the blessing on. Or at the very least, I want to wish him a longer life. I don't want him to go.

He is on another path. 'Sometimes I just want to get on with it,' he says.

* * *

I tap a knife against my glass so that it rings out, and eventually the rush and bubble of conversation subsides. The crowd turns to me. 'This', I say, 'is not my last supper, because I will still be here in the morning.'

It's a necessary thing to say. Despite initially accepting the invitation, Jerry is not here tonight. I had seen him the night before for dinner, at the end of what had been a tough week, complete with ambulance trips to hospital and a reorganising of his morphine supply. He wasn't up to a night out like this, and anyway, he said quietly, he wasn't sure it was the right place for him to be. Sarah had come with Molly and Todd, and I wasn't about to do a bunch of clumsy death jokes for their benefit.

Instead, I say, 'You will, however, all get to eat your way through my life so far.'

Pulling this together has not been straightforward. I have had to get food items couriered here; three of them have come from Northern Ireland. Wines had to be located and ordered. The choice of venue was much easier. Henry Harris was obviously the right man for the last course because he had made the first version of the dessert I had chosen, the one I had tried back at his restaurant, Racine. He also shares many of my tastes. I described the menu to him, and he laughed. He kept laughing. He was my man. Plus, the high-ceilinged room was available. They laid it out with three long tables, draped in crisp linen tablecloths. The glassware shined. Candles guttered.

We could begin.

Oysters

Three days before the big night, I received an email from the courier company. It announced that the oysters were due to arrive on the night of the event. That wasn't the plan. We had arranged for them to be there three days earlier, which meant the dinner would still fall before their use-by date. I was determined there would not be a repeat of the disappointment at the wine dinner. And now they were saying they were scheduled to arrive literally minutes before the dinner was due to kick off, which meant that if there was a delay, we wouldn't have them at all. They reassured us it was an administrative thing, a statement of the very latest they could be delivered. The next day, Henry texted to say he had them. Andrew Rooney's famed oysters had arrived.

And now here they were, creamy and glistening on the half shell, bedded down on crushed ice. The waiters placed them on a series of round spindle frames placed along the tables. They were everything I had hoped for and a little bit more. Rooney had boasted quietly to me about the size of the meat hidden away inside the shells, and he wasn't wrong. They were substantial, but not in a cloying, bullying way. They were the taste of the sea and memories of New Orleans. They were lunch with my old mum, when I was a child, and dinner in restaurants that sparkled, once I was old enough to pay the bill myself. They were a slap around the chops and an intense refresher. They were a reminder that I was alive.

Or at least they were to me. Some of my friends, the good, cultured, tasteful ones, swooned and gasped and declared them the best oysters they'd ever eaten. Quite right too. Others refused to eat them at all; they looked at them as if they were a piece of art they knew they were supposed to admire but didn't quite understand. For them, we had also laid on plates of mustardy celeriac remoulade with sweet-salty folds of pink Bayonne ham. For the non-meat-eaters, we'd made sure the two items were kept separate.

As the oysters started to slip down, I rose and tapped my glass again to announce the second wine. Back in the early 1990s, I said, I had decided it was time to develop a taste in wine beyond Thunderbird. Back then the thing had been New World Chardonnays, from Chile and Peru. 'Big oaked ones. We thought they were cool. They were so oaked they tasted like you were sucking on a log.' We drank them and felt like *K'nossers*, which my mother always said 'was Yiddish for connoisseurs'. In the sense that it was a choice based on taste rather than purely on cost, there was something to this. It was just quite bad taste. They were, by their nature, young wines that did not benefit from ageing. Indeed, any ageing might have softened them, rendering them subtle and crisp. That wouldn't do at all. They needed to be unsubtle and heavy. They would need to be modern versions of the past. I consulted the wine writer Olly Smith, who has many claims to fame, including being the lead writer on the stop-motion children's animated classic *Pingu*. He directed me to Montes Reserva Chardonnay 2016, from Chile's Central Valley.

One sip and I knew it was the thing. Doubtless somebody, somewhere thought this was classy. Once upon a time that person would have been me. To me, it now tasted like a timber yard. It tasted of bad ideas, vengeance and profit margin. But it also tasted of myself when young. I told the room to think of me as a young man in search of a modicum of good taste. I then said they should drink up and promised there was better to come.

Pat, Dave, Robert and I ran through 'Ain't Misbehavin'" from the playlist, a song we used to gig, then I handed piano duties over to Joe Thompson, from the Ivy Club, for 'Ghost Town' by the Specials, because I didn't know it. Neither did he, as it happened, but no matter. Robert had worked up a chord chart. We crashed through it like a stand of football supporters trying to intimidate the opposing team's fans. Pat led the lyric, with Ian dropping into a growl for the reggae toasting elements. If Jerry Dammers and Terry Hall of the original Specials line-up had been there, they would have had grounds to sue. Everything was going as well as could be expected.

Snails, bread and butter

In the 1970s a greedy teenager from Lancashire who wanted to be a cook went to work for a French chef called Yves Champeau at La

Normandie, in Birtle. The teenager's name was Simon Hopkinson – Hoppy to his friends – and he would go on to become regarded as one of the great chefs of Britain's late-twentieth-century restaurant revolution. One of the books he co-wrote, *Roast Chicken and Other Stories*, was eventually declared the most useful cookbook of all time, in a poll of chefs and food writers. In the mid-1980s he opened his first restaurant, Hilaire. Working alongside him in the kitchen was Henry Harris, who in 1987 went with him to open Bibendum on London's Fulham Road. It was part-owned by the wealthy design guru Terence Conran, who adored classic French restaurants and wanted one he could call home. Bibendum was shiny, polished and nose-bleedingly expensive. It served the best versions of familiar French dishes. Accordingly, on the menu was escargots de Bourgogne, made to the recipe Hoppy had first learnt at La Normandie. He later included the recipe in his cookbook *The Prawn Cocktail Years* (written with Lindsey Bareham), which celebrated the great food of a decade it had become fashionable to laugh at.

'It's still the best snail recipe,' Henry told me. 'Obviously, butter and garlic, though the garlic must be chopped rather than crushed or it burns. There are breadcrumbs in there and a dash of Pernod.' The problem was that Henry had only half a dozen dimpled snail platters and nowhere near enough tongs. We needed more. I called up L'Escargot on Greek Street, in Soho. They quickly agreed to loan us what we needed.

The snails arrived at the table fizzing and spitting from the oven, the shells under a sea-green, garlicky, parsley-flecked crust. A few people flinched. It turns out that some people don't eat snails. I find this baffling, but what can you do? I pointed those people to the burnished crust of the open-crumbed sourdough from the Brick House Bakery and the daffodil-yellow whorls of Abernethy butter. One friend sitting near me stuffed a lump of thickly buttered bread in her mouth. She turned to me, her jaw slack, and said, 'This butter.'

I said, 'I know.'

The snail refuseniks were not a problem because we had Dan. It's obvious that if you are the child of a restaurant critic, you are likely to have been exposed to a wider range of foods than most. My younger son had not been taken by all of those he had met. He hadn't touched the oysters, for example. But oh, how he loves snails. In northern Spain one summer I had watched him pick through dozens of them, pulling out the meat, picking at the crusted edges. He seemed absorbed by the process as much as by the taste. Now he set to work, demolishing tray after tray of Henry and Hoppy's finest. If there were any unclaimed snails left down the long table, they were passed towards us, where Dan received them gratefully. A heap of empty shells built up on his plate, until we gave him an overflow, and still he went on. This probably sounds like the bragging of an overly proud father. That's exactly what it is.

My boy!

We drank more of the terrible wine, mopped at the ponds of garlic butter with the Brick House bread, which was perfectly engineered for the job, and bashed through the playlist, going from Stephen Sondheim's 'Ladies Who Lunch' to a Latin-inflected 'Night and Day' to a raucous 'Cantaloupe Island'. Ian took over vocals for 'All of Me', the song which had got me started as a gigging musician. I had got an award-winning jazz singer to perform for free. Result.

Pig, chips and salad

A dinner party is never just about the night itself. It is also about the anticipation. It is weeks of fun. I play out particular moments in my head, adjust them for maximum impact and adjust them again. I imagine how my friends will react to the food and wine choices I have made, what it will make them think of me. Given what I do for a living I feel a certain weight of expectation upon my shoulders, which I enjoy. Journalists are, generally, amateurs who reach for authority by faking it over time. Each story we research provides instant, if shallow, expertise. We keep faking it, keep acquiring that shallow expertise, until the accretion of experience means we aren't really faking it any more. I'd had more hot dinners than they'd had hot dinners. They had the right to expect something good.

This pig course moment had to be good. I'd thought about this one in more detail than any other. I was sure it would deliver. Just to make sure, just to give it real theatre, I hired in eight cloches and the platters to go with them. I do love an old-fashioned bit of silverware. Then I emailed Peter Hannan in Northern Ireland and told him what I needed. He was eager to oblige.

With the snail debris cleared, the cloches were laid along the table in pairs. I took the crowd through the pig-eating fests that had been part of the story: from suckling pig at Pearl Liang to Tim Anderson's Japanese journey round a pig at Nanban to the celebration of extremities at St John. I got those who were present at each one to raise their hands. I wanted this to feel like a group effort, even though it wasn't. Finally, I said, 'But all of those, while brilliant, were just a little complicated for an event like this. Lift the cloches.'

As the lids came off, the room roared with laughter. One platter was laid with thick-cut sliced white bread; the other with Hannan's finest cured product, both streaky and back, cooked to crisp and bronzed.

'Make yourself a bacon sandwich.'

It had to be a bacon sandwich. A bacon sandwich makes everything better. It is soft and it is crunch. It is hot animal fat, just on the edge of melting on the tongue. There is salt and, with the right loaf, just a little sweetness. We had the right loaf, from a bakery called Bread Ahead. You can have tomato ketchup or brown sauce if you wish, for acidity. We had made both available. And yes, of course, we had options for non-meat-eaters, though I know many, many vegetarians and vegans who have been drawn from their own moral path by the smell of a bacon sandwich. It is food for when you are drunk and for when you are exhausted and for when it just happens to be Tuesday.

It is early-morning food and late-night food and hangover food and 'please make everything better' food. Even a bad bacon sandwich is good, and these were very good: we had asked Hannan for rindless bacon so nothing could get caught in people's teeth, and for it to be smoked, because why wouldn't you, if you had the choice? It deepens and intensifies the flavour.

I moved across to sit at a new table and made my own. This whole event was my answer to the death-row-meal question. But, as I layered a piece of bread with two pieces of burnished back bacon and then a couple of streaky rashers for extra crunch, I concluded that were I forced to choose one thing to go out with, a single food item, this would be it. Bring me a bacon sandwich, because with one of these in my hands everything else falls away.

We have bowls of rustling chips made from the Pierre Koffmann range of potatoes, and they are indeed as good as I had been promised. They are that ideal balance of crisp exterior and fluffy interior. They are not quite up there with those from Ken's, near my house, but we'd never have been able to have those here. We couldn't have transported them across town, and they needed to be made at Ken's shop. I was determined not to let the search for the perfect and the unachievable be the enemy of the good.

There were bowls of green salad, made using Kressi vinegar. That afternoon I'd shown Henry and his sous chef how it should be prepared. 'To be honest,' I said, adding two capfuls of vinegar to the olive oil and sliced spring onions at the bottom of a stainless-steel bowl, 'it's barely a recipe. It's just a thing.' Happily, they agreed it was a very nice thing.

To go with this there was one more wine. It was a nice wine. It was a properly lovely wine, and I'd bought more of it than anything else. In the early 1990s I had been sent by *Cosmopolitan* magazine on an organised press trip to Alsace-Lorraine to write a travel piece. There were twenty of us journalists, bussed around from Strasbourg into the countryside and out again. I ate my first Michelin-starred meals on that trip, at Au Crocodile and Restaurant Buerehiesel. There were quenelles of pike and platters of choucroute: sauerkraut laid with garlicky pork sausages and salted belly. There were intense chocolate desserts, executed with obsessiveness and precision.

One afternoon we were taken out to Hugel & Fils, a winery in the town of Riquewihr. It was founded in the seventeenth century by Hans Ulrich Hugel, a Swiss refugee from the Thirty Years' War. We were given a short lecture on their wines and introduced to their finest product, poured from long, dark-green, slim-necked bottles of the sort that I had once associated with overly sweet German wines. The Gewürztraminer was deep and floral. But it was the Riesling that stayed with me: it was crisp and bright while still being aromatic. It was like nothing I had ever drunk before. It was structured without being bullying. It was refreshing. It was the taste of adulthood achieved. After that, I started looking for Hugel on wine lists. I ordered a lot of it, when I could afford it. Tonight we had ten bottles of the 2012. It was the single most expensive item of the evening. I told the room the story and reassured them that this, at last, was the good stuff. I told them it went exceptionally well with a bacon sandwich. Dave Lewis thanked me and filled his glass. This was the one he had been waiting for.

And there I sat, surrounded by the rush and clamour of happy people talking and eating. I had chips. I had salad. I had a majestic bacon sandwich. I had a great wine. I didn't want any of this to stop, ever.

Dessert, water and one for the road

Somewhere deep into my second bacon sandwich I noticed a bottle standing lonely and unmolested on the table. It was made of clear glass and had a label that was half yellow, half a dull peach colour. In gold lettering was the year '1650'. It was the Châteldon sparkling mineral water, Louis XIV's favourite, the one I had decided was nicer to drink than all the other sparkling mineral waters I had ever drunk. I had been thrilled by the bubble size and viscosity.

Except here it was on the table and I hadn't even noticed it was there. I hadn't mentioned it. I poured myself a glass, took a swig and shrugged. It was just a bloody glass of fizzy water. I looked around the room. Some people were drinking it, some weren't. Absolutely no one was paying it the slightest bit of attention. I'd paid £70 for two cases, and that was with a discount. I had sweated and fretted over every detail, had imagined it all in context. This element now seemed completely pointless. There was, it seemed, a limit to just how interested and obsessed I could be by food and drink. I decided this was a good thing.

No matter. It was getting late, and we had the last bits of the playlist to complete. We took a quick break for a rendition of 'Come Fly with Me', then I forced everyone to sing 'Love Cats' from the song sheets. I wondered what the regular punters in the bar of the pub downstairs were making of this noise. Then I stopped wondering and, fuelled by Thunderbird and over-oaked Chardonnay and Hugel Riesling, carried on singing.

I had made huge efforts to get the right dessert. I had tried Mont Blancs in Paris and Tokyo and London. I had consulted recipes and methods. I had studied the history. It was one of those searches that ended right back where it began. It ended with the man who made the first one that had so enthralled me. The one he now served here, at the Hero of Maida, was even better. The Mont Blanc is a very simple idea: meringue, whipped cream, sweetened chestnut purée. And yet these three things combined could produce a hugely varied set of outcomes. I had long said that I was not seeking to create the perfect meal. It was not meant to be balanced or elegant. It was merely meant to be mine.

But as far as I was concerned, the Mont Blanc Henry Harris now served me really was perfect. It was better than any of those I had tried in Tokyo, including the good one sold by the Angelina concession there. It was better than any I had eaten before, and I have eaten many. The meringue had a crisp shell that gave way to a soft, chewy centre. The cream was whipped, but only until there was a lightness and cloud-like softness to it. It was about coolness, not the mouth-coating ballast of dairy fats. Finally, there was the indulgence of the lightly alcoholic chestnut purée, flavoured with a little Armagnac. A spoon bearing all three parts was a delightful, sigh-worthy thing.

Anna, my Italian friend, who had compared Thunderbird to sweet vermouth, looked at me, slightly damp-eyed.

'My grandmother used to make this,' she said. 'Thank you.'

I said it was my pleasure. It was all my pleasure.

There was one last drink, a way to toast my late parents and to recall the child I once was. I placed a bottle of advocaat and a bottle of cherry brandy on the bar and poured a blood and pus for as many as wanted it. The deep red of the brandy swirled and spider-webbed its way through the thick, yellow, boozy custard. I handed a glass to Dan, who took a sip and laughed, in the way I'm sure I did when I was his age and younger. It was soothing and rich. It was the way to settle ourselves after the night we'd had.

Finally, I sat down at the piano and both played and sang Billy Joel's 'Piano Man'. It was the sort of song we would never play as the quartet. The line between jazz and pop is often extremely artificial, but we all knew which side of the line this song sat on. I was also never likely to sing at a gig. Why would I do that when I had Pat?

But tonight it felt right that I should take on the job. As it happened, to my surprise, I did not have to sing it alone. I had printed out lyric sheets for both 'Ghost Town' and 'Love Cats' because I was sure most people would want to join in but wouldn't be quite sure of the words. I didn't imagine anybody would actually know 'Piano Man'. But then some songs just secrete themselves into the depths of our memories, don't they? Whether you want to recall them or not, whether you think you know them or not, they are there. The entire room sang along with me. We ended with a throaty, unforced cheer.

My last supper was done. I kissed a lot of cheeks goodnight. I thanked them for coming, for indulging me, for helping me finish what needed to be finished. I thanked Sarah, Molly and Todd for being there, and told them to send my love to Jerry back at home. We hugged. I sent Pat off ahead of me with our boys as I stayed on to settle the bill.

Zoe Laughlin, the *Kitchen Cabinet* colleague who had given me moral guidance on eating animals during the suckling pig dinner at Pearl Liang – all the hypocrisy I can live with – looked at me intently. She said, 'That was a great evening. If you die tomorrow, we'll all be furious.'

I told her I would try my very best to stay alive.

Jerry died in the early hours of Christmas Day 2018. He was fifty-six years old. It was not quite the good death he had hoped for. There was too much pain, both physical and emotional, for that. Nor was it slow and insidious, though that may have been a blessing of kinds. The end came quickly. During his last month the reporter in me made a mental note to find out what his last meal was. I told myself I would be doing so for the sake of completeness. I was telling his story, and that required detail. In the immediate aftermath of his death, however, nothing seemed more irrelevant than what he may or may not have eaten for his last meal. Instead, as we had often done during his illness, we fired up the stove and continued cooking, so that Sarah, Edith, Molly and Todd sometimes had dinner in the freezer, ready to heat up. It would be one less thing for them to think about.

A couple of days after Christmas, Sarah came around to collect the filled boxes of coq au vin and meatballs in tomato sauce that Pat had cooked for her. She sat at the kitchen table and, over a cup of tea, told us about his last days. 'I almost texted you while he was still alive to tell you about his last meal,' she said, unprompted.

'What was it?'

'Bolognese with a bit of pasta. That was his last full meal, a few days before.'

It is easy, in these circumstances, to imbue the smallest of things with significance, but this did have something of the pleasingly familiar and the domestic about it. Sarah had shown us her method for ragu the summer we all shared a house on Cape Cod, a decade earlier. It is essentially browned minced beef and lamb, with chopped tomatoes and an awful lot of good red wine, cooked down for hour after hour. I remember Jerry in the kitchen of our summer rental, grinning with anticipation, telling us just how good it would be, as long as we had the patience. He wasn't wrong. Sarah's ragu was deep and rich and savoury. A version of that recipe became ours.

And that had been his last supper. It wasn't symbolic. It wasn't a statement. It was just what Sarah had decided to cook that evening because she thought he might like it. I hope Jerry found it comforting.

One night, eighteen months after I had first been referred to the sleep clinic at Guy's Hospital, I sat on the edge of my bed and adjusted a set of straps designed to go over my head. I tightened the Velcro fastenings, then slipped them over my ludicrous hair so that the soft plastic mask they were holding fitted snugly over my nose. A long, transparent, corrugated plastic tube was clipped onto the end of the mask which led to a black, wedge-shaped box sitting on my bedside table. Inserted into one side of the wedge was a clear plastic humidifier that I had earlier filled with filtered water. A small screen on the front told me that the water had now warmed up. I checked the arrangement of straps was in place, slipped under the duvet, lay my head down on the pillow, turned off the bedside light, then reached across and pressed the button on top of the wedge.

On the screen a dial briefly showed air pressure rising swiftly from one to four (out of eight). Not that I needed the screen to tell me what was happening, because I could feel the air pushing up the tube and up my nose. It was a light, rather pleasant sensation, like a cool wind. Weirdly, for reasons I still don't understand, it forced me to keep my mouth closed. If the tube was off my face, the noise was significant: a fierce, rushing blast of air. Sealed to my face by the soft flanges on the nasal cup, it was all but silent. I closed my eyes and gently drifted off to sleep. I did not snore. Pat stayed in the bed alongside me, undisturbed.

It had taken months of fitful, fractured sleep and wretched days on the edge of exhaustion, uncertain when I might all but pass out, for me to conclude that something had to change. Finally, I contacted my consultant, Brian Kent, and said the NightBalance device was not working for me, not well enough anyway. He prescribed me an automatic positive air pressure (APAP) machine, the wedge that I had just switched on. It senses your breathing during sleep and responds to episodes of apnoea, when the airways attempt to close down and you stop breathing. By increasing the pressure, it keeps those airways open. Because they do not close, you do not stop breathing. And because you do not stop breathing, your body does not wake you repeatedly. I had avoided asking for one of the machines for many months. From what I had seen online, they appeared clumsy and obtrusive and extremely medical. The thought of them made me feel in some way frail and disabled. I felt like that until I realised that my dysfunctional sleep was genuinely disabling. It made me less able than I could be during waking hours. Sometimes you just have to wait until the medical problem is worse than any solution might be.

That very first night the APAP machine worked exactly as I was told it would. It stopped my airways closing. It stopped my body from mimicking the early signs of death. And when I awoke the next morning I felt refreshed for the first time in many months, perhaps even years. I didn't drift off to sleep during the day, let alone on the sofa in front of the television. My body might have been ageing. Bits of me might have become saggy and loose. But I was not dead. Not yet.

The day after my last supper, I carried a heavy canvas bag filled with cast-iron snail trays and stainless-steel tongs up to Soho and returned them to L'Escargot. Afterwards, I trudged through the rain to Chinatown's Gerrard Street, and the Four Seasons. They seated me in the basement, a utilitarian space of cream-coloured walls and strip lights. They poured me a small, handle-less cup of hot jasmine tea and gave me one of their thick laminated menus. As ever, its plastic edges were frayed and cracked, and the cover was crying out for a wipe-down with a wet cloth. I didn't object to any of this. It is the way of things at the Four Seasons.

I had been replaying the events of the night before over and over in my head, much as I had imagined them ahead of time. I had already received many messages from my friends telling me what fun it had been. They weren't wrong. Partly, I ascribed that to the live music. There is nothing like talented musicians working their way through great tunes right in front of you to make a room come alive. I had played too, which always made me happy. As to the menu, I had kept my word. It had not been the Platonic ideal of anything. Even if the Mont Blanc had been perfect, as a meal it really wasn't. It was bizarre. Both oysters and snails? A bacon sandwich as a main course? And, oh, that terrible Chardonnay. I had spent over a year chasing my own appetites, investigating the foods that made me feel most like myself, and the meal that resulted from it had been one huge, unbalanced bloody mess.

Then again, perhaps that messiness was a virtue? If you really were going to shape your last meal, surely you would just throw any sense of good taste away and do just that which pleased you? I had done what pleased me. I had told some stories. I had found out a little more about myself. The only problem was that the end result was so damn good, so much fun, that I didn't want any of it to stop. I didn't want it to be the last of anything. I certainly didn't feel any sense of closure.

I picked up the menu and, as I often did when I came here, began flicking through the pages, with their garish pictures in oversaturated colours. I could have stewed lamb brisket with dry beancurd in hot pot. I could have braised aubergine with minced pork, or double-cooked belly pork with preserved vegetables. I could have the mapo beancurd with minced beef.

But then I turned to the page headed 'BBQ dishes', and there they were, the shiny pictures of Cantonese roasted meats that always called to me: of belly pork with crackling like glass, of char sui pork the worrying colour of a dying sunset, of darkly lacquered birds, many and various. I loved these pictures. Just looking at them made me happy. When the waitress came, I gave her my usual order: the Cantonese roast duck, bone in, and the dry-fried green beans with minced pork and chilli, no rice.

One day I would order those other things. Really I would. One day I would explore the depths of this menu. Just not today. That was something for the future. That was something to look forward to. There would always be other times.

Life goes on.

In memory of Jerry Burden
1962–2018

For the full last supper menu and links to suppliers visit:
www.jayrayner.co.uk/news/jay-rayners-last-supper-menu/

Acknowledgements

An awful lot of people helped me with this book. Most of them are named in the text, and I am grateful to them all for giving me their time, expertise and, where required, their appetite. Others helped me, but their names didn't necessarily make it onto the page. In San Francisco I am indebted to my friends David Coulter and Kei Koyoma for guiding me through my toast tour and matching me slice for slice. In New Orleans Molly Petersen of the ACE Hotel made sure I was beautifully looked after and showed me the sights. I was assisted in my exploration of Paris by Oliver Mernick-Levene, Natalia Esteves and their guide PJ from Secret Food Tours/Essor. My trip to Japan was made manageable courtesy of help and support from Inside Japan Tours (and in particular James Mundy), Ann Scott Associates, the Mandarin Oriental Hotel, Tokyo, and ANA. I couldn't have eaten any of the pig dinners alone – or I could have done so, but it wouldn't have been anything like as much fun – so thank you again to my companions Ben Adler, Tim Anderson, Laurence Basset, Thomas Blythe, Jordan Bourke, Annie Gray, Tim Hayward, Miranda Hinckley, Zoe Laughlin, Barry Smith and Marc Webbon. Andi Oliver deserves an honourable mention for intending to come to all of the pig dinners, but not making it to any of them.

Henry Harris and his staff at the Hero of Maida must have another huge round of thanks for making the last supper itself such a success. Likewise, Will and Allison Abernethy of Abernethy Butter, Peter and Jim Hannan of Hannan Meats, Fergus Jackson of Brick House Bread and Andrew Rooney of Rooney Fish went out of their way to get their products to me for the big night. Dave Lewis, Robert Rickenberg, Joe Thompson, Ian Shaw, Malcolm Edmonstone and Jo Nichols literally played and sang for their supper. Markson's Pianos found a way to get a cumbersome keyboard up those stairs. Brian Clivaz and George Pell of L'Escargot made sure we had enough snail trays, tongs and forks.

A couple of passages of the text were adapted from pieces I wrote many years ago. My lunch with a Nazi was commissioned by the *Independent on Sunday* and my description of my interesting bus trip in Turkey by *Cosmopolitan* (UK). I am grateful to all the editors who have commissioned me over the years, providing me with a lot of the experiences that went into the memoir sections of this book, but in particular to Roger Alton, Marcelle D'Argy Smith, Lee Eisenberg, Sheryl Garratt, Gareth Grundy, Nicola Jeal, Allan Jenkins, Sue Matthias, John Mulholland, Ruaridh Nicoll, Vanessa Raphaely, Paul Webster, Greg Williams and Eva Wiseman.

Jonny Geller and his team at my literary agents Curtis Brown gave me impeccable support throughout the publishing process, as ever. Fred Baty at my publishers Guardian Faber not only proved an incisive and supportive editor, but also made a great personal sacrifice by attending the suckling pig dinner. He also leads a cracking team, including marketing supremo Maria Garbutt-Lucero and copy-editor Ian Bahrami. It must, however, be recorded that the initial idea which sparked this book actually came from another editor, Jack Ramm at Penguin. Thank you, Jack.

Finally, I must thank my family: my boys, Dan and Eddie, who are occasionally forced to tag along on bits of the research and to put up with my absences. But the last words of dribbling gratitude must go to my wife, Pat Gordon-Smith, who marries her moonlighting as a cracking jazz singer with her day job as an editor of uncommon wit, perspicacity and insight. She read every page of the text as it was written, kept me on the editorial straight and narrow with tact and grace, pulled me back from errors of judgement and kept pouring the wine. At the end of the process we're still sharing a bed, though that may have more to do with the fact that I sorted the snoring issue. She really is a saint.